New England
Humor

He seized the fellow by the scruff and the seat of his overalls, and pitched him three yards further into the river than he did upon the first trial!

New England Humor

FROM THE REVOLUTIONARY WAR
TO THE CIVIL WAR

Cameron C. Nickels

THE UNIVERSITY OF TENNESSEE PRESS • KNOXVILLE

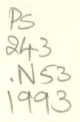
Frontispiece. "Taking the Starch Out of 'Em." Courtesy of the American Antiquarian Society.

Copyright © 1993 by The University of Tennessee Press / Knoxville.
All Rights Reserved. Manufactured in the United States of America.
First Edition.

Part of Chapter 2 was originally published as "Federalist Mock Pastorals: The Ideology of Early New England Humor" in *Early American Literature* 17 (1982): 139–51. It is used here with the permission of the publisher.

The paper in this book meets the minimum requirements of the American National Standard for Permanence of Paper for Printed Library Materials. ∞ The binding materials have been chosen for strength and durability.

Library of Congress Cataloging in Publication Data

Nickels, Cameron C.
        New England humor: from the Revolutionary War to the Civil War / Cameron
C. Nickels. —1st ed.
                p.   cm.
        Includes bibliographical references (p.) and index.
        ISBN 0-87049-804-5 (cloth: alk. paper)
                1. American wit and humor—New England—History and criticism.
2. American literature—New England—History and criticism.
3. National characteristics, American, in literature. 4. New England in literature.
I. Title.
PS243.N53 1993
817.009'974—dc20   93-320
                                                                                CIP

For my mother,
and in memory of my father and sister

Contents

Illustrations

Preface

On a Hudson River pier in Albany, New York, a Yankee "direct from the Green Hills" of Vermont initiated a throwing contest with a knot of city idlers determined not to be "beaten by a 'feller right strait out o' the woods, no how.'" One thing led to another, as they say, and when the Yankee allowed as how he could toss the leader of the group across the river, the "bully" bet ten dollars against it, with the following result:

> Without further parley, the Vermonter seized the knowing Yorker stoutly by the nap of the neck and the seat of his pants, jerked him from his foothold, and with an almost superhuman effort, dashed the bully heels over head, from the end of the dock—some ten yards out into the Hudson River.
>
> A terrific shout rang through the crowd, as he floundered in the water, and, amidst the jeers and screams of his companions, the ducked bully put back to the shore and scrambled up to the bank, half frozen by this sudden and involuntary cold bath.
>
> "I'll take that ten-spot, if you please," said the shivering loafer, advancing rapidly to the stakeholder. "You took us for green-horns, eh? We'll show you how *we* do things down here in York"—and the fellow claimed the twenty dollars.
>
> "Wal, I reck'n I wunt take no ten-spots jes' yet cap'n."
>
> "Why? You lost the bet."
>
> "Not edzackly. I didn't calkilate on deuin it the fust time—but I tell yeu, I kin *deu* it,"—and again, in spite of the loafer's utmost efforts to escape him, he seized him by the scruff and the seat of his over alls, and pitched him three yards further into the river than upon the first trial.
>
> Again the bully returned, amid the shouts of his mates, who enjoyed the sport immensely.

"Third time never fails," said the Yankee, stripping off his coat; "I kin *deu* it, I tell ye."

"Hold on!" said the almost petrified victim—

"And I *will* deu it—ef I try till to-morrow mornin'."

"I give it up!" shouted the sufferer, between his teeth, which now chattered like a mad badger's—"take the money."

The Vermonter very cooly pocketed the ten-spot, and as he turned away, remarked:

"We aint much acquainted with you smart folks daoun here'n York, but we sometimes 'take the starch aout of 'em' up our way—and p'rhaps you wunt try it on tu strangers agin. I *reck'n* you wunt," he continued, and putting on a broad grin of good humor, he left the company to their reflections!

"Taking the Starch Out of 'Em," by "the Young 'Un" (George P. Burnham), appeared twice in the *Spirit of the Times* in 1849, in Burnham's book, *Gleanings,* the same year, and was later reprinted in other periodicals of the time. Today, whether or not the story amuses us, we intuitively understand the humor intended by the triumph of the unsophisticated provincial over city types who think they are more "knowing" and "smart," because that humorous contrast has become a staple of popular entertainment and advertising. In other words, despite our reluctance to "explain a joke," we all do it, however unconsciously or automatically; we must, if we are to "get it." Which is to say that humor means something, some things—that it is a product of a culture, and its meanings can be fully understood only when we know some things about that culture, the contexts in which the joke or story appears. And finding those meanings can be, well, certainly fun, if not humorous. (I have long been taken with the ambiguity of that construction.)

We have a better understanding of "Taking the Starch Out of 'Em," for instance, if we see it as one example of a long, diverse, and popular literary tradition of New England humor that by 1849 had reached something of a peak. Standing at the center of that tradition is the rustic Yankee, identified most readily by his vernacular speech (intended as comic in itself) and ultimately by some action typically attributed to Yankees, in this case a trick.

Between the American Revolution and the Civil War, the rustic New Englander had become not only the most popular native characterization on stage and in print at home and abroad but also the archetypal American, the embodiment of the common man. He thus had an important role to play in a nation that from the 1770s had sought an identity separate from the mother country. The triumph, then, of the countrified Yankee in "Taking the Starch Out of 'Em" affirms not only rural shrewdness but also, implicitly, the superiority of indigenous American experience over qualities associated with English "civilization" and all that word had come to imply, such as culture, urbanization, and modernization.

How else to explain the meaning of the illustration, taken from the collected stories of the author, that accompanied the second appearance of the story in the *Spirit*? Here the Yankee gripping the hapless townie for another try at tossing him across the river is not the "tall, rugged built," "brawny, strong-looking" Yankee described in the story. Young, even baby-faced, not merely "decently clad," as the text describes him, but dressed in a swallow-tail coat, top hat, and striped trousers—inexplicably as far as the story itself is concerned—he is the rustic Yankee as Brother Jonathan, an early version of Uncle Sam, who would evolve, in large part, from New England humor. In rendering that illustration, artist D. C. Hitchcock surely thought that some readers would "get it." (Some might even have been amused with the notion that the bully had something in common with the archetypal Englishman, John Bull.)

But there is more to the story, because there is more to *this* story and what it means, and to New England humor and what *it* means. In *The Rise and Fall of American Humor* (1968), Jesse Bier states the matter succinctly when he speaks of the "adumbration" of Uncle Sam by the cracker-barrel philosopher Jack Downing, the most popular Yankee in New England humor: "This particular derivation of our venerable national image in the figure of the clown provides an exact commentary not only on our early confused exploration of a comic genre but on the question of self-definition fundamentally allied to a comic sense." Unfortunately Bier buries that insight in a chapter, titled "Early New England Humor," that dismisses Downing and most of New England humor as "a fit subject only for federal writers of the lean thirties, professional folklorists, and indefatigable students of 'American civilization.'" Over the

years and now in this book I have tried to answer that "question of self-definition fundamentally allied to a comic sense," and do so for the moment by
looking more closely at the contexts in which this story appeared and at the
story itself. In doing so, I see meanings at odds with its humorous "moral," as
Yankee Notions called it in an 1852 reprinting illustrated with a picture titled
"Goose Done Brown."

For all of its celebration of the kind of indigenous identity represented by
the vernacular values of the archetypal Yankee, the nation by 1849 had taken
on many of the attributes of civilization identified with English experience—
and often had done so enthusiastically. "Taking the Starch Out of 'Em," for
example, appeared in the *Spirit of the Times,* a New York weekly that once
claimed forty thousand readers and that was printed and then circulated to all
parts of the country with all that modern technology had to offer. Also, although acclaimed today for furthering the "big-bear," or backwoods, school of
native American humor, in its own time the *Spirit* had other and higher ambitions. As the subtitle announced, it was *A Gazette of the Literary, Fashionable and Sporting World,* and according to its 1835 editorial policy, addressed
not unsophisticated rustics and what they stood for but "gentlemen of standing, wealth, and intelligence."

The narrator of "Taking the Starch Out of 'Em" is just such a gentleman.
No bumpkin, he writes comfortably in a formal diction very different from the
lingo of both the Yankee and the city idler. Indeed, his witty plays on the word
"green" artfully and subtly underscore the rather simplistic, perhaps borrowed,
plot and presuppose alert and experienced readers, ones capable of registering
a variety of comic meanings. The *Spirit* valued sophisticated writing, because
like virtually all American periodicals, for all their literary nationalism, it hap-
pily printed as well "the choicest selections from the highest class of English
Belles-Lettres."

What we make of all this—or more honestly, what I do—is what the rest
of this book is about: a consideration of the texts of New England humor and
their many contexts in an effort to get some sense of their complex, because
often conflicting, often covert, meanings to writers and readers of the time. I
say "some" sense and "some" meanings because that is all we can know. However naïve it may be to think that we can understand those meanings com-

pletely, it is also naïve to think that we can know too little. Current scholarship emphasizing critical theory rightly cautions us to be aware of our own biases as scholars, but it errs and errs self-indulgently when it confuses ends with means—putting theory first, obscuring knowing with nomenclature, making too much of the "scholar" in "scholarship." There are some things we can know better than the readers and writers of the past if we look at the past with some sense of common sense.

I began my work many years ago in truly splendid isolation, the appropriate environment for an aspiring scholar, because so little had been written about New England humor. (See the Bibliographic Essay at the back of this book.) As a result I spent most of those years poring over nineteenth-century sources looking for New England humor that people read, but I looked too for what seemed to me just as meaningful: what they read *about* New England humor and what *else* they read at the same time, often on the same page. (Asked in a grant application to describe my methodology, I wrote that I sat in libraries and read as many nineteenth-century newspapers and magazines as I could. Got the grant.) My claims for what Americans thought are based on what they read.

True, I was inspired by the work of earlier literary historians, now out of fashion to some—Henry Nash Smith, John William Ward, Charles Sanford, Benjamin Spencer, Leo Marx, and Marvin Myers, to name a few—because they identified and gave close attention to primary sources. But more recent writing on the cultural history of the period has confirmed my sense that broad concerns—and that is the correct word—about nationalism, progress, and democracy dominated thinking about America at all levels of culture. Books by Larzer Ziff, Robert Winesburch, David Reynolds, Lawrence Buell, and Douglas Miller (again, to name a few) give fresh insights into nineteenth-century thinking on these matters and above all to the contradictions, the tensions they called forth in texts "beneath the American Renaissance," to use Reynolds's title. Buell in particular gracefully and meaningfully integrates popular Yankee humor and high culture, and finds, as I have, a telling, paradoxical division "between the impulse nostalgically to identify with the bygone or simplified life-style depicted and the cosmopolitan impulse to mock it as clownish or repressive." This is not to say that any of us wholly agree, but then what we scholars do is not, say, a tossing contest: there is nothing of too much importance, ultimately, at stake. The passion, the joy, is in the doing, not in what is done.

In regard to what I have done here, the first chapter, "New England Humor and the Dilemma of American Identity," is essentially an extended introduction to what I think New England humor is and above all an analysis of the historical contexts in which that humor was written and read. Chapter 2, "Early American Humor," considers the origins of a native humor in the colonial American experience and then those works, beginning in the Revolution, that clearly established the conventions of a tradition of New England humor that began in earnest after the War of 1812. In order to make some sense of that tradition, I have divided chapters 3, 4, 5, and 6 by genres, although in fact the genres appeared nearly concurrently. "New England Humor on Stage" deals chronologically with those actors who developed Yankee roles. Chapter 4, "New England Humor in Print," does not lend itself to chronological organization, so I have divided it into categories by types of stories. Although New England humor was primarily a written humor, pictures provided a varied and increasingly important dimension. Over the years, pictorial delineations were important in many ways, as chapter 5, "New England Humor Illustrated," reveals. The sixth chapter, "The New England Cracker-barrel Philosophers," is the longest because not only was cracker-barrel humor widely popular for many years but also, unlike with most humor in print, its authors are known and their lives well documented. As a result, we have the opportunity to examine in depth the evolving characterizations and the connections to the writers' lives—their literary aspirations and their responses to the contexts in which they wrote.

At the end of "Taking the Starch Out of 'Em," the Yankee, having done his best, puts on "a broad grin of good humor" and leaves "the company to their reflections." I begin this book—and will end it—in much the same spirit.

Acknowledgments

"Although this is a book about humor, it is not a humorous book."

I wrote that many years ago when I was convinced that I was going to "write the book" on New England humor. I was naïve about what it took to write "the book," *any* book, but not naïve about the kind of book I wanted to write. I have never been informed or entertained by scholarly books on humor that tried to be humorous in an effort, it seems to me, to overcome the conventional wisdom that people who write about humor do not have a sense of humor. (Writing about New England humor raises even more problems: people say things like "I bet that'll be a short book!" and I'm supposed to smile, if not laugh.) So now, completing my scholarly book (it has endnotes) on humor, how to respond to that devastating indictment? There should be some sort of certification, maybe a blood test. Is it enough that I created "American jokes"?

All I can say is that I was raised right, by parents who shared naturally the fun of irony and of humorous incongruity in general. As very young children, my sister and I listened to and later watched with our parents "Jack Benny," "Our Miss Brooks," "The Life of Riley," and all the rest. (My favorite television show is still "The Andy Griffith Show," and I am always ready for any bits and pieces of old "Saturday Night Live," "SCTV," and "Monty Python" shows that appear.) We also enjoyed together records by Spike Jones, Homer and Jethro, and Stan Freberg. Our parents actually encouraged their children to read— and they read as well—*Mad* (the comic book, of course) and the other masterpieces of EC Comics. Only later did I appreciate how these midwesterners integrated shtick from the movies of the Marx Brothers, Laurel and Hardy, and W. C. Fields into our lives. They taught us also to see the humor in the serious or ostensibly serious: in turn-of-the-century recitations and poetry, passages from Horatio Alger, presidential conventions, roller derbies, and professional wrestling. They were no doubt puzzled by, but did not discourage, my adolescent interest in recordings by Ken Nordine and the Beat poets, the latter a gift from my sister. Little wonder that I dedicate this book to them.

I grew up and have lived thinking of humor as sociable, as socializing, and over the years I found that writing a scholarly book about humor, despite the necessary isolation of the researcher and then the writer, is also a sociable enterprise. In acknowledging that, I must forgo my very early plan for a parody of this part of a book, which in my callow arrogance too often sounded like the worst performance by an Oscar winner. "I once was lost, but now I'm found," the gospel song goes, and the acknowledgments that follow represent an essentially chronological pilgrimage.

Librarians, curators, and archivists everywhere deserve their own paragraph: a scholar cannot thank them all, nor can they be thanked enough.

This odyssey began with a graduate paper at Southern Illinois University at Carbondale in a class on American humor taught by Howard Webb, a teacher so good that I would probably have gone on to do whatever he did. He also helped me to get my first teaching position, at Central Missouri State College (now University), which made it possible for me to spend a summer in New England, summer school at Harvard, where I found the kind of libraries—Harvard, Boston Public Library, Boston Athenaeum—and new friends—Don Bacon and Alan Kantrow—that confirmed my sense that this scholarly stuff might be as much fun as teaching or playing music.

Later, at the University of Minnesota, Edward M. Griffin did not direct, but he helped me mightily with the dissertation stage of my venture. More important, he continued to provide advice, encouragement, and friendship as I re-researched and completely rewrote that early effort. John O'Neill and Jeff Titon, friends from those days and now at Hamilton College and Brown University, respectively, continued their friendship, played music with and for me, and collaborated on scholarly projects of mutual interest.

My continued work in humor ultimately brought me into the company of other scholars in the field. John Harrison, J. A. Leo Lemay, David Sloane, Lawrence Mintz, Milton and Patricia Rickels, and Daniel Royot not only provided examples of their own thorough research and sound thinking but also willingly answered questions and above all gave the encouragement a scholar at a "teaching institution" needed.

And yet, at James Madison University, albeit after many years, my work has come to this, with the university itself granting support for summer research and an educational leave. At least as important, though, have been the assistance and companionship of colleagues here. Scott Suter, first a fellow musician, then a student, now a close friend and nascent scholar in his own right, has read parts of my work and passed on all kinds of relevant information. Colleagues in English—Robin McNallie, Jean Cash, and Mark Facknitz—and those in history—Sidney Bland and Chris Arndt—willingly and wisely read sections relevant to their expertise. I also appreciate the support of two department chairs, Mark Hawthorne and David Jeffrey, who thought my work worth encouraging.

In a rather different sense, I have to acknowledge too the many fine musicians in the Shenandoah Valley—musicians from many parts of the country, really—whom I have played with over the years. Their companionship took me willingly from my study, because I always returned inspired by their commitment to excellence, the notion that the effort to try to do one's best is also good fun. This book is why "Doc" usually had to leave early, folks.

As for my family, I thank my daughter Melynn Nickels Byerly and her husband, David (best friends as well as family), for the time they spent during a week at the Outer Banks reading one of these chapters. And finally I thank Sue, who reads everything I write with the rigor and love that she brings to teaching English to young Virginians.

James Madison University
Harrisonburg, Virginia

Chapter 1

New England Humor and the Dilemma of American Identity

Economic, social, and political causes certainly played their part in the American Revolution in the mid-1770s, but the American triumph in that conflict represented as well a logical fulfillment of the long-promised destiny of the New World. Political independence gave new impetus to the need for the new nation to reject English precedents and achieve indigenous attributes—attributes not only commensurate with political independence but also built on those political principles declared so fervently as the Revolution began. Even before that triumph was assured, Thomas Paine had anticipated that "the birthday of a new world is at hand" (*Common Sense,* 1776), and when the ultimate victory gave nation status to that "new world," the American nationalism it engendered reiterated the age-old terms of New World identity in light of the new political reality.

Nationalism at One with Democracy

In celebrating their military victory, Americans spoke of the "grand political Millennium" expected of a nation "designed to be the political redeemer of mankind,"[1] but in the two decades or so following the Revolution, they laid no foundations for these castles in the air. Not even the republican-inclined Jefferson had a plan to give substance to the revolutionary declaration that "all men are created equal," a phrase John Adams deemed a "glittering generality." In these years, Federalists held office, edited influential newspapers and journals, and set cultural standards. Although they shared an abstract faith in republicanism as America's contribution to world history, and sometimes even defended it as an auspicious contrast to Old World practice, they were unpenitently enthusiastic in denouncing what they considered democratic excesses. For them, state constitutions had already gone much too far, and the constitutional convention in 1787 was called in part, at least, to "clip the wings of mad democracy," as Henry Knox put it. In 1785 Noah Webster (*Sketches of American Policy*) had lauded American representative democracy as the model for the world, but rebellions such as Shays's forced him to recant: "This is the misfortune of republican governments," he admitted in the *Connecticut Courant* (20 Nov. 1786). "For my own part, I confess, I was once as strong a republican as any man in America. *Now*, a republic is among the last kinds of governments I should choose. I should infinitely prefer a limited monarchy."

But the American victory in what has been called our "second war of independence," the War of 1812, invigorated national self-consciousness and solidarity, and it marked a shift in political ideology that would endure for some time. The words of Albert Gallatin are often quoted because they capture so well the new nationalistic spirit: the end of the war "renewed and reinstated the national feelings and character which the Revolution had given. . . . the people are more Americans; they feel and act more as a nation," he wrote in 1816.[2] Secure as Americans might be in their twice-won political independence, and confident as they still were in fulfilling those time-honored promises of the New World, the military victory in 1815 gave a new sense of urgency to completing the separation from England by broadening the dimensions of an indigenous identity. In that spirit, the 1823 "Prospectus" for the *National Journal* voiced the need to develop native genius and talent because that would "at once render us really an independent people. . . . Until this is accomplished, we shall not be entirely free. . . . We do not govern ourselves while we permit others to think for us." The search for that independence fills the pages of American journals after 1815, virtually all of them begun to promote, identify, and judge native achievement. This kind of parochialism led J. R. Wright in the *Pioneer* (Jan. 1843) to take the Boston Athenaeum to task for exchanging a picture by Thomas Doughty for one by Thomas Cole. Americans should be "proud of Doughty as an *American* painter," Wright argued, whereas concerning the English-born Cole, "we do not like to see foreign artists receiving so great a share of public patronage." (Such an incrimination of the great Cole's patriotism did not go unanswered. "L.," in the *New World* (25 Feb. 1843) quoted Cole himself on the matter: "I would give my right hand could I but say I was born in America!") No feature of American life went unexamined to determine its native integrity and thus to measure its distance from English example. An essay on "National Postures" in the *New England Magazine* (Sept. 1834) identified a distinctly American way of sitting, and an article in *Putnam's* (Mar. 1853) titled "Are We A Good-Looking People?" concluded that we are.

The end of the War of 1812 also marked, although it did not also initiate, the beginning of a dramatic shift in American political ideology that would become one with the new nationalism. By 1815 the shrilly antidemocratic voices of the Federalists were stilled. Already languishing with the election of Thomas Jefferson in 1800, the party laid itself to rest with the Hartford Convention called late in 1814. After that, caustic references to the "Loaferism" and "jacobinical spirit" threatening the land, once featured so publicly in Federalist newspapers, were confined to the diaries of men such as George Templeton Strong. (For him, the Federalists had declined to a "mere commercial aristocracy.")[3] There were divisions on significant issues, of course: Jackson's attack on the Bank of the United States caused economic and political turmoil within his own party, and the various compromises on the issue of slavery over the years barely masked the divisions that would ultimately split the nation. But *democracy* was not the tainted word it had been; it did not evoke—it was not *used* to evoke—horrific images of mob violence and imminent takeover by the motley rabble. And no one confessed (publicly, at least) that a limited monarchy might be best after all. Indeed, Jackson's conservative political opponents took to calling him "King Andrew" to indict what they saw as his monarchical high-handedness, and in time they would enthusiastically and successfully adopt as their own the log-cabin style of Democratic electioneering. Historians debate the circumstances, motives, and degrees of democratic reform that took place following the end of the War of 1812, but undeniably changes were wrought—most notably universal (albeit white male) suffrage—and Americans could universally proclaim the prophecy of political exceptionalism and mission with a faith that something tangible had been done and more would be done to effect the political equality that seemed to give substance to revolutionary abstractions about the dignity and worth of the common man.

The invigorated democratic faith, then, was not only concomitant with the heightened sense of national self-consciousness in the decades following the War of 1812, but was verily conjoined in ways that it had not been in the years following the War of Independence. Democratic reforms seemed to mean fulfillment of the New World's old mission, but they provided as well the substantive basis for effecting the complete independence from England that was the more immediate concern, a concern intensified by British skepticism about American progress in that regard. The American West served much the same purpose by offering a virgin land that would ensure the continued growth of democracy and thus national identity. "We look to see yet in the West, a bolder and a manlier action of the American mind," wrote the editor of the *United States Magazine and Democratic Review* (July 1841), "which will scorn that emasculate imitativeness of England and English things that yet holds us in an unworthy thralldom, which will surrender itself more freely to the guidance of the genius of American democracy."

More viable, however, as examples of American exceptionalism than those millions of unsettled acres were those democratic "civil institutions," as they were called, that made democracy operative and that Americans believed confidently, smugly even, provided a genuine contrast to English practice. Those institutions were "new, peculiar," according to the editor of the *American Monthly Magazine* (Mar. 1837), and thus they stood "opposed in all their features to those of European nations," but he found wanting other features of a national identity. Given the uniqueness of America's institutions as well as her "vast and varied extent of territory," the editor continued, "the necessity of an independent literature is obviously very great," but "at the present moment we may be said to be in a state of mental vassalage to foreigners. With the yoke of political dependence, we have not yet shaken off the fetters of the mind," he admitted, voicing the same lament in much the same aphoristic form used by countless American writers. British observers delighted in baiting Americans with that disparity. Sydney Smith was the most notorious observer to do so. In his famous attack in the *Edinburgh Review* (June 1820), he not only asked, "Who reads an American book?" but posed a catalog of questions so rhetorical and so complete that it mocked America's pretense of complete independence.

Foreign commentators infuriated Americans. Smith so provoked the impetuous John Neal that he reportedly gave up the study of law in Baltimore to go to England and confront the British in the pages of their own reviews. And he did so (posing as an English observer), although according to another story he left Baltimore to avoid a duel. Ironically, in turn, Neal's own forthright opinions about America in the British journals provoked some of his countrymen to try to prevent his returning home.[4] At heart, though, Americans knew that reservations about indigenous fulfillment were just, that cultural independence had not been achieved. In telling a Harvard audience in 1837 that "our day of independence, our long apprenticeship to the learning of other lands, draws to a close" ("American Scholar"), Emerson echoed the sentiments of the age no less than he did a year later when he told a Dartmouth audience that "this country has not fulfilled what seemed the reasonable expectations of mankind" ("Literary Ethics"). Americans had few doubts that those expectations *would* be fulfilled, and they believed too that the means for doing so could be found in the egalitarian principles inherent in the country's political institutions; the logic of a national identity made one with a democratic ideology led relentlessly to that conclusion.

George Bancroft, whose premier history documented what he saw as the nation's long and inexorable democratic mission, stated fully and accurately that compelling logic: "If it be true," he announced in an 1835 address at Williams College, "that the gifts of mind and heart are universally diffused, if the sentiments of truth, justice, love, and beauty exist in every one, then it follows as a necessary consequence, that the common judgment in taste, politics, and religion, is the nearest possible approach to an infallible decision."[5] His fundamental worth already entrusted in political matters, the common man thus became the scale for measuring the native integrity of all other features of the American experience—"peculiarities," those features were called without censure. Europeans interested in America's future (and most of them were—above all the English) accepted the promise of a unique destiny for the New World—they had, of course, formulated it—and they believed too that it would be realized by what they considered the "great experiment in democracy." In the nineteenth century they came in droves to search out the palpable results of that experiment, to record American peculiarities, although they did not usually approve of them. Witness Trollope, Tocqueville, and Dickens. Sydney Smith too acknowledged the uniqueness of democratic institutions, but like so many of his countrymen, he was offended by American smugness, and in that spirit he ended his catalog of questions thus: "Finally, under which of the old tyrannical governments of Europe is every sixth man a Slave, whom his fellow creatures may buy and sell and torture?"

Most Americans tended to ignore that tragic incongruity, but dutifully and doggedly they answered all other real and imagined slurs, for pugnaciously nationalistic pride in the American experiment and sensitivity to criticism of it were themselves identified by English observers as "national peculiarities." And yet the very sweep and intensity of the American response suggest underlying reservations, not about the need or the potential, certainly, of an indigenous identity, but reservations, apprehensions even, about the true nature of the common man, who must act as the common denominator of that identity. Among Americans, James Fenimore Cooper faced the problem forthrightly and publicly—and he earned the acrimony of his countrymen for doing so. (Southern antidemocratic opinion served chiefly to defend another, different "peculiar institution.") He considered himself a democrat, but only in political terms, and thus he was not bound by the exigencies of egalitarian nationalism. "Democracy asserts the control of the majority, only, in matters of law, and not in matters of custom," he declared in the *American Democrat* (1838). That conclusion he premised on the belief that the "celebrated proclamation" of the Declaration of Independence was not to be taken literally. "All men are not 'created equal,'" he declared, "in a physical sense, or even a moral sense, unless we limit the significance to one of political rights." Most Americans would not deal with this crucial issue so forthrightly.

"If it be true," Bancroft had posited, that "the gifts of mind and heart . . . the sentiments of truth, justice, love and beauty exist in everyone"—only if that premise is true does "the common judgment in taste, politics and religion" become "an infallible decision." Logically, at least, Bancroft and nearly all other Americans assumed the truth of that premise. They had to, for to question that premise was to undermine the foundation on which American identity had been so irrevocably laid; however, the conditional structure Bancroft used to pose the proposition does not prove the crucial consequence of his premise. Revealingly, that structure indicates a necessarily implicit, covert, uncertainty about the nature of the mass of common men, the one issue vital not only to making political democracy work but also, in turn, to ensuring the native integrity of all other features of the American identity. Considering the prospects of an indigenous American art, a writer in the *American Review and Metropolitan Magazine* (1843) came about as close as most Americans could to addressing the problem directly: "In a democracy like our own, where the right of government emanates from the people—where every social or legislative appeal is made to the people—all our hopes and fears are bound up in the condition of the mass." In the words "and fears" lie the crux of the dilemma.

The Yankee and American Nationalism

Beginning with the war of revolution and up to the Civil War, the figure of the rustic Yankee appeared in New England humor as the American stereotype, embodying not only the distinguishing features of the national identity but also the hopes and fears that identity engendered. The figure first appeared as the representative American in the writings of Loyalists who used the terms *Yankee, Jonathan,* and *Brother Jonathan* satirically to identify those who fought for the American cause. Early literary characterizations subsequently appeared in various British and American versions of "Yankee Doodle," in Royall Tyler's play *The Contrast* (1787) and its imitators, and in a series of mock pastorals written by Federalist writers in the 1790s—the early New England humor of the next chapter. Just why the Yankee came to be considered the typical American and why he was given the names Jonathan and Brother Jonathan have eluded those who have researched such questions—nor do we know the origin of the word *Yankee.*[6] The designations stuck, though, and following the War of 1812, characterizations of the rustic Yankee proliferated dramatically in form and number in New England humor, and he was widely accepted as the most popular American character type in print and on stage as the appropriate embodiment of the American experience. Whether Jonathan or Brother Jonathan, he was the American counterpart, usually the antagonist, of the English figure of John Bull, his acknowledged ancestor (see fig. 1.). "Jonathan may be described as the finishing model of the Anglo-Saxon, of which John Bull is the rough cast," concluded the patriotic author of "Are We A Good-Looking People?" in *Putnam's*. The figure of Uncle Sam, born in the War of 1812, owes much to the delineations of Jonathan, whom Uncle Sam replaced as the national prototype during the Civil War.[7]

The rustic Yankee did become the iconic American between the Revolutionary War and the Civil War, although why he did is not clear. But why was humor the most popular medium for delineating the type? The answer lies first in a conventional form of humorous incongruity and then in the unique import the American experience gave that incongruity. The *humor* of New England humor typically lies in the incongruity of the inferior, the provincial—the individual who stands outside of and in contrast to a more genteel, modern system of social and cultural values. Humorous incongruity can occur in two resolutions to that contrast: the comic triumph of those values because the outsider has pretensions to them or simply never fathoms them, or the comic triumph of the outsider over values presumed superior. Both have long been sources of humor in the folklore and belles lettres of many nations, but the American experience charged them with new meaning, for the new nation struggled to—as we have seen, it was compelled to—define itself in terms of the contrast between the provincial experience of the New World and the genteel values of the Old World.[8]

It is above all as a rustic that the Yankee appeared as an appropriate representation of the American position and served the purposes of New England humor so well. As a rustic, he stood emphatically free of influences derived from the city, where, it was believed, foreign values and practices tended to prevail and inhibit, even to corrupt, native growth. From those rural origins come the other indigenous, distinguishing features of the Yankee—his homespun dress, manners, and speech. Outside European experience, a provincial, the rustic Yankee embodied the American common man who had become the principal element in the experiment in democracy and thus who, more significantly, seemed to give substance to the hope of achieving an indigenous national identity.

However, the literature of New England humor renders two very different judgments of the rustic Yankee and the identity he had come to represent. The literature abounds with stories that judge favorably the rustic attributes of the

Yankee and thus find him an exemplary representation of the American ways of doing and seeing. Although unworldly and unrefined, the Yankee in many stories possesses a natural good sense and shrewd practicality that triumph in peddling schemes, ingenious trades, and Yankee tricks that even Southern victims could at times admire. In other stories, his rustic judgments expose the conventions of genteel, urban society as artificial and ridicule artistic taste as affected. Identified as such values were with European experience, the Yankee's rustic superiority reaffirms the American escape from that experience and assures independence from it. The ostensible ignorance of the rustic Yankee masks his native genius, often to disarm those people seen as his social and intellectual betters, which heightens the humorous triumph over them.

But another, quite different judgment of the Yankee appears in countless stories that treat the Yankee's rustic peculiarities as humorously inferior. In a nation showing the first, prophetic, signs of industrialism and urbanization, for example, the rustic already represented a comic anachronism. Machinery overwhelms him, often injures him, and in the city he is awed by the diversity of people and activities, confused by modern conveniences, and duped by more knowledgeable city types. Other stories portray his ludicrous, often belligerent, inability to appreciate or even comprehend things artistic, and in circumstances that require emotion and sensitivity—love, for example—his rude speech and manners become crudely and humorously inappropriate.

In rendering those two judgments, the literature of New England humor reflects a profound American dilemma about a national identity postulated on rustic attributes as representative of the American common man: those attributes provided the most clearly identifiable qualities of an indigenous identity; yet, the more identifiable and thus indigenous those qualities were made, the more vividly rustic they were made—and they were in New England humor—the more clearly they represented social, cultural, and even political distinctions that were patently undesirable.

The manifestations of that dilemma are diverse and the dimensions of it complex, but they can be illustrated for the moment by a page from the *New England Galaxy* (16 June 1826). In one corner there is a brief, untitled poem narrating the triumph of someone called a "plebeian" over the citified pretensions of "Carlos." The poem concludes,

External show and specious grace
Are nought but ribbons, cambric lace.
A rustic garb and artless mien,
Conjoined with worth is often seen.

A conventional kind of romantic faith certainly, but the sentiment appears time and again in many forms in nineteenth-century America as a rejection of urban, that is to say "foreign," affectation and an affirmation of rural worth, the touchstone of indigenous definition.[9] The consciously nationalistic intent is clear in this case in the name assumed by the poem's author, "Uncle Sam." Further consideration of the poem and the context in which it appears, however, reveals implicit reservations about the judgment it makes. The poem overtly values the natural simplicity of the artless rustic over the show and grace of "Carlos," but the formal language used by the author—"specious," "mien," "conjoined"—and the formal poetic form indicate a commitment on the part of "Uncle Sam" to sophisticated, artful cultural traditions that the rustic, by definition, does not understand.

That judgment of rustic character is represented on the same page as the poem by a letter from Abram and Sarah Strickland advertising for the return of their wayward sons, Joe and Sam. According to the parents, the boys have gone "one to Nue yak and won toe Bowstown ware tha are gitten in two bad hab bits sich az plain keards paw paw go in toe thea tres sir curses byin lot try tickets and sevrul uther ah tickles two newmrus to men shun." Here, the humor is directed at the rustics' moralistic ignorance of what they consider city evils, ignorance that is underscored by the grotesque illiteracy, which in this case exemplifies the rustic artlessness lauded by "Uncle Sam" only to mock it. The letter is, in fact, part of a series of rustic Yankee letters from Joe and Sam Strickland and their family that the *Galaxy* had helped popularize, and for the most part, the magazine had used these characterizations and others like them to ridicule ignorant rusticity generally and more specifically to stigmatize the democratic constituency of Andrew Jackson.

The implicit contrast of values represented on this page from the *Galaxy* can be illustrated further by another example from the Strickland humor and, in subsequent chapters, by the tradition of New England humor as a whole.

Like some New England humor, some of the Strickland humor does affirm, not mock, what Henry Nash Smith calls "vernacular" values to "designate not only the language of rustic or backwoods characters but also their ethical and aesthetic [and inherently political, I would say] assumptions they represented." Taking his cue from Santayana, Smith sees in the tradition of native American humor a contrast with and an escape from a genteel tradition of inherited, European values that in Smith's view tended to dominate and enervate the indigenous authenticity of American life. In the native-humor tradition, says Smith, "uncouth manners and speech could easily become a mask for homely wisdom and rugged honesty that were an implicit indictment of empty elegance and refinement."[10] That is the case with Zachariah Strickland's letter in the *New England Galaxy* (6 May 1826) reporting his first visit to the "oppery," the "Babbler of Seville." He cannot understand a word the performers sing, and when his nephew Joe tells him that virtually no one else in the audience can either, Zachariah asks with homespun good sense, "If thay dont understand it ses I, what do they cum to the oppery for? O becaze its the fashion ses Jo, they cum for to larn for to talk about sentiment and taist." Such sophisticated pretense has no place in Zachariah's vernacular scale of values. "Now I dont know but twas good taist for dandys, but twas no taist for me. Id rather hear Mr. Hastings sing mear or old hundred, than the trilling and squealing of all the Italyons or Apollyons in the univarse," he decides.

Here the rustic morality contrasts favorably to more worldly values— Yankees singing hymns are superior to foreigners "squealing" opera—and the illiteracy in this case gives further credence to the artless, rustic point of view. In its affirmation of vernacular values and rejection of "empty elegance and refinement," the letter from Zachariah Strickland illustrates not only Smith's thesis about American humor but also the terms for national identity set out in the poem by "Uncle Sam." Exactly that contrast of values lies at the heart of New England humor and American identity. As the letter from Abram and Sarah Strickland indicates, however, New England humor also reflects a tacit— and, as we shall see, often a not-so-tacit—affirmation of a genteel cultural tradition and ambivalence about, often forthright criticism of, democratic politics and the consequent egalitarianism that had assumed so crucial a place in the search for American identity. Even Zachariah Strickland's letter requires a final consideration in this regard. It must be assumed that the author of that letter is not himself a rustic semiliterate, if for no other reason than the pun in "babbler" of Seville. That pun effectively satirizes the opera, but it is not conscious on the part of the persona, for Zachariah's tone is solemnly moralistic, not playfully witty. Thus although the characterization created by the author is used to satirize sophisticated values, the writer himself, *as* a writer, has, like "Uncle Sam," some commitment to literary and cultural values very different from those represented by the rustic persona he creates.

The Yankee as Representative American: At Home and Abroad

To ascribe some serious social-political-cultural significance to the tradition of New England humor is not to deny that it was intended primarily to entertain, to be humorous. As humor, however, it expressed serious issues of the time and in laughter relieved the tensions those issues created. The many and varied ways that New England humor expressed those concerns and relieved those tensions will be dealt with in following chapters. For the remainder of the present chapter, I will look at how the dilemma over national identity posited in egalitarian terms was reflected in American responses to writings by English travelers and reviewers *about* the rustic Yankee and New England humor.

America and Americans fascinated the English at the end of the eighteenth century and above all in the early decades of the nineteenth century, as democracy seemed to give real promise to a meaningful American independence. Curious visitors from England—and some from other countries as well—made the trip across the Atlantic to identify and evaluate American developments.[11] Concerning the burning question of who read an American book, one observer facetiously suggested that Americans had not yet produced a national literature because they were too busy doing battle with the large and plentiful mosquitoes considered indigenous to New World nature.[12] Most travelers, though, were seriously interested in the effects of democracy on the more personal features of the American character—the speech, customs, manners, and even the physiognomy of the new, democratic man and woman. (Courtly Old World opinion usually had it that American women were exceedingly attractive.) Having observed and recorded at length, the travelers returned home to publish their findings for their equally curious but less traveled countrymen. Reviewers of the travel books gave still wider currency to these opinions, and they used the opportunity to tender their own. (Sydney Smith did so in his review of a statistical study of the United States.) Curious, believers in the New World destiny though they were, British observers were not loathe to find life in the former colony wanting in too many respects, at least according to many Americans.

Notoriously thin skinned as Americans were when it came to admonishments from the once-mother country, their responses were as varied as they were unrelenting. Satire of English travel books in the form of *mock* travel books became for a time a kind of literary genre in its own right. Charles Jared Ingersoll in *Inchiquin, the Jesuit's Letters* (1810), and James Fenimore Cooper in *Notions of the Americans* (1828), created fictitious visitors with more kindly views of the American experience; in a more humorous vein were *John Bull in America, the New Munchausen* (1825), by James Kirke Paulding, and *Travels in America* (1833), by Asa Greene, who posed as a former barber of the English king. Also, caricatures of obnoxious travelers appeared in American books, plays, and cartoons, with Mrs. Frances Trollope as the traveler of choice, not only because her *Domestic Manners of the Americans* (1833) was especially irksome to Americans but also, surely, because her name served the ends of satire so well. In an early survey of these "British Travelers in America," as his essay was titled in the *Monthly Magazine* (Dec. 1826), John Neal, himself posing as a British observer, concluded archly, "Anybody may go to America, and therefore nobody goes, or, to speak with more propriety, nobodies go."

In their search for indigenous American peculiarities, these English observers often found in the delineations of the Yankee in New England humor examples suited to their generally jaundiced point of view. It was the English, after all, who first designated Yankee Jonathan as the stereotypical American and who continued to portray him as such long after Uncle Sam had become the more respectable, and in America the more widely adopted, national type. "The history of the Yankee is the history of the Republic," wrote "Q.Q." in the *New Monthly Magazine* (Oct. 1836). "The character of the Yankee has influenced and continues to influence that of every part of the nation, and their name, from a provincial designation, has become among foreigners, the popular appellation of the whole people."[13] That conviction perhaps explains why New England humor was so popular in England—more popular than backwoods humor, Nils Enkvist argues in his study of American humor in England—with stories and cartoons appearing in newspapers and magazines. *Punch* and *Fun*, for example, first borrowed from American sources, then turned to their own creations to satirize Americans more effectively, "particularly their bragging, their crude manners and brutality, as well as their questionable business methods," Enkvist says.[14] English publishers reprinted editions of New England humor, which were reviewed and quoted copiously, as were American ones; English editors assembled their own anthologies of what they considered *Yankee Humor and Uncle Sam's Fun*, or *American Broad Grins*, as two were titled. On stage, English character actor Charles Mathews, after a visit to the United States, performed his *Trip to America* in London in 1824 (it featured the American Negro and Irishman as well as the Yankee), the same year he performed the Yankee lead in Richard Peake's *Jonathan Doubikins: or, Jonathan in England*. American actors who specialized in comic Yankees subsequently appeared regularly in English theaters. In drawing on New England humor for illustrations of American character in their travel books, English visitors used examples that their countrymen would find comfortably consistent with those in other sources. American readers, however, were not at all pleased to have their character so identified and so impugned, as they saw it.

Americans objected strenuously to the many English travelers who repeated stories of the rustic Yankee's legendary shrewdness (*'cuteness*, it was called, a variation of *acuteness*) as representative of the American character itself. As Jane Mesick writes in *The English Traveller in America*, the Yankee "bore the brunt of this accusation because he was looked upon by his countrymen as the embodiment of 'smartness' in trickery and business," and travelers, in return, recounted stories they had been told "of wooden nutmegs, or of watches sold at auction without works or of common sheep with Merino wool sewed upon them."[15] When New Englanders told such stories, they perhaps did so to lead on the outsider, itself a conventional Yankee trick, and people from other parts of the country may have told the stories to express their own prejudices against the New Englander. Traveling in the western territory of his own country, Massachusetts-born Timothy Flint bristled at the tales a Kentuckian told of Yankees who sold pit-coal indigo, wooden nutmegs, and gin made by putting pine tops in alcohol.[16] As for the appearance of such stories in travel books, Captain Frederick Marryat, whose own *Diary in America* (1839) proved him no friend of the country he visited, identified Americans themselves as the reason that they were so often misrepresented. "There is no other country perhaps, in which the habit of hoaxing, is so common," he observed. "Indeed, this and the hyperbole constitute the major part of American humor. If they have the slightest suspicion that a foreigner is about to write a book, nothing appears to give them such pleasure as to try to mislead him."[17]

Appearing as these stories do in travel books, they seem authentic reports of the American character in action, and certainly the travelers intended that they be so understood; however, such stories were also a staple of printed New England humor, which was surely the source for many of the oral versions.[18] All of the specific tricks and trades mentioned by Mesick and Flint, for example, appeared in print to entertain American readers, not to dupe English travelers, who nevertheless borrowed them. Henry Cook Todd's *Notes Upon Canada and the United States* offers a telling example. To illustrate the native skill of the legendary Yankee peddler, Todd reports that "one of those dealers honestly confessed to me, . . . 'I trust to *soft sawder* . . . for getting my clocks into a house, and to human *natur* for its staying there.'"[19] Despite the apparent folk authenticity of this, Todd had, in fact, added it to the second edition of his book in 1840, lifting the example and the aphorism, including the italics, from Thomas Chandler Haliburton's Sam Slick story "The Clockmaker," which had appeared in the *Novascotian* in 1835 and then in book form in 1836. Given the popularity in England of New England humor in general and of the Sam Slick stories in particular, one must wonder at the audacity of this kind of interpolation, but no English reviewer appears to have called the practice into question. Americans would, however.

Reading such stories in the pages of their own newspapers and magazines, Americans could enjoy them as indicative of a rustic, apparently native, genius, especially when that genius triumphed as it very often did over some starchy representative of the Old World, preferably an Englishman or Dutchman. But Americans took self-righteous umbrage when those same stories appeared in

English travel books and other publications as indicative of—as indictments of—the American character. John Neal, the inveterate defender of that character, took the issue to the offenders themselves in the pages of the London *Monthly Magazine* (Dec. 1826) in order to expose what he called the "strange errors" that prevailed in England "touching America and the people of America, and which have grown up out of the testimony of British travellers in America." According to Neal, one reason for such errors was that certain kinds of stories, "while they are either untrue in every part or greatly exaggerated, are reported by the Travellers in America, as if they know them to be true."

Only a few months earlier he had taken up the matter at greater length in another English publication, the *New Monthly Magazine and Literary Journal* (Sept. 1826), in an essay forthrightly titled "The Character of the Real Yankees; What They are Supposed to Be, and What They Are." The confusion about that character, Neal admitted here, had its origins at home. In America, except for New England, "the people of every state regard the people of every other place lying to the east or north of their own, either as already Yankees or as a sort of qualified Yankee." (It could be said that the belief is prevalent in the South today.) Also, he admitted, Yankees are notorious peddlers. Little wonder then, Neal suggested, that Europeans have much the same perception of New Englanders; and although some do "entertain a more favorable idea of the American character," he said that "in every case they confound it with the Yankee character."

That confusion, however, was closer to home than Neal acknowledged, for Americans too used the term *Yankee* and the peculiarities of character it represented in two very different, contradictory ways, given the all-compelling need for national self-assertion. As Cooper pointed out in *Notions of the Americans,* "The term has two significations among the Americans themselves, one of which may be called its national and the other its local meaning."[20] (In all fairness to British travelers, some of them made the same distinction.) In terms of its local meaning, New Englanders exulted in the title and thus found stories of Yankee ingenuity as evidence of regional superiority; Americans from other regions saw it as a term of reproach and no doubt enjoyed the same stories as evidence of that judgment. In the face of British use of those same stories as indictments of the American character, though, virtually all Americans adopted the national signification of *Yankee,* used the term, and defended it as stoutly as they did the national identity it stood for. Outside of the United States, Cooper says, "even the Georgian does not hesitate to call himself a Yankee. The Americans are particularly fond of distinguishing anything connected with their general enterprise, skill, or reputation by this term."

In addition to their interest in the American character, English observers were concerned about changes in the mother tongue that had taken place in the new nation, and they often saw in the speech of the rustic Yankee an indigenous language, but one indicative of what they considered a declension from proper English. In *Travels through Canada and the United States* (1816), John Lambert wrote a brief, humorous narrative made up of the "many curious phrases and quaint expressions" that he says he heard among New Englanders. The narrative device was a common one, and Lambert put it to a common use when he concluded, "Colloquial barbarisms like the above, among the peasantry of a country, are excusable, but when they are used in composition by writers, they become disgusting. I could collect hundreds of others equally absurd, which have been invented by Americans who are desirous of introducing what they call an *American language.*"[21]

Despite Lambert's initial claim that he "heard" such barbarisms, the examples in his narrative, his reference to their use by writers, and his claim that there are hundreds more that have been "invented" by Americans suggest that his sources may well have been more literary than oral. Americans of the time were every bit as eager, even anxious, about establishing a national language as Lambert's sarcastic italics would indicate. In the nationalistic enthusiasm following the Revolutionary War, "it was even seriously proposed to have a new language," James Russell Lowell wrote in the *North American Review* (1849). "The existing ones were all too small to contain our literature, whenever we should get it. One enthusiast suggested the ancient Hebrew, another a fine new tongue of his own invention." Enthusiasm for the cause did not diminish, but later Americans could rely on what had become a more indigenous basis for linguistic independence. The editors of the *Southern Literary Gazette* in 1828 called for a *"dialect of our own"*—ironically echoing Lambert—"a language as American . . . as the principles and opinions which it should embody."

To English readers, at least, New England humor provided that dialect in its characterization of the stereotypical common American man, the rustic Yankee, and they took it to be authentic. Many Americans, although they believed in the distinctiveness of an American language and could be amused by the literary dialect in New England humor, were uneasy when it was measured against conventional standards. British judgments in the matter aggravated their uneasiness. In an article titled "Yankeeisms" in the *New England Galaxy* (18 Nov. 1825), "Peter" struggled with exactly that dilemma: "We 'abrogate' provincialisms, but the boors of our back villages are the only true, unadulterated, uncontaminated pronouncers of our native English. . . . The facility of the press 'honours these corruptions' or improvements as the case may be." The piece is ostensibly an attempt to defend indigenous speech against aspersions—"We wish only to vindicate Yankee pronunciation against the laugh and jeer so often cast upon it"—and the words "unadulterated" and "uncontaminated" auger well for the cause of indigenous identity. In syntax and word choice, however, the author vacillates between lauding rustic speech as native and denigrating it as boorish. Even the quotation marks around the word "abrogate" suggest conflicting commitments: given the subject matter, do they apologize for the learned word or for the judgment it denotes? Certainly they draw attention to the word. And should the press be praised for honoring "improvements" or damned for fostering "corruptions"? With the qualifying phrase "as the case may be," "Peter" seems to acknowledge his quandary.

Whatever the case was, the press, in printing humorous stories of the rustic Yankee, did give currency to Yankee speech and other peculiarities that English travelers recorded as authentic. Joseph Buckingham, writing on "Yankeeisms" for the *New England Magazine* (Nov. 1832), objected to these British versions of American speech.[22] It was "somewhat amusing," he began, to read a book "professing to contain specimens of what the authors are pleased to consider Yankee dialect; that is, I presume, the customary use of language among the Americans." Among foreign writers, John Galt, Charles Mathews, and Mrs. Trollope were the chief offenders, and Buckingham was clearly no longer amused when he concluded that their distortions of the American language are "downright stupid lying and misrepresentations, and evince neither wit nor humor." Although Buckingham admits, as did "Peter," that the source of these misrepresentations lies close to home, there is no doubt in his mind whether the public press honored "improvements" or fostered "corruptions." His fervent words on the matter deserve to be quoted at length:

> Even some of our own writers do not seem to know when they have got to the proper limits of burlesque; but, as if there could not be too much of a good thing, cram into the mouth of one man, all the queer, cant phrases they ever heard, either at first or second hand, from all the uncouth fellows, idiots included, that they ever met with in the course of their lives, doubling the stock to boot out of their own invention, and send the crambo out to the world, as a caricature of Yankeeisms; witness, for instance, Joe Strickland and Enoch Timbertoes.

As editor of the *New England Galaxy* in the 1820s, Buckingham had guarded against the insidious influence of vernacular speech at home. The *Galaxy* (26 Oct. 1827) praised the calendar of the *Old Farmer's Almanac for 1828* as "a better thing than it has sometimes been, when it contained slang in a distorted dialect, intended for the yeomanry of New England." The almanac was widely read, the complaint continued, "and thus these vulgar, vile and cant words become to the farmer's family legitimate English." Yet at the same time, also as editor of the *Galaxy* in the 1820s, Buckingham had made that publication a veritable anthology of New England humor, including letters from Enoch Timbertoes, and he had fostered the popularity of Joe Strickland, whom he would later consider a "caricature of Yankeeisms." In doing so, he ignored the implications that such characterizations had upon an indigenous identity. British observers who took those characterizations as authentic (although one must wonder if they did so with knowingly malicious delight) made those implications clear, and the objections of Buckingham and other Americans indicate not only their sensitivity to English opinion but also their predilection for standards of taste and propriety inconsistent with the egalitarian identity that the rustic Yankee personified.[23]

Given the British interest in the American experience and their penchant for finding the character of the rustic Yankee illustrative of that experience, little wonder that British reviewers should see in New England humor and later in native American humor in general a source of information about America and praise that humor as an indigenous literary form. (Little wonder too that many Americans would be uneasy about British opinions on the subject.) In a review of Thomas Chandler Haliburton's two-volume anthology *Traits of American Humor* (1852), the *Irish Quarterly Review* (Mar. 1852) saw it as a way of learning something of the "manners, the domestic lives, and the various provincial dialects, as well as the humor of the Americans." An article in *Eliza Cook's Journal,* reprinted in the *Eclectic Magazine* (June 1855), thought American humor would provide "more accurate notions of the character of the people to whom it belongs than from the graver, which have a greater likeness to the books of the old world," and further saw American humor as "a department of the national literature quite distinct from anything we have in Europe."

Interest in a native American speech in particular had always been high among the English, and as we have seen, the New England Yankee provided a lingo that they confidently assumed to be authentic. In his travel book-cum-novel, *The Stranger in America,* quoted at length in the *Quarterly Review* (Apr. 1838), F. Lieber predicted that the Charles Augustus Davis series of Jack Downing letters would be "a curiosity to the philologist some hundred years hence, when the true Yankee idiom will have given way, as all provincial languages in time do." A mere forty years later, another *Quarterly Review* article, reprinted in *Littel's Living Age* (16 Mar. 1867), praised the same book because it "provided us with the first authentic specimens of the wonderful tongue which forms the actual colloquial dialect of the United States." These observations lack the explicit sarcasm of earlier commentators, but sensitive as they were to English judgments, most Americans could not have been pleased with the condescending implications of certain words, such as "provincial," that British observers persistently used. To many Americans, such slang was not so much a reflection *of* the national character as it was a reflection *on* it. Timothy Flint for one tried earnestly to set the record straight. Writing in the British *Athenaeum* (4 July 1835), he told its readers that the "collection of phrases, which has recently figured so much under the name of the Downing dialect had had its day," and English travelers who expected to find it "the common speech of the people, would be surprised not to meet any trace of these ludicrous barbarisms." The Downing slang, and the Crockett too, were literary creations, "at least eight parts invented fiction to two parts which ever had real existence in the mouths of the people at large." The tenor of Flint's remarks are part of his larger effort in these "Sketches of the Literature of the United States" to defend America from "those English observers, who have been among us, and who have returned to attempt to degrade and vilify us at home, as wholly destitute, not only of literature, but a taste for it." Americans at large, he assured his English readers, not only spoke correctly but also had good taste.

Particularly exasperating to Americans was the popularity that the Sam Slick series of books enjoyed among English readers. The creation of a Nova Scotian judge, Thomas Chandler Haliburton, the many stories of the clockmaker and peddler, beginning with *The Clockmaker* in 1836, sold well enough on both sides of the Atlantic (there were also editions on the continent), but they sold best in England. According to Clarence Gohdes, "The enthusiasm for American humor in England was incited by the popularity of Sam Slick, and throughout the latter half of the century cheap reprints of his work were readily available."[24] But why so popular? Haliburton scholars have seen a direct link to English travel books: V. L. O. Chittick says that "Haliburton's peddler was to them [English readers] the living embodiment of all they had heard of America from the travel books of their countrymen," and little wonder, if Walter Avis is correct in concluding that Haliburton "seems to have been widely read in the writings of the numerous British travelers who had given much space to the quaint barbarisms of the colonial."[25] Certainly English reviewers saw the Sam Slick books as accurate a source of information as they assumed the travel books to be. To a reviewer in the London *Times* (27 Nov. 1840), the third series of *The Clockmaker* stories was even more reliable. "No modern book can give a better insight into the politics, prejudices, manner, modes of thinking and acting of the inhabitants of the United States than this." Other commentators felt much the same way. To *Bentley's Miscellany* (Mar. 1843) the stories were "faithful transcripts of human nature in America," and a reviewer of *The Attaché* in *Chambers' Edinburgh Journal* (26 July 1843) elaborated on just what that human nature consisted of: "With all his shrewdness, and good as well as broad humor," Sam Slick was "a thorough American, imbued with an unconquerable conviction [quoting Sam] 'that a free and enlightened citizen of the United States is the best of the whole universe.'"[26]

American readers, however, might well have questioned the reasons behind the English fondness for Slick as the representative American, for Haliburton, a Tory of the oldest school, had made the Yankee an ironic caricature of the "free and enlightened" nation that Americans were so unpleasantly vain about, according to British observers. The *Times* reviewer of *The Clockmaker* stories saw that as yet another example of the accurate rendering of the American character. Sam Slick "has performed a most worthy office to them [the Americans] in holding up for their inspection and improvement a mirror in which are reflected all their absurdities, illiberality, nationalism, narrow-mindedness, and ignorance." Another review in the same newspaper (12 Dec. 1840) liked "the contrast between the clear-sighted way in which the American is made to view the ridiculous points of English democracy, and his total blindness of the kindred absurdities of the United States." These comments described precisely what Haliburton was up to in these books, especially *The Attaché* series, but most English reviewers dismissed the many political implications, giving their attention to what they considered its humor and its accurate delineation of American peculiarities.

For obvious reasons, Sam Slick was not so popular in the United States, although some reviewers seemed grateful for the kinder remarks of the British reviews.[27] The *Knickerbocker* (Oct. 1843) admitted that "many of his so-called *Yankeeisms* are only specimens of cockney dialect; yet he has more genuine wit than is to be found in all the 'down-east' letters which have been inflicted upon the public *ad nauseam* any time these three years," and *Harper's Magazine* (Apr. 1852) went as far as to say that "scarcely any native writer has succeeded better in giving what is termed the true Yankee dialect." Few would agree with the accuracy of the dialect, however, and many found Sam reprehensible in taste and politics and not at all authentic in either speech or character. C. C. Felton, writing in the influential *North American Review* (Jan. 1844), found the character of Sam Slick "badly conceived . . . an incongruous mixture of impossible eccentricities." Felton agreed to the presence of a certain wit, but he could not abide the dialect that pleased so many English readers. "His language is a ridiculous compound of provincial solecisms, extravagant figures, vulgarities drawn from distant sources, which can never meet in an individual, and a still greater variety of vulgar expressions which are simply and absolutely the coinage of the provincial writer's own brain." Felton had prefaced these observations with the premise that "Sam Slick is no proper representative of the Yankee," and he concluded them soundly with the judgment that Sam "has no organic life in him; that he is an impostor, an impossibility, a nonentity." James Russell Lowell agreed. Writing in the Introduction to *Biglow Papers, Second Series* in 1867, Lowell says, "I had always thought 'Sam Slick' a libel on the Yankee character, and a complete falsification of Yankee modes of speech." Later scholars have thought so too.[28]

Convinced as they were that New England humor faithfully recorded what they considered the authentically American experience, English reviewers hailed it as the first fruits of an indigenous literary tradition. The phrase "native American humor," which twentieth-century scholars have taken as their own, was in fact first used by a nineteenth-century English writer. The review in the April 1835 *Quarterly Review* of Davis's Downing letters observed that "since Washington Irving's delightful genius first revealed itself in the Knickerbocker, we have met with few specimens of native American *humour* calculated to make any very favorable impression on this side of the Atlantic, with none, in our humble opinion, approaching, by many degrees, to the merit of this homespun production." Other reviewers did not use the phrase "native American humor," but they clearly distinguished such "homespun productions" from those that seemed to derive from an English literary tradition.[29] (With many, Irving did not fare so well. In November 1837 a writer in *Blackwood's* saw in the humor of Sam Slick salvation from "the Washington Irving style, which to us tastes like a composition of treacle and water, sickly and sweet . . . and has utterly spoiled the viscera of American penmen.") Even as late as 1866, Leslie Stephen, writing in the *Cornhill Magazine* (Jan. 1866), saw most American literature as still imitative, but he concluded that the one distinctly original product of the American mind was American humor, "which has a flavour peculiar to itself. It smells of the soil, it is an indigenous home growth."

All of this was not to say that English reviewers thought that native American humor was good, that is to say respectable, literature, only that it did not imitate English example. Most reviews implied that distinction, but one in *Eliza Cook's Journal* (reprinted in the *Eclectic Magazine*, Sept. 1854) made it perfectly clear. "The Humor and the Fun of the United States *are* really national and original, but," it continued, "we cannot call this fun Wit, for it has no polish or refinement in it." In that distinction lay the dilemma for Americans of the age, for although they believed that a "national and original" literary tradition would prove at last their cultural independence, they had serious reservations about the very qualities that would make American literature native. "The vital principle of American national literature must be democracy," John O'Sullivan decreed in his *United States Magazine and Democratic Review* (1837), and Francis Parkman elaborated on that principle in the *North American Review* (Jan. 1852) in arguing that "with few exceptions, the only books which reflect the national mind are those which emanate from, or are adapted to, the unschooled classes of people." But for many other Americans, a literature founded on such principles was incompatible with standards of literary worth they found difficult to abandon, even for the cause of nationality.

Writing on "National Literature" in the *American Monthly Magazine* (1829), "P.Q." acknowledged the assumption that to create a native literary tradition "every page must be made to smack of the national character," which meant that "republicanism must peep out at every line, and the glories of popular institutions must be shouted to the skies. . . . These rules demand, in every American work, a copious admixture of American peculiarities." Popular literature, "the current literature of the day," did just that and was thus "national," but not only was that literature "limited, local, transient," but worse, the national peculiarities it contained were "in fact, only the peculiarities of the unpolished and uncouth." If P.Q.'s tone suggests that he would not be sympathetic to "republicanism" in any form, consider then Theodore Parker, whose liberal credentials as transcendentalist and abolitionist would appear sound enough. In his essay on Emerson in the *Massachusetts Quarterly Review* (Mar. 1850), Parker distinguished between "two grand divisions" of American literature, the "permanent" and the "transient." The former, he said, "is almost wholly an imitation of old models," and therefore "there is nothing American about it." "Transient" literature, on the other hand, "is commonly stronger and more American," but, he had to concede, "it is often coarse and crude. The permanent literature is imitative; the other is rowdy." In that conclusion, Parker succinctly expressed the dilemma felt earlier by "Peter" in writing about "Yankeeisms," and one might ask again, much as he had done, whether the popular press should be praised for proliferating "transient" literature that seemed to bear the unmistakable stamp of native "peculiarities" or damned because that literature was "crude and coarse." Newspapers, which proliferated New England humor, tended to laud it for the apparently native genius it represented, but the more learned journals usually insisted on a higher standard of taste and indigenous achievement. "Is there an American school of writers?" E. W. Johnson asked in the *American Whig Review* (June 1845). "None," he answered, "unless they who degrade and vulgarize the tongue and taste of the country by performances, the whole merit of which consists in their adoption of particular local slang (such as was employed in Major Downing's letters, or in the lucubrations of Sam Slick) are the models of a new and noble literature that is to be for us." New England humor, represented so well by the characterizations of Jack Downing and Sam Slick, undeniably was "new" enough, but it was not "noble" at all. Nor could those literally on the frontier of American culture avoid such distinctions. According to a reviewer in the Cincinnati-based *Western Monthly* in 1835, "The Jack Downing and David Crockett taste, which has been gaining favor even in polite circles, for several years past, is one which should not be encouraged; and we think it far from creditable to the nation, that it has so far been introduced into our literature, as to be spread through the newspapers and periodicals."[30]

Time and again between the Revolutionary War and the Civil War, Americans deplored any semblance of deference to British opinion, berating themselves for it as inconsistent with the complete independence they had so long and so fervently sought. "Why do we, like an overgrown booby, persist in remaining tied to her apron strings?" asked the *New England Magazine* (Nov. 1834) in an essay titled "English Strictures Upon this Country." The question seems aptly put, for in the American relationship with the parent country there was much that was adolescently ambivalent. As for the substance of the question—why indeed? One reason was that Americans were far too sensitive to a long history of British condescension that judged them as uncouth provincials and errant children. As early as 1779, Charles Brockden Brown had begun the

United States Magazine to promote native culture as a way of demonstrating that Americans were "not so many Ouran-Outans of the world" but "able to cultivate the *belles-lettres,* even disconnected with Great Britain." In subsequent years, that motive would call forth many efforts in many forms.

The second war of independence invigorated the national self-confidence and self-consciousness, yet Americans were no less sensitive to British opinions, especially when they seemed to be aspersions cast against what British observers too often implied were the unsavory effects of the "new, peculiar" democratic institutions that had become the touchstone for measuring the native integrity of the American experience. At heart, though, Americans had persistently nagging doubts about those institutions, and certainly about the pervasive egalitarianism that indigenous identity made requisite. Above all, in aesthetic matters they were not comfortable with a scale of values derived wholly from and thus embodying that identifying egalitarianism. At the same time, however, the nationalistic imperative made it difficult to acknowledge an implicit commitment to genteel, Old World standards of taste.

"'America is stuck with its self-definition put on paper in 1776, and that was just like putting a burr under the metaphysical saddle in America—you see, that saddle's going to jump now and then and it pricks,'" Louis Rubin writes, quoting Robert Penn Warren. Rubin finds here, in this "discomfort," what he considers "The Great American Joke": "The contrast, the incongruity between the ideal and the real, in which a common, vernacular metaphor is used to put a somewhat abstract statement involving values—self-definition, metaphysical—into a homely context."[31] New England humor, in fact a national humor, did not resolve this dilemma in the nineteenth century, but it brought together the irreconcilable alternatives, and relieved in laughter, if only momentarily, the tensions, the "discomfort," they generated.

Chapter 2
Early American Humor

"The palm of wit has been unjustifiably withheld from our countrymen by foreigners," complained the editor of *The Chaplet of Comus,* a collection of humor published in Boston in 1811, "and even some of our own writers have intimated that no good thing of a humorous kind can come out of New England." And although the patriotic editor promised "more specimens of American *humor* than in any other publication," he padded his anthology with anecdotes about Samuel Johnson. Sensitive as they were to foreign fault finding when it came to native achievements, Americans had, in fact, not considered an American humor as particularly significant to their general concern for the cultural independence that would justify what had been won politically.

True, jest books may not be the best place to expect this. Although they were not mere imitations of English jest books, a recent scholar seeking to correct an earlier judgment that they were concedes a high degree of borrowing and imitation: "An American jest book does not imply a book of particularly American humor. On the average, for every story with an American setting in these books, there are two or three more properly located in Great Britain."[1] Much the same is true of the humor in early almanacs. In his fine anthology and commentary on the subject, Robert Dodge says that few of the stories "had yet gone through the process of Americanization," that Americans unsatisfied with "jokes about English people and places . . . had to find their own characters to apply the stories to." He devotes a chapter to the rustic New Englander but says there was "seldom a specifically Yankee type to unify the body of almanac stories. Rather, the almanacs seem to present a body of stories waiting for a hero."[2]

That would change after the War of 1812, called forth by the nationalism of that war and democratic identity, when a tradition in the truest sense began: numerous examples and diverse ones, but with common, identifiable conventions that were widely circulated and imitated, generating further development of the tradition. Those conventions originated in the humor between the Revolutionary War and the War of 1812, what I call early New England humor:

"Yankee Doodle," *The Contrast,* and Federalist mock pastorals. These were not written to contribute consciously to an indigenous humor, but they did respond to newly national cultural and political conditions, and they were available to humorists of the later tradition. Still earlier, colonial humor was not available to later writers, but it shows an evolving American consciousness of New World experience and ways of expressing it humorously that clearly prefigure the conventions and the political and cultural concerns of the New England tradition.

Colonial American Humor

The earliest colonial humor recorded the provincial-New World, urbane-Old World contrast so central to native American humor, to much American literature, really. Nathaniel Ward's *The Simple Cobler of Aggawam in America* in 1647 had English literary origins and satiric intent, but the title identified the speaker as a humble provincial, and one, as the contents made clear, who spoke with comic audacity of mending "his Native Country, lamentably tattered, both in the upper-Leather and sole, with all the honest stiches he can take."[3] In the seventeenth century, only one book could compare with Ward's in "mirthful, grotesque, and slashing energy," according to Moses Coit Tyler[4]—George Alsop's 1666 humorous promotional tract, *A Character of the Province of Mary-Land.* In it Alsop exploited to the hilt the comically satiric contrasts between Old World and New—the geography, its native Indians, the character of the colonists—with England the butt of the fun. Although uncouth outlanders, for example, Marylanders are shrewd enough to take in the better bred sons of the mother country. "Alsop used America as a satiric device in ridiculing England," W. Howland Kenney writes. "From the hardened and hardy colonists, living among seven-foot-tall Indian giants in harmonious, industrious plenty, we look back to a cowardly, overcrowded and foppish England, too torn by war and ignorance to realize the possibilities of her own colonies."[5]

Based on much the same contrasts as Alsop's work, but something of an antipromotional tract, is Ebenezer Cooke's *The Sotweed Factor* in 1708. In it an English sotweed factor (tobacco agent) reports a long and scurrilous catalog of New World, provincial peculiarities—"a whole menagerie of American types," Leo Lemay says: "The hard-drinking, illiterate planters, their sloppy and sluttish wives, the hypocritical religious Puritans, quack doctors and lawyers, half-tame Indians, drunken justices."[6] But are these the object of what the title admits is a "Satyr"? Or is the factor, who is so often the comic victim of frontier provincials and the vicissitudes of the frontier itself? According to Larzer Ziff, "The unspoken models of magistrate, yeoman or innkeeper against which the Marylanders are measured and found wanting are, clearly, to be located in England," whereas to Lemay—and other scholars lean to varying degrees in the same direction—the poem satirizes English assumptions of superiority to provincial life and character.[7] More important and less arguable (more important and less arguable too than whether Cooke and Alsop are "American" or "English" writers) is that both writers identified certain provincial, New World peculiarities of character, behavior, and geography and contrasted them humorously to English experience.

Benjamin Franklin gave those contrasts a new direction, one that anticipated even more clearly the later tradition, by turning them inward to colonial concerns and thus giving them new political meaning, with provincial characteristics coming to stand for what we would now call democratic ones. Only sixteen and submitting his Silence Dogood letters anonymously to his brother's Boston newspaper, the *New England Courant,* in 1722, Franklin drew his New England widow with literary skill and an understanding of human nature that belied his years. Silence Dogood is a complex, round character whom the young apprentice printer not only used for specific political satire but also explored the many dimensions of.

In the tradition of many an eighteenth-century heroine, Silence had married her master, but only after he had "made several unsuccessful, fruitless Attempts on the more topping Sort of our Sex."[8] Franklin's acumen about human nature and his ability to delineate it in literature are clear in the widow's self-satisfied, underlying assumption here: only a homespun, honestly plain woman such as herself is suitable for marriage after the more "topping" kind have been sampled. At the same time, though, she unconsciously reveals that she appeals only to a man who does not appeal to, who has been rejected by, more topping women.

For the purposes of political satire, the rural New England widow is a democrat, a self-proclaimed "mortal Enemy to arbitrary Government & unlimited Power," and the least encroachment was apt to make her "blood boil exceedingly." She is the enemy too of corrupting luxury, pretentious manners, and useless learning, all of these political targets represented by the Boston establishment of the Mathers but also appropriate to the countrified democrat that Franklin had created. Also, albeit stereotypically, the New England widow is far from silent, for she has "a natural Inclination to observe and reprove the

Faults of others, at which I have an excellent Faculty." That inclination is appropriate to her satiric role, but at one also with her family name, derived from Cotton Mather's popular *Essays to Do Good* (1722). That Dogood is her *married* name also connects her to the Mather family with comic irony, given her anti-establishment proclivities and the sexual ones of her late husband.[9]

Franklin, however, was interested not only in the political purposes the rustic persona might serve with her homespun, honest opinions but also in the humorous possibilities of the rustic as an *ironic* persona. In what has become the most often reprinted of the Dogood letters (the seventh), Silence takes up the complaint among foreigners that "good poetry is not to be expected in New England." In doing so, she takes on a decidedly American role, but then Silence herself unwittingly reveals the reason for the dearth of worthy literature by praising so highly and analyzing in such detail a patently bad elegy. A typical stanza reads as follows: "Come let us mourn, for we have lost a Wife, a Daughter, and a Sister, / Who has lately taken Flight, and greatly we have mist her." The widow's "I will leave your Readers to judge, if ever they read any Lines, that would sooner make them *draw their Breath* and Sigh, if not shed Tears" is the ironic persona at its best, the words of the persona coming as close as they can get to being those of the writer, but with very different meanings. To aid colonial poets, she concludes by sharing "A RECEIPT to make a New England Funeral ELEGY," an appropriate gesture for the homey widow who blithely assumes that rendering deep emotion into verse is as easy as, well, pie.

This letter is reprinted often today because the characterization is so complete and the satiric point so universal, given that homespun elegies still endure in daily newspapers. The judgment of the untutored philosopher, however, is not consistent with her typical political stance—learning here does have value—but perhaps young Franklin wanted to show that he knew the difference between literary gold and dross, even if his rustic persona did not. Although warned against becoming a poet, he had literary inclinations that could not be gainsaid. Taken together, Franklin's "Silence Dogood Papers" rank with the best colonial humor, not because he first turned the earlier contrasts inward and made them "American," nor because he followed English models less assiduously than had Alsop or Cooke, but because he wrote so well.[10]

As good as they are, though, as sharply as they prefigure the later tradition of the Yankee cracker-barrel philosopher—nothing so good, so complete, would appear until the 1820s—they were not known to writers then; nor was the remarkable work of another colonial writer of early cracker-barrel humor, John Adams. A future president, Adams struggled, as had Franklin, with an early inclination to write verse: "Law and not Poetry, is to be the Business of my Life," he admonished himself in his diary in 1760.[11] Prose satire better satisfied that inclination, and his first published work was a letter by a barely literate New England farmer, Humphrey Ploughjogger, published in the *Boston Evening-Post* (14 Mar. 1763). Five more letters appeared in Boston newspapers over the next four years, as Humphrey offered his opinion on a variety of political and social issues.[12]

With Ploughjogger's phonetic dialect, Adams went further than Franklin had in representing vernacular speech and thought in print. "I Arnt book larnt enuff, to rite so polytly, as the great gentlefolks, that rite in the News-Papers, about Pollyticks," he says, but there is more real principle in his low speech than in the "high-flown Words" of more learned correspondents. That distinction sets up other contrasts of value. In the city for the first time in fifteen years, the bucolic Humphrey finds "grate alterashons both in the plase and peple, the grate men dus nothin but quaril with one anuther and put peces in the nues paper aginst one anuther." In contrast, life in the country is simpler and more virtuous: "There is not hafe such bad work amungst us when we are a goin to ordane a ministur as ther is amungst these grate Fokes," he says, and observes that "Bostun peple are grone dedly proud" in dress in contrast to back-home and down-home modesty.

With a letter in 1765 and two in 1767, Adams charged that conventional urban-rural contrast with new meaning in resurrecting the rustic Yankee to speak out on the Stamp Act and its subsequent political implications. In his influential "Braintree Instructions" of 1765, Adams had argued learnedly that the tax was unconstitutional and economically burdensome, but with the words of Ploughjogger, he made the arguments more down-to-earth. To Governor Francis Bernard's dire predictions that trade would cease if custom-houses closed for lack of stamped paper, for example, Humphrey responded with a brand of patriotism that had its home in rural virtues:

[Trade] only makes rum and such things cheap, and so makes folks drink toddy and flip instead of cyder, when they an't half so good and holsome—and it makes us all beaus, and dresses us up fine—We got into a way on't o late,—our young men buy them blue surtouts, with fine yellow buttons and boughton broad cloth coats jackets and breeches—and our young women wear calicoes, chinces and laces, and other nicknacks to make them fine—But the naughty jacks and trollops must leave off such vanity, and go to nitting and spinning—

Adams's letter was not only reprinted in a New Hampshire paper but also inspired a response in kind by a "Jeffrey Snob, Esq."[13]

In the last two letters, Humphrey added his voice to the many critics of "Philanthrop" (Adams's friend Jonathan Sewall), whose letters defended Bernard's position on the Stamp Act. The Yankee farmer reduces to absurdity the notion that those who attacked the governor would, in Philanthrop's words the Yankee quotes, "induce contempt in the minds of the People" for authority. And when Philanthrop refused to acknowledge him, the democratically inclined Ploughjogger broadened the political implications of the issue with the reproach that "the poor Man's Council is always despised by the great and larned." (Playing upon the word "poor," Adams then cleverly reversed the argument with Humphrey's concern that the controversy "seems to have made the poor Man a most crazey.") Ploughjogger concludes the letter with two illustrative anecdotes taken from his on-the-farm experience, homey parables that entertain while they instruct, as later cracker-barrel philosophers would find.

John Adams's Humphrey Ploughjogger letters are a significant departure from the humor of the time. In contrast to other essayists, "whose use of the rustic signature was little more than a ruse to mask their identity," Helen Saltman says—and, I would add, more in the English tradition—"Adams creates a well-rounded character. Adams's use of New England dialect and phonetic spelling for political satire anticipates later writing in the tradition of American humor."[14]

Colonial satire writers over the years relied less and less on English models for their humor and tried their hand at a rustic character that represented a way of life different from that of the mother country—still a provincial way of life, but one increasingly thought of as "American." That character was not wholly or consistently an affirmation of American experience, however. As Kenney says, satire is "always a double-edged weapon," and in reference to Alsop and Cooke he concludes that the "democratic satire of British ineptitude in the wilderness was implied but overshadowed by the initially stronger desire to discredit new world barbarities. The early tendency was to ridicule the extent to which the colonists fell short of being British."[15]

The point is well taken but needs to be taken further. Franklin's seventh Silence Dogood letter, the recipe for an elegy, pokes fun at not just the Yankee widow's rustic taste in literature but also the tacit assumption that "bad" literature, by aesthetic standards implicitly British, is somehow "good" if it is indigenous. As for Humphrey Ploughjogger, he speaks contemptuously of "high-flown Words," but his usage ameliorates over the letters, he becomes increasingly self-important, and he draws attention to the fact that he spells "better and better." Compared to his first letter, his last is nearly standard English. Helen Saltman suggests that in the later letters, Adams was too well known as Ploughjogger, "or he may have wanted to argue from a more elevated position."[16] Or there may be no "or" about it: self-conscious about being known as Humphrey Ploughjogger, Adams wanted to make the Yankee more like *him*. As did Benjamin Franklin, John Adams recognized the limitations of the rustic persona and made them a part of the characterization itself. Their humor reflects a way of thinking, a sensibility that was increasingly American. They followed English models less slavishly than had Alsop and Cooke—Franklin and Adams can be read today with only historical, not literary, footnotes—and they created a characterization consistent with an American identity. That what they wrote was not known to writers of the later tradition of native humor is less significant, ultimately, than the fact that they anticipated so clearly not only the conventions of that tradition but also the dilemma inherent in it.

"Yankee Doodle"

Surveying American humor before 1775, Walter Blair writes, "As its history reveals, the process of recognition by American writers of the literary possibilities of native characters was a lengthy one and also a fairly complicated one. . . . Though some evidence concerning the process is no longer discoverable, enough evidence exists to point to a process of the sort one would expect—a slow accretion of details until at last native figures came to be generally regarded."[17] The recent resurrection of Adams's Ploughjogger letters, along with Richard Beale Davis's discovery of unpublished Southern humor in the same vein,[18] tends to substantiate rather than contradict Blair's notion of a "slow accretion of details." The Revolution quickened that process, but there was no revolution, really, in American humor.

The works I call "early New England humor" are transitional, a bridge between colonial humor and the New England tradition that began after the War of 1812. From origins in British and American colonial history and popular literature, "Yankee Doodle" became the most popular song of the Revolution and figured in Royall Tyler's play *The Contrast* in 1787, which provided literary precedent for the mock pastorals of Tyler's Federalist literary and political circle. From this early New England humor evolved the New England rustic Yankee as an identifiable type that would be "generally regarded" as the representative American, a characterization that would embody both the hopes and apprehensions of the American experience.

A regional type that came to have national significance, the literary Yankee evolved from the various versions of "Yankee Doodle," a song that antedated the Revolution. That conflict popularized the song first among British soldiers and then among Americans, and both adapted it to their respective causes.[19] At first it was "a song composed in derision of the New Englanders, scornfully called Yankees," according to William Gordon in a "letter" dated April 1775,[20] but with the Battle of Bunker Hill in June of that year, the name "Yankee" and the song became identified with the American cause. "The name [Yankee] has been more prevalent since the commencement of hostilities," Thomas Anburey wrote in 1777. "The soldiers at Boston used it as a term of reproach, but after the affair at Bunker's Hill the Americans gloried in it. *Yankee Doodle* is now their favorite paean, a favorite of favorites, played in the army, esteemed as warlike as the Grenadier's March—it is the lover's spell, the nurse's lullaby."[21]

Like many Revolutionary War songs, English and American versions of "Yankee Doodle" made use of the age-old contrast between New World provincialism and Old World sophistication. Written after the American siege of Quebec, the British "A New Song to the Tune *Yankee Doodle*," in the *Bath Chronicle* (21 Nov. 1776), satirizes the lowly origins of American officers, called "Yankee leaders," in contrast to the elite, formally trained British officers. Benedict Arnold (not yet a traitor) is as brave a man "as ever dealt in horses," the British song begins, "and now commands a numerous clan / Of New-England Jack-asses." By the end of the third stanza, Arnold is exposed as a coward, as is Nathaniel Greene, "a blacksmith by his trade, Sir; / . . . Tho' he's a Colonel made, Sir." Other American officers comically vow to treat the English in ways appropriate to their prewar trades: the butcher Jophen says he will flay them alive; the tanner Ogden promises to tan their hides; Gullege, a cobbler, swears by his shoes to leave none alive; and Thayer, a barber, says he will shave them alive. The concluding stanza condemns them all soundly, yet admits to some frustration on the part of the British:

> 'Tis thus, my friends, we are beset,
>   By all those d——n'd invaders;
> No greater villains ever met,
>   Than are those Yankey leaders.

Another British version, "Yankee Doodle's Expedition to Rhode Island," published in Tory James Rivington's *Royal Gazette* (3 Oct. 1778), also ridicules the Continental army's lack of Old World polish, describing the Americans as "a tattr'd crew" and "a swarm of Rebels and of fleas, / And every other vermin," whose spirits, in the face of British strength, must be bolstered by large quantities of "Yankee Rum." The song also represents one of the earliest published uses of the name *Jonathan* to designate satirically those who fought in the American cause. Americans did not adopt *Jonathan* (or *Brother Jonathan*) as quickly as they did *Yankee*, but they responded as readily to English attacks in song as they did to those in battle. "The Dance," printed in 1781, follows the metrical form of "Yankee Doodle" and gives the American side of the New World-Old World contrast, deriding as it does the formal military tactics and handsome uniforms of the English army as comically inappropriate to American frontier terrain and soldiering:

> Though men so gallant ne'er were seen,
>   While sauntering on parade, sir,
> Wiggling o'er the park's smooth green,
>   Or at a masquerade, sir.
> Yet are red heels and long-laced shirts
>   For stumps and briars meet, sir?
> Or stand they chance with hunting shirts
>   Or hardy veteran feet, sir?[22]

Several years later, after the decisive battle against the British at New Orleans, Americans again exploited the contrast to their advantage in the most popular song to come out of the War of 1812, "The Hunters of Kentucky."[23]

Other American versions of "Yankee Doodle" became popular during or shortly after the Revolution but deal with more general topics. "Yankee Doodle, or (As now Christened by the Saints of New England) the Lexington March," has nothing to do with the war except for the title. The lack of any references to the war, the unrelated stanzas, and the obscure sense of many lines would indicate that the verses predate the Revolution and that it is a compilation from more than one, possibly folk, source.[24] Together the verses evoke various aspects of rural New England life, at times with comic intent. Pumpkin pie, a sugar dram sweetened with molasses, and Apple Lantern are straightforward enough, but a "pinch of snuff and a drink of water" described as a "Yanky's supper" must be a comic allusion to New England parsimony. Certainly the lines (expurgated in the Sonneck facsimile) "Two and two may go to Bed, / Two and two together, / And if there is not room enough, / Lie one on atop o'to'ther" indicate a ribald attitude toward bundling. That same spirit also inspires the racy version of the Yankee's visit to the city in the admonition "Do not let the Boston wags, / Feel your Oyster Basket." Although some of the lines are not very complimentary about rural New England ways, there is no reason to assume that these verses were the work of a British officer intent on ridiculing American troops, as nineteenth-century commentators were wont to argue about early versions of "Yankee Doodle." "The Lexington March" does poke some good-natured fun at the New England rustic character and life, but Americans themselves, New Englanders among them, enjoyed poking just that kind of fun at curious rustic Yankee ways.

What appear as only disparate hints of comic possibilities in "Lexington March" are made manifest in what became the most popular, and the "standard," version of "Yankee Doodle," variously titled "The Yankey's [or Yankees] Return from Camp," "The Yankey's Return to Camp," and "The Farmer and His Son's Return from a Visit to Camp."[25] Like "The Lexington March," this version evokes aspects of New England rural life in general and shares some specific similarities, as in comparing the size of a fiddle to a hog trough. The "Visit to Camp" stanzas, though, have a clear narrative—a story with a beginning, middle, and end—and they develop a single characterization of a comic rustic Yankee related unmistakably to the humorous Yankees in the later tradition of New England humor. Central to the humor is the rustic Yankee's account of a military camp. An awed naïf, he has never seen things of such kind and number, and measured by his narrow perspective, everyone at the camp seems rich and extravagant to the point of wasting more than most people have—at least the people he knows. The folks at the camp eat enough molasses every day to last a country household all winter, he observes, and they do not save it for special occasions but "eat it when they're amind to." This is not the point of view of the superior Yankee moralist condemning excess and profligacy; the humor here, as in so much of the song, resides in the rustic's attempt to find some kind of understanding of a world that overwhelms him, and does so with comical consequences.

Much of the humor in that attempt is verbal. The Yankee describes all of the sights in a quasi-New England vernacular, for although words such as "nation," "tarnal," "deuc'd," "pockily," and "snarl" and contractions such as "on't" are not exclusively New England usages, they all became part of a conventional Down East vocabulary that authentic or not, was humorous in the nineteenth century. Other descriptive words reflect his rural origins in other ways. The crowd of men and boys, for example, is "as thick as hasty pudding," and a gun is as "large as a log of maple." The most entertaining source of verbal humor is the Yankee rustic's description of what he sees but does not understand. Struggling to use the vocabulary of his familiar rural world to describe the unfamiliar world of the military camp in phrases such as a "crooked stabbing iron" and a "pamkin [pumpkin] shell as big as mother's basin," the Yankee comically conflates two fundamentally incompatible realms of life, rural domesticity and militarism. In turn, his metaphors become riddles for the reader to interpret as a bayonet and a mortar—or is it a cannon? An elaborate example of this kind of humor is the Yankee's description of a drum, which extends the metaphor into a comic conceit:

> I see a little barrel too,
> The heads were made of leather,
> They knock'd upon't with little clubs
> And call'd the folks together.

These figures of speech, humorous in themselves, also characterize the Yankee narrator as hopelessly and, for the reader, comically naïve. Overwhelmed by a world he does not understand and cannot make comprehensible, the rustic becomes the comic victim of that world at the climax of the narrative. Told that the "long graves" the soldiers are digging are for him, he retreats to his country home, and we find him there, in the last stanza, "lock'd up in mother's chamber."

Although an "American" version of the song, this text portrays the rustic Yankee with comic condescension, creating humor at the expense of his innocence of a world beyond his own rural ken and kin as well as at his inept attempts to make some sense of that world. Humor of this sort was not new to the American literary experience—it looks back, for example, to Ebenezer Cooke's *Sotweed Factor* and to Franklin's "recipe" for a New England elegy in the Silence Dogood letters—but with its embodiment in the character of the rustic Yankee in the "Visit to Camp" version of "Yankee Doodle," we find unmistakable beginnings of the New England humor tradition.

The Contrast

By the early nineteenth century, "Yankee Doodle" had become a truly national air, a popular vehicle for expressing the pugnacious nationalism inspired by the War of 1812. Through the end of the eighteenth century, however, the song and the characterization of the comic rustic Yankee were the literary property of Federalist writers. These writers portrayed the rustic Yankee in the tradition of the comic naïf of the "Visit to Camp," with condescending amusement, as did Royall Tyler in *The Contrast* and Thomas Green Fessenden in "The Country Lovers." In other works, however, they went further, caricaturing rustic Yankee speech as barbaric and the vernacular figure himself as the personification of the American common man in whom Jeffersonians placed the democratic faith that these Federalists abhorred.

Royall Tyler's delineation of Jonathan in *The Contrast*, produced in 1787, is not merely the best characterization of the comic Yankee before 1815 but one of the best in the tradition of New England humor as a whole. F. O. Matthiessen called the play "the brightest comedy written by an American until the twentieth century," which, it must be confessed, may say something about the comedy written in the nineteenth century.[26] As with virtually all American writers of his time, Tyler's primary aim was to create a work of indigenous American literature, one based on native subjects and national themes (the play appeared in the same year as Joel Barlow's attempt to provide the country with an epic, *The Vision of Columbus*), and like these writers, Tyler used conventional, borrowed forms for literary representation of native materials. The plot and characterizations of *The Contrast* typify those of the eighteenth-century English comic drama, as do the thematic contrasts declared in the title. "It is only an adaptation, to fit the circumstances of a young republic, of the perennial concerns of social comedy—the differentiation of hypocrisy and sincerity, of surface and show and inner worth," writes G. Thomas Tanselle, Tyler's modern biographer.[27] Nevertheless, these perennial concerns served Tyler's nationalistic intent well, for he used them to represent in his play the dichotomy between Old World vice and New World, now "republican," American virtue.

The story of an American named Dimple illustrates the corrupting influence of Europe. Once a "ruddy youth who washed his face at the cistern every morning, and looked eternal love and constancy," Dimple was metamorphosed by his travel in Europe into "a flippant, palid, polite beau, who devotes the morning to his toilet, reads a few pages of Chesterfield's letters and then minces out, to put the infamous principles in practice upon every woman he meets."[28] The aptly named Colonel Manly, in contrast, is untraveled—it is his first time in a city—and his righteous condemnations of contemporary mores and fashions are to be seen as honest and unaffected. Thus the exemplar of American virtue in the play is Manly, not Jonathan, as many scholars today would have it. In the *New York Journal* (19 Apr. 1787), an observer more contemporary to Tyler made no mistake: "The striking Contrast, in this piece, is between a person who had made his tour of Europe, studied the *bon ton*, with his *galloned* attendant . . . and an heroic, sentimental American Colonel, with his honest *waiting-man*."[29] By literary tradition, the Jonathan figure was a comic bumpkin, and Tyler's characterization is in that tradition[30]; by political inclination, Tyler judged the rustic Yankee in ways consistent with the Joseph Dennie circle of Federalist writers to which he belonged. In his study of that circle, Harold Ellis writes, "The typical Yankee farmer or trader, the Jonathan of Royall Tyler's *The Contrast*, shrewd and honest often unlettered and uncouth, whom as Uncle Sam or Brother Jonathan we have adopted as our national prototype, represented to Dennie nearly all the evils of American life which he desired to eradicate."[31]

In *The Contrast,* Jonathan is at times brave and stoutly independent, but most of the time Tyler makes us laugh at his bucolic ignorance of urban life, his descriptions of it, his wholehearted acceptance of fashionable norms, and his general lack of sophistication and refinement. He willingly accepts the instructions of Jessamy, Dimple's valet, on how to court the servant girl Jenny according to the modern standards of "gallantry," as Jessamy puts it. Jonathan's misunderstanding of the word as "girl huntry" may well suggest a subtle satire of sophisticated courtship, but the satire is unconscious on the part of the Yankee, for Jonathan himself stoops to fashionable folly. In courting Jenny, he must talk as much as he can about "hearts, darts, flames, nectar and ambrosia—the more incoherent the better," Jessamy instructs him, but Jonathan's rendering is crudely countrified. Rushing to Jenny and kissing her soundly, he shouts, "Burning rivers! cooling flames! red-hot roses! pig nuts! hasty-pudding and ambrosia!" Rebuffed with a slap from the city girl, Jonathan decides to return to the country life he knows. Certainly Tyler satirizes the artificiality of fashionably foreign courtship here, but Jonathan's behavior offers no acceptable alternative. Just as with Jessamy's efforts to coach him in the proper way to laugh, Jonathan willingly embraces the silliness and thus dramatizes comically the foolishness of doing so.

Tyler found humor not only in the inadequacies of the rustic in matters that require feeling and sensitivity, such as romance, but also in his ignorance of, and comic efforts to explain, things beyond his limited experience. In what must be *The Contrast's* most famous comic scene, Jonathan gives his account of unwittingly attending a play. Intending to see a knife-eating "hocus-pocus" man, Jonathan wanders instead into a theater in which *The School for Scandal* is being performed.[32] "So I went right in," he reports, "and they shewed me away, clean up to the garret, just like a meeting-house gallery. And so I saw a power of topping folks, all sitting round in little cabbins, 'just like father's corn cribs.'" His notion of what happens next is innocent to the point of thickheadedness. "They lifted up a great green cloth and let us look right into the next neighbor's house," he says, and reports the action of the play as though he had been watching a real family. This sort of humor is of course akin to the young Yankee's account of a military camp in "Yankee Doodle," which Jonathan quotes at one point. In various forms a rustic's description of a play, a ballet, or an art exhibition became a popular source of native humor in the nineteenth, and even the twentieth, century. For Tyler, however, as for many later writers, the situation also provided the opportunity to satirize the rural Yankee's narrow moralism. To Puritan Jonathan, the theater is "the shop where the devil hangs out the vanities of the world upon the tenterhooks of temptation," yet he eagerly seeks out the knife-eating man, and his comparison of the theater to a meetinghouse, like his comparison of a city girl (in fact, a prostitute) to the deacon's daughter back home, indicates that the difference between urban vice and rural virtue is much narrower than his simplistic rural morality supposes.

Throughout the play, Jonathan's attitudes and actions provide a humorous, thematic contrast to similar attitudes and actions on the part of Manly, and thus heighten Manly's position as the indigenous moral arbiter of the work. Like Jonathan, Manly has never been to a city, but he is not ignorant of or gullible about city life. He may not attend a play, and certainly not by accident, but he would know what one was; he would also know what a statue was and would not describe it as "two marble-stone men and a leaden horse that stands out in doors in all weathers," as his servant does. Manly would also have recognized a prostitute for what she was and not mistake her for a deacon's daughter; and above all, he would never ape the artificial fashions so central to the play's nationalistic theme. As a talented, if amateur, dramatist, Tyler effectively represented these contrasts not only in actions but in speech. To the modern ear, certainly, Manly's moralistic pronouncements sound stiffly formal and artificial, but that does not mean, as has often been contended, that Tyler satirizes Manly, the one character in the play he most closely resembles. Like Manly, Tyler served as an American officer who participated in quelling Shays's Rebellion, a service that brought him also for the first time to fashionable New York less than a month before he wrote *The Contrast.* Moreover, as Frederick Tupper writes, Tyler's style in "moments of stately eloquence or of high morality . . . is straightway vitiated by all the artificialities of the stilted contemporary jargon."[33] Jonathan's colloquialisms, countrified analogies, and malapropisms offer no satisfactory alternatives in Tyler's play. They are more exaggerated than the pithy slang of Van Rough, and Jonathan's lingo is as outlandishly unrefined and laughable as Jessamy's is refined and laughable. For Tyler, rustic speech and the rustic point of view were not appropriate to the national seriousness that was the raison d'être of his comedy.

Federalist Mock Pastorals

Judged by theater standards of the time, five performances of *The Contrast* within a month in New York, followed by performances in other cities, must be considered a success. Other plays with comic rustic Yankees appeared—such as *The Better Sort* (1788), *The Traveller's Return* (1796), and *Tears and Smiles* (1802)—but none delineate the character as fully or as well as Tyler's work.[34] Early New England humor found wider circulation in a different form in the 1790s with a series of humorous poems portraying love-struck Yankees and featuring rustic New England speech and customs. Except for the pioneering work of Jeanette Tandy's *Crackerbox Philosophers in American Wit and Humor* (1925), these poems have received little notice from twentieth-century scholars of New England humor. Yet Tandy correctly observed that "the New England rustic verse of the seventeen-nineties must be considered of equal importance with the early comedies in the formation and diffusion of the tradition of the comic Yankee."[35] Tandy, and others after her, called these poems "anti-Della Cruscan," linking them with the work of Joseph Dennie and his circle that parodied the florid poetic effusions of the Della Cruscan school, popularized in England by Robert Merry. These New England poems, however, differ in style, and more significantly, in intent from the anti-Della Cruscan efforts.[36] Differences in form are apparent in the following examples from (1) a Della Cruscan poem by Sarah Wentworth Morton, (2) an anti-Della Cruscan poem by Royall Tyler, and (3) a rustic Yankee courting poem by the pseudonymous "Tommy Squintum":

1

    Blest Poet! whose Eolian lyre
    Can wind the varied notes along,
    While the melodious Nine inspire
    The graceful elegance of song.
    Who now with Homer's strength can rise,
    Then with the polished Ovid move;
    Now swift as rapid Pindar flies,
    Then soft as Sappho's breath of love.

2

    O Thou, who with thy blue cerulean blaze,
    Hast circled Europe's brow with lovelorn praise;
    Whose magic pen its gelid lightening throws,
    Is now a sunbeam, now a fragrant rose.
    Child of the dappl'd spring, whose green delight
    Drinks, with her snow drop lips the dewy night.

3

    Ah *Rompa,* thou snug little jade,
    Come listen to *Tommy's* sweet strain,
    Art thou so insensibly made,
    That *Tommy* must praise thee in vain?
    Thine eyes like a dollar doth shine,
    Thy nose like a water-spout is,
    Thy lips are reder than wine,
    And sweeter than treacle to kiss.

Tyler's verse more clearly burlesques both the spirit and poetic conventions of the flowery "Boston style," as the American strain of Della Cruscanism was judged. The Yankee poem would seem more in the tradition of the mock pastorals of John Gay and, particularly, Robert Greene. Compare, for example, the following passage from Greene's "Doron's Ecologue, Joined with Carmella's":

    Thy lips resemble two cucumbers fair,
    Thy teeth like to the tusks of fattest swine;
    Thy speech is like the thunder of the air;
    Would God, thy toes, thy lips, and all were mine!

These distinctions are not merely reductive quibbles, for identifying differences in form is helpful in distinguishing meaningful differences in intent. In England the Della Cruscan controversy had ideological implications, for although his poems had only vaguely political import, Robert Merry, as a champion of the French

Revolution, aroused the ire of William Gifford, who dispatched Merry and his Della Cruscan coterie with the *Baviad* (1791) and the *Maviad* (1795). In America the flamboyant, bombastic style of Della Cruscanism appealed to a native penchant for expansive rhetoric that blurred political commitments. Federalists and republicans alike wrote Della Cruscan and anti-Della Cruscan poems, which appeared in the literary columns of the newspapers of both political parties.

Whereas the Della Cruscan poem provided an example of false taste that was both imitated and parodied without let or hindrance, the Federalist mock pastoral provided a much different poetic vehicle, one with latent potential for political satire for antidemocratic ideologues and cultural reactionaries. In the tradition of the English mock pastoral, the Yankee poems juxtaposed idealized rural life to the ostensibly "real" peculiarities but charged them with the potent symbolic meaning they had assumed in American politics and culture. These Federalists shared not at all the Jeffersonian faith that the laborers in the earth were God's chosen people, and they saw in the rebellions named for Shays, whiskey, and Fries ominous examples of agrarian mob politics. The long travails of the French Revolution in the 1790s intensified their fears and provided examples of rampant libertarianism, which Federalist writers lost no opportunity to equate with any form of political dissension in America. They were unable, Wilford Binkley says, "to distinguish frontier agrarianism from proletarianism *sans-coulottes.* So they railed futilely at the refusal of virile agrarians to submit complacently to the rule of their betters."[37]

In their mock pastorals, caricatures of low American Irishmen and Dutchmen also appeared as comic suitors, representative of the volatile, loutish, foreign-born constituency that unscrupulous democratic politicians could manipulate for their radical ends, but Federalist writers' most popular satiric figure was the rustic New England Yankee. These writers stood their Federalist ground against democratization in any form, and in part their poems provided a way of ridiculing the low speech that they feared would become the orthodox and indigenous idiom. True, they argued for a tradition of national letters distinct from the English, but they guarded against the inroads of democracy in cultural matters as vigorously as they did against those in political ones. Even Noah Webster, though a sound enough Federalist politically, went too far for many with the Americanisms authorized by his famous dictionary. In some poems offending usages are ridiculed as "provincial phrases," identified with italics, or explained in supercilious notes. The title of one mock pastoral, "Cant Phrases" (also titled "Yankee Phrases"), which appeared in more than a half-dozen newspapers, illustrates the concern.[38] A prefatory note to the poem in Dennie's *Port Folio* (12 Mar. 1803) complains specifically of an American propensity for proverbs: "This debasement of the dignity and eloquence of diction, is not less justly than humorously ridiculed by a Yankee bard who thus jeers the woeful insipidities of the simple style." And what was the "simple style"? According to Thomas Green Fessenden, it meant "exaggeration of thoughts expressed by colloquial barbarisms, mixed with occasional pomposity of diction."[39] Offending "meter mongers," as Fessenden called them, included Southey, Wordsworth, and Burns, who were surely no less suspect for their liberal political sentiments than for their literary innovations.

The firm line the Federalists drew between the ridiculous and the sublime in language can be illustrated by passages from two poems, both appearing, as if for that purpose, on the same page of Dennie's *The Eagle; or, Dartmouth Centinel* (25 Aug. 1774):

A Pastoral

    Florella, all blooming and fair,
        Thy cheeks red potatoes outshine,
    Thine eyes, like a wild-cat's, n'er flare,
        But diffuse "mellow lustre" divine.
    Thy limbs straight as hay-poles appear,
        And thy hand soft as soup grease to touch,
    Should I grasp, though you bid me forbear,
        I am sure I should squeeze it too much.

The Rural Beauty, A Village Ode

    Lift the window, lift it high—
        Who is she that's tripping by?
    It's my little sprightly Sue,
        With pouting lips and eye so blue,
    Dimpled cheek and cloven chin,
        Taper arms, and waist so thin,
    O'er her neck her tresses strewn,
        Curl'd by nature's hand alone.

The grotesque conceits of the first poem ironically mock the feelings and locutions promised by the title, "A Pastoral." There is no such mockery in (or of) "The Rural Beauty," by Royall Tyler. Although it also describes physical features of a bucolic young lady, that description is not comically grotesque, for it is rendered in an idiom that was, for these writers, sufficiently homespun but still properly decorous.

Although countrified language provided a target for satire, it served most often as a weapon for the Federalists's attack on the whole character of the common man—his customs and manners—as represented by the rustic Yankee. A conspicuous example of the technique appears in a different kind of poem, not a mock pastoral (untitled, in the *Port Folio,* 10 July 1802), in which a Southern slave enthusiastically anticipates the license he will enjoy under Jefferson's doctrine "dat all man's free alike are born." The dialect itself is intended to question that axiom of the democratic faith.[40] In the Yankee mock pastorals, dialect is used in much the same way, although the satiric intent is not so transparent. Typically in these poems, the rustic professes his feelings for a rural maid in terms appropriate to his earthy experience but therefore comically inappropriate to the higher sentiments usually associated with love.

Thomas Green Fessenden's "Peter Periwinkle, to Tabitha Towzer," in the *Farmer's Weekly Museum* (20 Aug. 1798), begins

My Tabitha Towzer is fair
  No guinea pig ever was neater,
Like a hackmatak slender and spare,
  And sweet as a musk rat, or sweeter!

Subsequent stanzas feature a similar rustic analysis of different parts of Tabitha's physiognomy. These bucolic figures of speech clash incongruously with the Yankee's rhetorical intention of expressing devotion and intense emotion, and the author of the poem evokes laughter at the Yankee's failure to perceive the discrepancy between what he thinks his words mean and what they mean to the reader. For example, not only does the rustic fail to see the contradiction in the comparison of "sweet" and "musk," but in his ignorance and passionate enthusiasm he compounds the travesty with the comparative "sweeter." In the course of the poem, these rude, ludicrous metaphors ultimately dehumanize the loved one, portraying her (to the reader, at least) as grotesque and unworthy of the conventional romantic effusion. That fact provided the subject for a reply to Peter, "Tabitha Towzer's *comic-tragic response* to Peter Periwinkle" in the *Farmer's Weekly Museum* the following week. As Tabitha puts it,

> Can the guinea pig's querulous squeak,
> > With Tabitha's converse compare?
> Does Peter the hakmatak seek,
> > To tell him the form of his fair?

Although her perspective is as earthy as Peter's, she has the good sense to question the appropriateness of his countrified conceits.[41]

Such metaphors were popular and facile, but some poems went beyond the limitations of that poetic device. In the anonymous "Jonathan to Jemima" (*Port Folio*, 15 May 1802), Jonathan voices his passion for Jemima as he surreptitiously watches her milk a cow.[42] His interest is clearly sexual.

> I look'd right at your cheek and chin,
> > And all from where your gown had fell,
> It made me think of fifty things . . .
> > But you won't like it if I tell.
> . . . .
> I wish that I had been a weed,
> > That almost to your bosom grew;
> Or if the cow's teat I had been,
> > Then should I have been press'd by you.

He nearly falls into a fit as he watches Jemima milk the cow's teats; he feels "all over," as he puts it in his rustic New England way, and he cannot sleep. He even attempts suicide, but with the rope around his neck, his practical, unromantic good sense triumphs over idealized romance, and he decides the girl is not worth it. The poem ends with his offer of a Yankee trade for her hand.

In characterization, narrative, and humor, "Jonathan to Jemima" goes beyond the limited opportunities of the foolish conceits of "Peter Periwinkle, to Tabitha

Towzer," "A Pastoral," and Tommy Squintum's "Ode to Rompa," but the judgment of rustic Yankee character and manners is no more endearing. A prefatory editorial note to the poem sheds some light on how it should be read. At first blush, the note appears genuinely uncertain about the poet's intent by suggesting that the lines "seem to sneer at the charming simplicity of Wordsworth's 'Lyrical Ballads.'" But, it adds, "whether this species of sarcasm, applied to the elegant work in question, be fair or not, the Editor [Joseph Dennie] will not now stay to settle; but will only add that the subsequent stanzas are very faithfully descriptive of *rustic* love in New England." Given the stanzas that follow, the irony of the ostensibly objective preface is clear: the poetic form, the language, and the characterization are hardly "elegant," and Jonathan, cast as the rustic pastoral lover overwhelmed with feeling, appears ludicrous and more comically ignoble than Peter Periwinkle or Tommy Squintum. Also, the apparent objectivity of the first part of the note seems to offer some assurance that the subject matter is accurately delineated, but given the content of the poem, that assurance actually underscores the poem's burlesque of "*rustic* love in New England," as the editor sarcastically designates it. Like the other Yankee mock pastorals, "Jonathan to Jemima" represents the Federalists' judgment of the *real* nature of those "cultivators of the earth" who were, according to Jeffersonian ideology, the salt of the earth as well.

Although not strictly a courting poem, Royall Tyler's "Ode Composed for the Fourth of July" in the *New Hampshire and Vermont Journal* (19 July 1796) goes further in cataloging rural New England customs and characterizations that appear to ring with authenticity:[43]

> Squeak the fife, and beat the drum,
> Independence Day is come!!
> Let the roasting pig be bled,
> Quick twist off the cockerel's head,
> Quickly rub the pewter platter,
> Heap the nutcakes, fried in batter.
> Set the cups, and beaker glass,
> The pumpkin, and the apple sauce;

> Send the keg to shop for brandy;
> Maple sugar we have handy.
> *Independent,* staggering Dick,
> A noggin mix of *swinging thick*;
> Sal, put on your russet skirt,
> Jotham, get your *boughten* shirt
> Today we dance to tiddle diddle.

Subsequent descriptions of staggering drunkenness and other excesses alone suggest that the poem is not "merely a lively injunction," as Walter Blair would have it, "to stock up on brandy, put on 'boughten clothes,' give Sambo, the fiddler, a drink and proceed to drink deeply and dance gaily."[44] The political intent of the poem seems unmistakable in the concluding lines:

> Come, here's the French—and Guillotine,
> And here is good 'Squire Gallatin,
> And here's each noisy Jacobin.
> Here's friend Madison so hearty,
> And here's confusion to the treaty.
> Come, one more swig to Southern Demos
> Who represent our brother negroes.
> Thus we drink and dance away,
> This glorious INDEPENDENT DAY!

Here Tyler invokes the specter of the French Revolution, drawing a parallel between it and the intemperate behavior of America's own homespun and boisterous Jacobins. This tactic, like the ironic toasts to Gallatin and Madison—staunch supporters of Jefferson's growing Democratic Republican party, which opposed the Jay Treaty—and the jibe at hypocritical Southern "Demos" were all conventional Federalist sallies in the American political wars of the mid-1790s.

More specifically, the poem must be read in terms of the long, impassioned political controversy aroused by the Jay Treaty with England, which reached President Washington for his signature in March 1795 and which was not fully implemented for more than a year. Each stage of the treaty's progress through the branches of government provoked petitions and demonstrations by republicans, actions Federalists perceived as the work of turbulent and seditious Jacobins acting under the influence of powerful French spirits. Violent anti-treaty protests erupted in major cities, but like other Democratic Republican—Federalist disputes, the issue in many respects reflected fundamental differences between agrarian and urban interests. The republican *Chronicle* of Boston persistently claimed that the "Country Brethren" represented a united, anti-treaty constituency; the Federalist *New Hampshire and Vermont Journal* just as persistently denied that was true in New Hampshire, but averred that in Connecticut it was the "low country members of the legislature who were generally averse to the treaty" (2 Feb. 1796).

The following story from the *Federal Orrery* (27 Aug. 1795) describes one of the more colorful protests, which took place in the rural village of Rye, New Hampshire, in August 1795.

> The TOWN of Rye, four miles from Portsmouth (N.H.) turned out last week, every man, woman and child in the Parish, to express *deliberately* and *legislatively* their sentiments on the treaty. After having given many brilliant specimens of popular eloquence, in the meeting-house, they adjourned to *Squire Quorum's* barnyard, where as an effigy of Mr. Jay, they erected a ten feet rail with a pair of *Stag's horns* affixed to it, emblematic of his political cuckholdom! They then capriciously saluted the pole with the most *convenient* implements in the yard; after which they stuck it full of pitch-pine knots, set fire to them, and danced around the blaze, singing the *Indian war-whoop.*

Amusing and harmless as the story may seem today, such behavior was deemed "contemptible" by the Exeter, New Hampshire, *Weekly Visitor,* which generally strove to be politically independent; staunchly Federalist newspapers reprinted the story without comment. The *New Hampshire and Vermont Journal* did not reprint it, but the editor surely counted on his readers' knowledge of events with the reference to "the petty town of shriveled Rye" as one of the few hotbeds of the anti-treaty feeling that could be found among the "Country Brethren" of New Hampshire (13 Oct. 1795).

These events provide the background for modern readers to understand the significance of the subtitle to Tyler's poem as it appeared in the *New Hampshire and Vermont Journal* and subsequently in many other Federalist newspapers: *"Calculated for the meridian of some country towns in Massachusetts, and Rye in New Hampshire."* (The Kennebec *Intelligencer* italicized only "some" and "Rye" in the subtitle.) Written as it is for the Fourth of July, 1796, shortly after the treaty had been fully implemented, the poem is a celebratory satire of events that had begun a year earlier. When the substance of the treaty, which the president had tried to keep secret, was published in the republican *Aurora* in Philadelphia late in June 1795, republicans made the celebration of the Fourth of July that year the occasion for initiating the year-long anti-treaty, anti-Federalist protests. In dozens of localities, Jay was hung in effigy and speeches were made against the treaty, much as described in the concluding lines of Tyler's poem. Although it was published in July 1796, Tyler's "Ode Composed for the Fourth of July" recalls the events of the Fourth of July 1795, looks back upon the events of a year that had begun so ominously for Federalists, and stands as a triumphant, satiric summary of those events.

The most prolific Federalist writer of poems satirizing New England customs and character was Thomas Green Fessenden, whose *Original Poems* (1806) contains mock pastorals of various kinds, most of them published earlier in different forms. The best and most popular of these—the best and most popular of any Yankee mock pastoral—is "The Country Lovers," which appeared in broadside form (as "Jonathan's Courtship") as early as 1795 and which was subsequently reprinted in newspapers, almanacs, and broadsides; the longer version in *Original Poems* was reprinted into the nineteenth century.[45] As Nathaniel Hawthorne put it in an essay on Fessenden in the *American Monthly Magazine* (Jan. 1838), "The effort in question met with unexpected success; it ran through the newspapers of the day, reappeared on the other side of the Atlantic, and was warmly applauded by the English critics, nor has it yet lost its popularity." That persistent popularity was bolstered by the fact that by 1838 the comedy of Yankee courtship had become one of the major conventions of native humor in the New England tradition in print and on stage, but the poem's popularity owes much to Fessenden's artful rendering of the subject as well. "The Country Lovers" is longer than the other Federalist mock pastorals, and with its fully developed characterizations and sense of plot, it resembles a short play.

And yet Fessenden was certainly no less passionate than his fellow Federalist writers in his scorn for rustic American life and the American common man represented in the rustic Jonathan. The tone of the poem is at best condescending—as the name of the leading character, Jonathan Jolthead, would suggest—and examined within the context in which it appeared, the poem must be read as implicitly satiric in intent. As an appropriate poetic vehicle for "The Country Lovers," Fessenden chose the verse form of "Yankee Doodle," which he calls in a footnote a "low musical air," and which served him and other Federalist writers well for satiric, anti-Jacobin delineations of American Dutchmen, Irishmen, and rustic Yankees. Like the rustic Yankee of the most popular version of "Yankee Doodle," who fails to comprehend the events at a military camp, Jonathan Jolthead is foolishly naïve. Sal, his girl, asks him:

> "Are you the lad who went to town,
>   Put on your streaked *trowses,*
> Then vow'd you could not see the town,
>   There were so many houses?"

Shamefaced, he must admit to the truth. Though a brief exchange, the situation echoes Royall Tyler's humorous treatment of Jonathan's first visit to a city, which became a popular source of New England humor in the nineteenth century. The political overtones of the characterization can be seen in the "streaked," that is to say "striped," trousers that Sal so indelicately, and, it would seem inexplicably, draws attention to. The reader of the 1790s would have recognized them as *sans-coulottes,* the trousers, typically striped, worn by French revolutionaries to identify their ardent republicanism. Jolthead espouses no political ideology here, but for Fessenden, his foolishness casts sufficient doubt upon the character of the American democratic man that the Jonathan figure had come to represent.

The primary source of humor in "The Country Lovers" is Jolthead's thick-headed ineptitude as a lover, which also echoes Tyler's treatment of the subject in *The Contrast* and, again, anticipates its popularity in later native humor. Forced by his mother to court Sal, the Deacon's daughter, Jonathan faces the task with dread because he is afraid of women. "I'd rather lie in stack of hay, in coldest winter weather," he grumbles to himself. At the Deacon's house he acts the fool, prattling and gossiping with Sal's brother to put off being alone with her. Sal sees through him, though, and taunts him about being sent by his mother, his trip to the city, and his father's offer of a bull calf as a wedding gift, suggesting that his father had better "keep his bull calves at home." Finally frightened by his quavering trepidation, she throws a pail of water over the spineless bumpkin. Within the context of this particular narrative, the refrain borrowed from "Yankee Doodle" becomes an ironic sexual indictment of the bucolic lover's ineptitude:

> Yankee doodle, keep it up,
> Yankee doodle dandy,
> Mind the music, mind the step,
> And with the girls be handy!

Like other poems of this kind, "The Country Lovers" is not just a literary exercise in the mock pastoral, nor merely a good-natured delineation of local color, but rather a satire of rural life as the basis of political power and the source of an indigenous cultural identity. The events of the poem are "really based on fact," Fessenden claims in the full title of the poem, and a review from the English *Anti-Jacobin* quoted in the back of *Original Poems* may have had "The Country Lovers" in mind when it praised the collection as "principally worthy of attention for the accurate delineation of rustic manners in New England." To underscore that authenticity—which, as in other poems of this kind, marks the true satiric target—Fessenden explains the manners in footnotes, italicizes colloquial usages, and in the preface to *Original Poems* assures his readers that "the peasantry of New England as described in my poems, will be found to bear some resemblance to what they are in real life." His judgment, however, is clear: "I will not assert, that I have not, in some instances, *caricatured* the manners of the New England rustic," he emphasizes in the preface, an antidemocratic tract that mercilessly scourges democratic politicians who manipulate the all-too-willing yeomen of America.

By the turn of the eighteenth century, the Federalists's mock pastorals had nearly run their course in the newspapers, although they continued to appear in collections such as *The Spirit of the Farmer's Museum* (1801), *The Spirit of the Public Journals* (1805, 1806), and Samuel Kettell's *Specimens of American Poetry* (1829), and later in nineteenth-century anthologies. Their end reflects not only the limitations of the imitative form that many of the poems had followed, particularly the dactylic catalogues of country conceits, but also the decline of Federalist political influence signaled by the Adams-Hamilton division and the unpopularity of the Alien and Sedition Acts, a decline sealed by the triumph of Democratic-Republican ideology with the election of Thomas Jefferson in 1801.

Although the specific form of the mock pastorals had had its day,[46] the delineations in these poems, along with the characterizations in versions of "Yankee Doodle" and *The Contrast,* had cast traditional sources of humor into American molds for native purposes. These conventions include a literary dialect, comic rustic courtship, and the humor of the rustic naïf and his efforts to explain what he does not understand. Other, perhaps more truly indigenous, peculiarities of Yankee character, such as peddling and pulling "Yankee tricks," appeared in print less often, but they too would become conventions in the tradition of New England humor. A different kind of Yankee peculiarity, according to the Portland *Eastern Argus* (19 Nov. 1807), was "to give a Yankee answer," in reference to the New Englander's tendency to avoid answering a question, often by asking one in return. As Royall Tyler put it in his mock travelogue *The Yankey in London* (1809), "An Englishman puts and answers a question directly, a New-Englander puts his questions circuitously and always answers a question by asking another." The anecdote he uses to illustrate the fact is one of the few examples of New England humor to find its way into the *Chaplet of Comus.* Like the other peculiarities, Yankee answering would soon find its way into countless stories and characterizations in the New England tradition of native American humor.

A harbinger of the true dimension of that tradition and of the role it would play in American culture can be found in a comedy published in 1815, David Humphreys's *The Yankey in England.* As the title indicates, the play addresses what surely must be seen as *the* American theme, but in making Jonathan Doolittle, the rustic of the piece, the title character, and in allowing him to represent the American position in that theme, Humphreys gave the role a new and meaningful purpose. Doolittle opens the play, alone on stage, having just liberated himself from impressment to an English ship. Hired as a footman by a fellow American, significantly named Newman, Doolittle, like Jonathan of *The Contrast,* objects to being called a "servant." Humphreys, however, makes a whole comic scene of the Yankee's egalitarian, American refusal to wear livery and to be ordered about. Doolittle's nationalism is resolute, even belligerent, and he refuses also to be awed by royalty, leveling Old World aristocratic pretensions with his earthy description of a countess as being "as nice a critter as ever trod shew's leather" and his report of seeing "the King himself and all his cattle." Such commentary seems worthy of Mark Twain's own Yankee some sixty years later. At times, it is true, Doolittle's bucolic ignorance makes him the butt of low comedy: he calls his daily journal a "diarrhea" and, like Jonathan Jolthead of "Country Lovers," he says he could not see the city because of all the houses. However, although Humphreys was a political antagonist of Jeffersonianism, he does not use the rustic figure as the satirical embodiment of the evils of democracy but treats the rustic attributes comically, often favorably, and as possibly desirable New World alternatives to Old World traditions and values.

The significance of Humphreys's work to the literary history of New England humor, however, lies not so much in the play itself, a clumsy piece, really, that never became part of the repertoire of Yankee theater. The published version also included an introductory essay, "Sketches of American Character," and a concluding glossary of some three hundred "Yankee" words. With the former, Humphreys attempted to answer the "assertion which has sometimes been made, that there exists no national character in the American people," and although much of his analysis of "three distinct kinds of characters frequently to be met with in America" is difficult to follow, his description of the rustic Yankee is detailed and worth quoting:

> The character of the Yankey, from whom the play derives its name, is little understood in several parts of America; still less in Europe.
>
> Although this Yankey, whose characteristics in the abstract are designed to be personified in Doolittle, may be fairly a subject of risibility on account of his dialect, pronunciation, and manners; yet his good qualities, even in the estimation of a rigid censor, will, doubtless, more than compensate for his singularities and failings.

Made up of contrarieties—simplicity and cunning; inquisitiveness from natural and excessive curiosity, confirmed by habit; credulous, from inexperience and want of knowledge of the world; believing himself to be perfectly acquainted with whatever he partially knows; tenacious of prejudices; docile, when rightly managed; when otherwise treated, independent to obstinacy; easily betrayed into ridiculous mistakes; incapable of being overawed by external circumstances; suspicious, vigilant and quick of perception, he is ever ready to parry or repel the attacks of raillery, by retorts of rustic and sarcastic, if not of original and refined, wit and humor.[47]

In so carefully detailing the "contrarieties" of the rustic Yankee character, in balancing what he sees as the indigenous virtues of the character with defects inherent in the Yankee rustic's naïveté and lack of refinement, Humphreys anticipated the fundamentally dual nature of that characterization in the New England humor tradition. As for the glossary of words that appears along with the printed version of the play, it is the most complete early recording of New England literary dialect, one that later writers would use as a source for their own characterizations of the Yankee.[48]

Thus only four years after the editor of the *Chaplet of Comus* had lamented in 1811 the assertion that "no good thing of a humorous kind can come out of New England," things had changed, or would very soon. David Humphreys's use of the rustic Yankee in the theme of his play, his analysis of that characterization as part of an effort to define, in order to defend, the existence of an American character in general—these together give some sense of the dimension of the tradition of New England humor soon to come and of the significant, complex place of that tradition in the national self-consciousness.

Chapter 3

New England Humor on Stage

In his 1832 *History of the American Theatre*, William Dunlap declared Tyler's characterization of the rustic Yankee in *The Contrast* as "Jonathan the First . . . unsurpassed by its successors." Given the national self-consciousness of the 1830s, however, Dunlap could not altogether approve of the kind of characterizations rendered by Tyler or his successors, taking them all to task for their assumption that "a Yankee character, a Jonathan, stamped the piece as American, forgetting that a clown is not the type of the nation he belongs to."[1] Writers of Dunlap's time would struggle some with exactly that dilemma, but as for those earlier characterizations, they were, without question, only stage clowns. Jeanette Tandy calls the character of Humphrey Cubb in Samuel Low's *The Politician Out-witted* (1788) "the most elaborate copy of [Tyler's] Jonathan,"[2] but Humphrey does not come close to the comic proportions of that character. For the most part, Cubb spouts nonsense, what with his interminable malapropisms and his witless inability to understand the language of his betters. (Called a "boor," he thinks it is "boar"; called an "illiterate lubber," he thinks it is "literary lubber.") The character of Nathan York in James Nelson Barker's *Tears and Smiles* (1808) comes off no better, and for reasons Barker himself admitted to. In a letter to Dunlap he wrote that the actor Joseph Jefferson had "put in for" a Yankee character—and "such a Yankee as I drew!" Barker confessed. "The truth is, I had never seen a Yankee at the time."[3] Imitators of Tyler kept the character of the Yankee alive and on stage, but just barely. None of the material became part of the extensive repertoire of New England theater humor that flourished between the 1820s and the 1850s.

Charles Mathews: English Actor, Yankee Character

Ironically, it would seem, the first popular and influential contributor to New England theater humor was an Englishman, Charles Mathews. Yet not so ironical, perhaps; it was English actor Thomas Wignell who first acted Tyler's Jonathan, and Mathews's work was in part an English answer to the new, pugnaciously nationalistic direction that David Humphreys had given the Yankee role. Like Wignell, Mathews was a popular character actor, but one who specialized in one-man shows featured as "At Homes" or "Trips to" various places. In 1822 he sailed for America to perform and to gather American material for a new production, and wary as Americans were of British travelers, they were all the more apprehensive of someone who could bring native peculiarities to life. In that regard, the *New England Galaxy* (7 Feb. 1823) speculated upon Mathews's return to England and his anticipated use of American materials, and an article in the *Edinburgh Scotsman,* reprinted in the *Galaxy* (17 Sept. 1823) from the *New York Post,* gave some portent of that use: "Poor Jonathan! [Americans] It is hard enough to have his follies and blunders pickled and preserved and exhibited cut and dry among his enemies—and all this by a man he had feted and flattered." Americans had little to fear, however, in Mathews's first effort, *Trip to America,* a three-and-a-half-hour performance that opened in London in March 1824 to great success from an audience curious about the New World characters he portrayed—the Negro, the American Dutchman, and the Yankee, Jonathan Doubikin (later, an *s* would be added to his name), among others (see fig. 9). It was, says Clarence Gohdes, "a spectacular medium of transatlantic humor," a success that can be measured not only in performances in and around London but also by the large number of published editions: one London publisher alone printed thirty of them, and four were published in America in 1824.[4] These are not, however, complete texts of the performance but descriptions of the scenes, with a few lines and some songs. In one of the Yankee scenes, Doubikin tells a story about a hunting trip with his Uncle Ben, a story Mathews had heard in America from painter John Wesley Jarvis and actor James Hackett, a circuitous and ultimately pointless story that became a standard piece in Yankee theater[5] (see below, Yankee Theater Stories) and in newspaper humor, as did his "Militia Muster" skit. In another story, Jonathan searches for his slave, Agamemnon, a runaway he bought from his Uncle Ben, and the description of the bargaining is a thinly veiled satire of American democratic pretensions:

"Uncle Ben," says I, "I calculate you have a Nigger to sell?" "Yes, I have a Nigger I guess. Will you buy the Nigger?" "Oh yes! if he is a good

Nigger, I will, I reckon; but this is a land of liberty and freedom, and as every man has the right to buy a Nigger, what do you want for your Nigger?" "Why, as you say, Jonathan," says Uncle Ben, "this is a land of freedom and independence, and as every man has a right to sell his Nigger, I want sixty dollars and twenty-five cents."

Hardly an authentically New England story, of course, for states there had abolished slavery, but the dialogue does represent Mathews's and many of his countrymen's distaste for what they considered the hypocritical pride Americans took in their experiment in democracy.

Most of the material of *Trip to America*, however, fails to express emphatically enough the distaste of a man who wrote in his memoirs of his visit to America, "If this be the effect of a republican form of government, give me a monarch, even if he be a despot."[6] Mathews acted out his real feelings in a play he wrote with Richard Peake, *Jonathan Doubikins; or, Jonathan in England*, which Mathews opened in September 1824.[7] In some respects, the play may be seen as an answer to the nationalism of Humphreys's *The Yankey in England*, which provided Peake and Mathews with a glossary of Yankee words as well as specific lines and scenes. In Mathews's rendition, the archetypal republican becomes an unmitigated racist. On seeing the black maid, Blanche, at the dinner of the Englishman Sir Leatherlip Grossfeeder, Jonathan confides in his journal that "English members of Congress drink tea freely with their female niggers." Also, appearing again as a slaveholder, he tries to sell his slave Agamemnon to the highest bidder. "It hurts my feelings to part with him," he admits, "but durn it, I want the dollars, and perhaps he will git a boss that won't thump him so much as I have done."

In the final scene, Mathews attacked the Yankee trickery that Americans called 'cuteness and liked to think of as an indigenous virtue and that the English preferred to judge a national vice. It had been reported that the promised fortune of Mary, Sir Grossfeeder's ward, had been wiped out by the failure of a New York bank. Jonathan, though, admits at the end that his Uncle Ben had been merely indulging in a little Yankee speculation and put the story of the failure in the newspaper in an attempt to buy cheap stock in Baltimore. *Jonathan Doubikins*, then, represents a forceful attack on the Yankee figure as the embodiment of the American experience. To the British eyes of Charles Mathews, Francis Hodge writes, "Jonathan was an uncouth, stupid, witless, dishonest, stubborn, easily insulted, unmannerly braggart, lost in a civilized society, a Negro beater, and a mockery of a true democratic society."[8]

Americans, of course, did not take the performance sitting down. John Neal, writing in *Blackwood's* (July 1824), had already taken Mathews mildly to task for *Trip to America*, claiming, as Americans were wont to do on such matters, that the characterizations had been "got up in a solitary chamber out of novels, newspapers, and books of travel." With *Jonathan Doubikins*, though, Mathews went too far in his attack on American character and institutions, and until replaced by Frances Trollope in the early 1830s, Mathews was for many Americans the most reprehensible of English visitors and reporters. "It would be dangerous for our inimitable Mathews to revisit America because of his far-famed delineation of the Yankee," English traveler Henry Cook Todd observed.[9]

American Actors Take the Stage

Mathews, a skilled actor and unsympathetic to so much that Americans would have liked the Yankee to stand for, went on to other roles after the 1820s. But in America, native actors responded to the growing popularity of New England humor, both on stage and in print, and made the character the leading national type to appear on stage at home and abroad through the 1850s. Today, however, it is difficult to capture that stage tradition very satisfactorily because its success relied more on the individual talents of the actors who played the role of the Yankee than it did on the text of the plays, which usually served only as a vehicle for those talents. In addition (probably as a result), only a small percentage of the plays are extant, most of them in manuscript in England, where American performers had to comply with the Licensing Act of 1737 and file a copy of their performance with the Lord Chamberlain.[10] The few published plays that are available, however, represent some of the most popular characterizations and illustrate the telling features of the comic Yankee on stage. Many actors played the part of the Yankee over the years, but three gave the role its international fame and developed nearly all of the material in the Yankee theater repertoire: James Hackett, George Handel Hill, and Danforth Marble. Given the close connection between stage humor and the actors who played the role, it is appropriate to look at the stage tradition in terms of the careers of these performers.

Most scholars of American drama agree that the identification of the actor as a specialist in New England comedy and the Yankee character as a permanent feature in native theater began in 1825, with Alexander Simpson's playing of Jonathan Ploughboy in Samuel Woodworth's *The Forest Rose; or, American Farmers.* Little more was heard from Simpson, but the play remained popular with leading actors such as Hill and Marble, as well as with others less well known. In California, Louis J. Mastayer strode the stage as Ploughboy for more than forty performances; in London, in 1851-52, Joshua Silsbee entertained audiences in the role for more than a hundred nights, the longest single run of a Yankee play[11] (see fig. 14). The published version of the play, however, provides what seems only a weak outline of the characterization that entertained so many theatergoers for so long.

Jonathan Ploughboy appears amiable and somewhat simpleminded with his country courting and native inquisitiveness, but he has none of the comic vigor of the earlier characterizations by Tyler or Humphreys. The theme of the virtuous American triumphant over high-stationed but low-minded English-men finds fulfillment in the character of William, not Jonathan. The Yankee is too easily tempted by gain—ill-gotten at that—to be exemplary, although the situation does provide a source of comedy that would entertain for some time. Hired by the Englishman Bellamy to kidnap Harriet, Jonathan finds himself torn between Puritan morality and Yankee parsimony, a dilemma further complicated by the fact that he does not plan to go through with the crime. "But will it be right to keep the money, when I don't intend to do the job?" he argues with himself. "Now if I was at home in Taunton, I would put that question to our debating society, and I would argue the affirmative side of the question." That kind of dilemma would become an important part of many printed stories of New England 'cuteness and trickery, and George Hill would develop the New England debating society into a different form of Yankee theater, the comic lecture.

James Hackett

Although James Hackett never included *The Forest Rose* in his repertoire, he was the first American actor to take advantage of the growing popularity of the Yankee rustic in the 1820s to become the first star of New England comedy and the first American actor to play the Yankee in England. As actor, theater

manager, and sponsor of play-writing competitions, he was responsible for
material that became standard fare in the tradition of the stage Yankee. His
performance in *Sylvester Daggerwood* in 1826 included imitations of leading
actors such as Edmund Kean and Charles Mathews, and versions of Yankee
stories such as the tale of "Uncle Ben," which Mathews had told in *Trip to
America*. Mathews, in fact, provided Hackett with many ideas for comic material
and technique early in his career. Undaunted by a singularly unsuccessful performance of *Sylvester Daggerwood* in 1827 for a London audience (it lasted one
night), Hackett in 1828 rewrote the Yorkshire character of Solomon Gundy in
George Colman's *Who Wants a Guinea?* (1805) and made it into a rustic Yankee
role. Solomon was given the appropriately Yankee surname "Swap," sometimes
"Swop," and the play became *Jonathan in England*.[12] By shortening the original
action and strengthening the role of Solomon, Hackett turned the conventional
romantic play into a vehicle for his still-growing talents as a Yankee actor.

Solomon Swap became one of the most popular characterizations with
Yankee actors—Hill and Silsbee most notably—and Hackett himself played it
for more than five hundred performances. Actor and theater manager Sol
Smith considered the play "the beginning of what may be termed the Yankee
Drama in this country, leading to the writing of many Yankee plays."[13] Solomon
Swap is not the bumbling Malaprop of Colman's original; he is more assertive,
and thus his character tends to dominate the scenes he appears in but not the
play as a whole. Solomon speaks characteristically rustic dialect and uses the
kind of earthy, outrageous comparisons that delighted audiences and readers
of native humor throughout the century. The Yankee speaks of a dog's tail "so
short you can't tell whether it's been cut off or driv in"; he describes the
housekeeper as "about as fit to be cook as a hog is to wear a side-saddle," and
he tells an obstreperous Englishman that his "soul is leetler than the leetle end
of nothing whittled down to a pint." Solomon also plays a typical Yankee trick
upon the Yorkshire servant Andrew Bang:

> *Swap.* Say, have you got five shillings?
> *Andrew.* Yes; I ha' gotten a guinea. (*Showing it.*)
> *Swap.* Well, come, I'll trade watches with you, unsight, unseen.
> *Andrew.* Noa! will ye, tho'?
> *Swap.* Yes; but mine's a first-rate watch, double patent, pinch-back.

Now, I'll gin my watch—(*aside*) it hain't got no insides—for yours, if you'll gin me that guinea boot.

Andrew. I be to gi' you *my* watch and a guinea for yourn—doane! *Swap.* (*Gives watch and takes guinea—Andrew going—Calls him back.*) Here, where's your watch?

Andrew. I ain't got no watch. I be Yorkshire. [*Exit R. chuckling.*]

Swap. Well, I rec'on that Bang don't know more than the law allows.

A good example of Yankee 'cuteness, which English travelers liked to attribute to Americans in general, the scene is enriched by Bang's notion that he has outfoxed the Yankee.

Another popular role Hackett originated was that of Joe Bunker in *Down East; or, The Militia Muster*, first played in 1830, a piece inspired by Mathews's muster skit in *Trip to America*. Popular in America, at least, for neither Swap nor Bunker found favor in London in 1832 when Hackett again tried to entertain London audiences with his comic abilities. The English, perhaps too used to Mathews's delineations of American character, did not like the interpretations of the American-born Hackett. According to one reviewer, "Many of the barbarisms introduced to tickle the ears of Jonathan were perfectly unintelligible to an English audience and fell still-born"; another suggested that the American actor "certainly might be more worthily employed than in exhibiting an extravagant caricature of his fellow-countrymen's peculiarities."[14] It may well have been his lack of success abroad that prompted Hackett in 1833 to take Mathews's *Jonathan Doubikins* and change it from a satire of America to a play showing the triumph of an ingenious rustic Yankee over his English cousins.[15]

George Handel ("Yankee") Hill

James Hackett had retired from active development of the stage Yankee by the mid-1830s, although he continued a long acting career, gaining distinction, for example, with his portrayal of Falstaff. No doubt Hackett felt the challenge from other Yankee actors such as George Hill, whose performance of Solomon Swap in 1832 was so popular that Hackett got an injunction against Hill's playing the role. (Hill responded by returning to George Colman's English version of the play, which Hackett himself had adapted.) Hill had begun his acting career early, at the age of fifteen, with an entertainment "in imitation of the great Mathews," he writes in his autobiography.[16] His career developed slowly, with his singing comic songs, telling occasional Yankee stories, touring theaters in many cities, and playing the parts assigned to the stock comedian. By the early 1830s, though, he was appearing in full-fledged Yankee roles: Jonathan Doolittle in William Dunlap's *A Trip to Niagara* in 1831 and Jonathan Ploughboy in Samuel Woodworth's *The Forest Rose* the next year. Another Yankee piece, written for him by Woodworth, *The Foundling of the Sea,* proved unsuccessful, as did *The Inquisitive Yankee.* With the character of Jedediah Homebred in Joseph Jones's *The Green Mountain Boy* early in 1833, however, "Yankee" Hill, as he came to be called, found his first popular and original New England role.[17]

The leading quality of Jedediah's character is his independence, an undaunted confidence in himself that cheerfully prevails despite the condescending amusement other characters take toward him. Although he wants a job from Bustle, an innkeeper, he refuses to restrain his natural and pesky curiosity about the slightest thing. "I say, captain, that's a pretty seal you've got there, shines like a brass kettle—chain tu. Gilt or gold, you?—looks expensive either way. Got a watch fastened on the end of it, I s'pose that's gold tu; how much did it all stand you in?" he asks. No matter who asks him his name, he reveals it only after a maddeningly circuitous explanation that has something of stream of consciousness about it:

> Well, you must know father's name was Jethro, when he was alive; but the old gentleman's dead; yes, he died, as near as I can remember, jist about the time Uncle Jonah was chosen into general court, that's over four years ago. I had the measles then. Yes, I'm right. Well, father he married Temperance Stowell—that was before I was born. She was kind of half sister to Uncle Jonah's wife. Uncle Jonah's a whole team; you ought to see him. He's a widower, he is, so he stays on our old place, and takes care of things now, and sees that mother don't want for nothin'. Now my old gentleman is dead.

Throughout the piece, Hill plays up Jedediah's rambling narratives, wariness, and inquisitiveness, all of which had become conventional peculiarities of the Yankee rustic character on stage and in print by the 1830s.

Like so many Yankee delineations, on the other hand, Jedediah embodies qualities that appear not so pleasantly amusing, qualities that suggest a satirical, or at least condescending, characterization of the rustic New Englander. Rejecting his rural home, Jedediah sets off for the city to see the fashions and "get ahead" in the polite world by learning formal English. He labors comically over parts of speech, fails to understand them, yet is fully confident of his achievement. "I've been larnin' grammar with blue covers, and how to talk out the words like city folks with their genteel sort of pernounsation," he brags. His exchange with Bill Brown, the black servant, shows him up as a bullying coward. Determined to poke fun at Brown—"just to let him see I ain't skeer'd of nobody"—he starts to run when the servant answers the insult, and turns to fight only when he sees Bustle coming on the scene.

Green Mountain Boy was an immediate hit with American audiences, but when Hill made his first tour of England in 1836, he chose the role of Hiram Dodge in Morris Barnett's *The Yankee Peddler; or, Old Times in Virginia,* a vigorous Yankee character and one less foolish than Jedediah Homebred.[18] Jedediah perhaps resembled too closely the boorish, slave-abusing Jonathan Doubikins whom Mathews had earlier shown to English audiences. Americans could be pleasantly enough amused at the foibles of the Yankee character, but they were incensed when English observers used them to indict the American character as a whole. Hill's plan to take his talents to England, in fact, was seen as an opportunity to present a "truer" picture of American life. A testimonial letter read at a dinner given the actor before leaving for the mother country charged him to answer English aspersions: "*The Yankee character.* It has been perverted and maligned by the Halls and Trollopes of Europe. If through the modesty of our countrymen its beauty has been 'hid under a bushel,' may it be seen 'on the house top' and conspicuous on the *Hill.*"[19]

Hill took the charge seriously, writing just a few days before he appeared on the London stage, "It's more of a job than I thought for when I started; but I'm in for it, and for the honor of Yankee land I will put my best foot foremost."[20] He had little to fear, though, for either his talents or the honor of Yankee land, because he would play Hiram Dodge throughout England, Scotland, and Ireland to audiences that loved it. So did the reviewers, nearly all of them praising his acting and drawing particular attention to the humor of the language. "The principal attraction and peculiarity of the performance was the quaint, dry humor of the actor, and the many odd phrases and similes interposed throughout the dialogue," the *London Globe* reported.[21] Certainly the play is full of the kind of incongruous exaggeration that Mark Twain saw in the art of Artemus Ward and others as characteristic of native American humor. Hiram's description of a cow with a tail "so crooked you could bore a hole with it" is standard fare; less conventional and more subtle is Hiram's story of Hopeful Perkins, "a dreadful proud man—used tu keep a dog with such a curly tail that it couldn't keep its hind feet on the ground." Or he tells of a grandmother so weak that she had to have three or four mustard patches to get the strength to draw her last breath. Perhaps the *London Chronicle* had such lines in mind when confessing that "some of the Yankeeisms were beyond our conception."[22]

The Yankee Peddler is one of the few plays in Yankee theater that attempts to integrate the comic Yankee into the main action of the drama. Hiram Dodge guides the two plot lines of the three-scene farce: the horse-racing rivalry between Fuller and Jennings and the romance between Fuller's daughter, Maria, and Charles, a suitor her father opposes. Also, Hiram is one of the few stage depictions of the Yankee peddler, and he is a master of the type. He audaciously returns to Fuller's plantation despite the Southerner's mortal antipathy to Yankee peddlers since Hiram had sold him a pony with a glued-on tail. "But I don't feel a bit consarned about that," Hiram admits. "I should think I was duin my dewty if I could sell him one of my cleanin' cakes, made out of flour and soft-soap. I'd like to git him to eat bout half a one, and I'll bet my head agin nothin', he'd be clean scour'd out in the mornin!—ha, ha, ha!"

Hiram also acts as the consummate Yankee trickster, playing all contending sides for his own gain with a native ingenuity worthy of praise. He is first paid to carry Jennings's challenge of a horse race to Fuller, who hires the Yankee to ride his horse. Seeing Charles and Maria secretly kissing, he gets five dollars not to tell, then gets ten dollars more from Fuller to tell where Charles has gone—though he gives the wrong direction. In retaliation, Fuller asks him to carry a note to his overseer telling him to give the bearer a hundred lashes. Seeing through the hoary trick, the Yankee gives the note to a servant who is then so disabled by the beating he cannot ride Jennings's horse in the race. Persistently in control of the action, Hiram rides Jennings's horse and arranges for Charles, disguised, to ride Fuller's; he wins when the Yankee tumbles from his mount.

Pleased with winning, Fuller offers Charles anything he wants, and the young man naturally takes Maria. The play does not end, however, on this conventionally romantic resolution; the Yankee has the last word. Fuller, thinking that Hiram is dead from the fall, declares that he would give forty dollars were he alive once again. "Jest fork over," says Hiram, rising in triumph from the stretcher. By the end of the play the Yankee is fifty-seven dollars richer and has the hand of Jerusha, the rustic Yankee servant he has courted comically throughout the play. "Hitch your team to mine," he tells her. "We can drive down the hill of life quite easy, without putting any drag on."

A hit in England, Hill played the role of Hiram Dodge on his return to America in March 1837 in cities all over the country: New York, Albany, Philadelphia, Baltimore, Richmond, New Orleans, Louisville, Cincinnati, and others (see fig. 11). His performance in Washington, D.C., drew letters of praise from John Quincy Adams and Henry Clay. At the same time, however, he began to suffer from a nervous depression that so debilitated him in Philadelphia that he had a physician on hand to check his pulse and look at his tongue every time he left the stage. A second voyage to England in 1838 revived his spirits for a time, what with continued success with audiences there, playing *New Notions, Seth Slope; or, Done for a Hundred,* and *Wife for a Day.* Queen Victoria and other nobility attended one performance, and Hill even made a short trip to Paris, where he gave two performances and attended a masquerade ball disguised as his favorite character, the rustic Yankee. Back in America, Hill had to contend with ill health and the economically depressed state of the American theater in the early 1840s. He tried theater managing for a time, and for a few months he seriously considered a late career in medicine. On stage he tried a variety of Yankee pieces that survive only as titles on playbills in nineteenth-century newspapers and in the essentially statistical histories of American theater written in that century. Hill's last major contribution to the stage tradition of New England humor was the role of Solon Shingle in Joseph Jones's *The People's Lawyer* in December 1842, a play that foreshadows major changes in Yankee theater.[23]

The plot of *The People's Lawyer* follows the pattern of later melodramas or Horatio Alger's novels more than it does the typical Yankee play. No conflict here between a father and his daughter on the choice of a husband, nor is there a contrast between rural virtues and city vices. The story concerns the plight of Charles Otis, a poor but scrupulously honest clerk who antagonizes his employer, Hugh Winslow, by refusing to testify falsely to witnessing a client's check. Winslow fires him, despite Charles's need to support his widowed mother and his younger sister, Grace, whom Winslow wants to marry. With the help of another clerk, John Ellsley (profligate son of a wealthy father), the villainous Hugh Winslow gets Otis falsely arrested for stealing his watch, then offers to drop the charges if Grace will marry him. In court, things look bleak for young Otis until the people's lawyer, Robert Howard, steps in, takes over the case, and forces Ellsley to admit his deception. At the end of the play, Howard reveals himself as the secret admirer of Grace, who agrees to marry him.

Solon Shingle, the Yankee of the piece, differs from previous Yankee stage characters. He does not have the youthful exuberance of a Jedediah Home-bred or the "go-ahead" spunk of a Hiram Dodge, and the conventional sources of stage comedy are treated indirectly and more moderately. Solon, for example, admits that when he is in Boston, he does not know "a string of sausages from a cord of wood," but his naïveté about city life does not make him appear foolish. And although he speaks a kind of New England dialect, there are no outrageous rustic similes or exaggerations, and, as in the following example, his circumlocutions are restrained: "I've got a case in court about a brindle cow, and Squire Dingle asked me how I was going tu sware, and I told him I should sware like lightening agin him; these are revolutionary times—my father fit in the revolution, that is, he druv a baggage wagon."

Even in a scene in which he gets covered with lampblack and flour and then frightens himself by accidentally firing a revolver, Solon does not become the caricature that many comic Yankees seem to have been. Through it all he maintains a quiet sensibility and an awareness of his own limitations. "If ever anybody catches me inside a Court House agin I'll agree to be proved non pumpus—and that means a tarnal fool, according to law books," he admits. Older and more sedate than earlier characters, Solon Shingle prefigures Harriet Beecher Stowe's Sam Lawson and Rowland Robinson's Uncle Lisha later in the century. Like them, he seems something of an anachronism, and he has little of the foolish pretensions of the more youthful Yankee figures that characterize New England humor through the 1840s.

Considered by most of his contemporaries to be the best Yankee actor of his time, George Handel Hill died at the age of forty in 1849. Unlike Hackett, Hill had devoted his acting career to Yankee theater, bringing more than forty Yankee plays to the stage and originating countless stories, which were retold and reprinted after his death. Even early in his career, an article reprinted in the *Courier and New York Enquirer* (7 Aug. 1833) said that as a Yankee actor, Hill was unrivaled—better than Mathews or Hackett.[24]

Danforth Marble

Hill's only competition came from an actor who started his career a few years later, Danforth Marble. Although only a year younger than Hill, Marble was still a stock actor yearning for leading roles in tragedy and melodrama when Yankee Hill's star began to rise in the early 1830s.[25] Not until 1836, when Hill was on his second trip to England, did Marble play the role that first gave him real fame, Sam Patch. No text of *Sam Patch the Yankee Jumper* remains, but it seems to have provided the usual vehicle for Yankee stories and comic business, although the real attraction may have been the portrayal of Sam's leap over Niagara Falls, with Marble staging jumps of nearly forty feet. His career followed the pattern for successful Yankee actors, with tours through the major cities of the United States, but Marble tended to favor the cities of the West, which may have had something to do with his Yankee taking on some of the characteristics of the frontiersman. For material he could rely on plays others had staged before him—*The Forest Rose, Sylvester Daggerwood, The People's Lawyer,* and *Jonathan in England,* for example—but in 1838 he opened *The Vermont Wool Dealer,* written for him by Cornelius A. Logan, one of the few Marble plays that became a major piece in the repertoire of Yankee theater.[26]

The brief farce is essentially an extended story of comic Yankee courtship that had become so popular in the New England humor tradition. Deuteronomy Dutiful arrives in New York from Vermont to sell his load of wool. During the boat trip, he had been smitten by the handsome Amanda, who has an equally handsome fortune, which, the Yankee admits, is one of the main reasons for his interest. She is pursued for the same reason by Captain Oakly, who takes offense at Dutiful's courtship and challenges him to a duel. The Yankee is also challenged by Amanda's father when he reads a note the Vermonter had sent to her, and although no coward, Deuteronomy refuses to be called out. In his courtship of Amanda, the Yankee first acts nervously circumspect about his intentions and talks around the real business at hand:

Hokey! for your sake, I'd do anything on airth—I'd almost swear never to eat no more clam chowder! On one condition, though, that we bring our business immediately to the conclusion that it must eventually arrive at. I'm every way a match for you—my family is good, none better in Varmont. My grandfather was one of the first settlers in our part of the country—bought up pretty nighly one third of the hull country. He was sent to our State Legislature—old Michael Dutiful— you must a'heern on him—he was my grand-father. Well, Mike, he married old Squire Holliday Harrindon's daughter, Harrietta, as like a gal as ever drove a pair of oxen, so they say that seed her when she was young and spry, but when I seed her, her face was furrowed like a new plowed cornfield. She had only one eye and two teeth, or two eyes and one tooth, I don't know which, but Harriet brought suthin' consider- able to the old man when he married her; she had an all-sufficient quantity of quilts and blankets—in fine, I hearn say she warn't short of body clothes, nyther.

Typical Yankee circumlocution according to the conventions of popular hu- mor, but when Deuteronomy gets to the matter of the proposal itself, he approaches it with Yankee economy and practicality:

Well, you see, I haven't got time to make a long courtship of it, because my business is all out o' kilter, and has to go on in Varmont without me; besides, this seems to be a pretty dear tavern, and you know every dollar I spend in staying here courtin' you, is so much out of your pocket after I marry you, for I swan, if you don't marry me right away, I'll charge the extras to you—I will—honor bright.

Despite Deuteronomy's belief that he is a match for Amanda, that his family is good, his courtship of the girl is also comic because the rustic is so obviously an inappropriate suitor to the genteel girl, and she arranges a trick to cure him of his presumption and to punish Captain Oakly for his jealousy, a trick similar to the one used on a Yankee in *The Forest Rose*. Telling Deuteronomy that she will elope with him that night dressed in the clothes of her black servant, Betty, she actually sends the servant girl in her place. At the end of the play she promises her hand to the captain, and Deuteronomy, admitting "I'm rather flummoxed," offers to treat the party with some champagne he has traded for in the city.

To Francis Hodge, Deuteronomy Dutiful illustrates the differences he sees between the kind of Yankee character delineated by Dan Marble and that portrayed by George Hill. Marble's Yankee he calls a "Western hybrid," less a clearly drawn New Englander than a composite American, "part Jonathan, part Davy Crockett, part Mike Fink."[27] It is not merely that the character lacks many of the typical New England traits, but that his hard-nosed pugnacity is akin to the character of the frontiersman. "Haven't I seen that impudent face of yours somewhere else?" Oakly asks him, to which the Yankee replies, "You haven't seen it no where but on the front of my head and I guess it ain't loose." And when Amanda's trick is revealed, he jumps about the stage shouting extravagant backwoods oaths: "I'll whip the hull boodle of you at once. (*Skipping about.*) Make me mad and I'll lick a thunder storm. . . . Git my dander up and you'd think it was the Cape Cod sea sarpent in convulsions." Many writers confused New England peculiarities with frontier ones, but Marble's persistence with such characterizations suggests that he preferred the composite type. (See fig. 10.)

Even more clearly a Western hybrid is Lot Sap Sago, in *Yankee Land; or, the Foundling of the Apple Orchard,* another popular play written for Marble by Cornelius A. Logan.[28] Lot first appears on stage in hunting attire complete with a rabbit in his game bag, and he plays the role of the frontier hunter throughout the play. "I've shot woodchucks enough, if they was all harnessed up, to work a steamboat," he boasts, and his story of one particular hunt would do justice to Crockett himself: "[I] shoved a bullet through his head with such all-fired force that I driv the ball clean through, and picked it up behind him." Chided that sending a bullet lengthwise through the body of a large bear seems "stretching" it a bit, Lot continues without pause, "Why, yes, I had to stretch considerable.—I had to gin the trigger an almighty hard pull." Lot proceeds with the details of the fabulous hunt:

Why, you see, there was nine of us, including your father, and we surrounded that animal. When he seed himself hemmed in, he wanted to sneak out the worst kind. He kept turning round and round, jest to make us think he wanted to chastise his tail; but he was only looking for an opening to get out of. I know'd what was passing in that feller's mind; so I jest stretched out jest so. He come towards me, and I blazed away. I meant to hit him in the eyeball, but that crocodile hunter's gun was crooked, so I bored a new hole in his nose. That staggered him; and just then your father let slip, and that wound up his airthly affairs; and Harvy and I had him skun and slung on our shoulders before the sarpent know'd he was hurt.

Lot also acts as the frontiersman in his treatment of Manikin, a foppish city type who pretends to vast scientific knowledge of nature, although he does not know a lizard from a fox, and Lot accords him the rough horseplay that a greenhorn deserves by frightening him with incredible stories and giving him a particularly unruly horse to ride. "As soon as the beast found the foolish critter astride on him, he knowed he had a simpleton on his back; so he give one loud snort, and set off full chisel," Lot reports. He then describes what happened when he took off the saddle and tied the rider's legs underneath the horse: "And when he got into town, he had no more sign of trousers on his legs than the horse had. I stowed him away in the bunk in the bar room at the tavern, and told the landlord there to give him a strong dose of pepper sarce and molasses, to settle his internals—that's the last we shall see of him."

His New England qualities are thinly sketched: he courts with some comic results, exasperates and confounds the other characters with his Yankee 'cuteness, and is given the stage direction *Yankee story* (although no stories are printed, as they probably varied with performance and performer). Unusual for a Yankee theater play is the rustic's integration into the plot, a complex one that includes blackmail, imagined crime, mysterious pasts, and the ultimate reunion of parents, spouses, and children. At the end, Lot thwarts an attempt on the life of Sir Cameron Ogleby, who, it turns out, is Lot's natural father. (Harvey Ashton, the conventional romantic lead, is revealed as the legitimate son and heir.) Thus the Yankee himself becomes "the foundling of the apple orchard" of the subtitle.

Yankee Land, like *The Vermont Wool Dealer*, was among the most popular plays initiated by Marble, and he played both of them in England when he toured there in 1844-45. Typically, English critics did not care much for the plays themselves, but most had high praise for the actor's comedic talents. Many noted the admixture of Yankee and frontiersman peculiarities, but it bothered them little, for the favorite "Yankee" of the English reading public was Thomas Chandler Haliburton's Sam Slick, who in the 1840s was himself becoming something of a Western hybrid. A reviewer in the *London Morning Post* (5 Oct. 1844) made that connection, saying of Marble, "This is a genuine Yankee article, manufactured in the States"—genuine because it had "the right *Sam Slick* stamp." As so often the case with the English reception of New England humor, however, the apparent accuracy of a given delineation of the rustic Yankee provided the opportunity to level some arch sarcasm at the national experience he represented. Thus a reviewer for the *Era* (13 Oct. 1844) saw the two plays as written not only for "the special purpose of introducing Mr. Marble . . . to an English audience" but also for "developing the outré notions, clothed in the marvelous diction of the new world."[29] On the other hand, Marble's considerable acting skills could not redeem a hastily written version of the Sam Patch story, an utter failure that brought to an end the actor's career in the mother country.

One more of Marble's plays deserves attention here, because although it seems never to have had the popularity of his other works, it is unusual in its depiction of Yankee character, and it reads today as one of the most truly humorous of the New England comedies. First performed by Marble in Buffalo in 1841, *Ebenezer Venture; or, Advertising for a Wife* was, according to the title page, written "expressly for the peculiar powers of Mr. D. Marble," by Lawrence LaBrée.[30] The play is unusual because the humor is not superadded to the plot; rather, the plot derives from a convention of New England humor that goes back to *The Contrast* and "The Country Lovers," rustic Yankee courtship. Much of the same could be said of Marble's first hit, *The Vermont Wool Dealer*, but in that play, the Yankee's efforts were thwarted by a more genteel suitor, Captain Oakly. In *Ebenezer Venture* the Yankee is the leading character, and he courts comically but successfully a woman who is his social better. The story goes as follows: Ebenezer comes to New York to visit his uncle and his family, and learning it is the fashion to advertise in the newspapers for a wife, Ebenezer places such an ad for himself. Emma, his cousin, tricks him by disguising herself in a veil, answering the advertisement, and accepting his proposal. When he takes her to meet his aunt and uncle, she throws off the disguise and reveals the trick, although she still holds him to his proposal. Two other sources of comedy are provided by his reacting to the city (he thinks Europe must be unpopulated) and his being taken in by a confidence man.

Although a foolish rustic Yankee at times, Ebenezer is not the farfetched buffoon that many stage characterizations appear to have been. Throughout the play he exudes an endearing kind of bucolic enthusiasm. "Uncle Jo, how du you du?" he says in greeting his city relations. "Aunt Sarah, how are yew? pretty middlin', I s'pose? Lor bless my eyes! if there ain't Em! She's grown as slick as a peeled carrot, and there's them ere everlastin' blue eyes, tew! Gosh molley! Well, folks, I've cum to see you all, and have a stop." Because Ebenezer's role is not an artificial addition to a melodramatic or romantic plot, the humor too, although conventional, becomes a natural extension of the Yankee's character. There is little to suggest that Ebenezer is the Western hybrid that Deuteronomy Dutiful or Lot Sap Sago are, although references to a steam churn that can make twenty pounds of butter out of a gallon of sour milk or to a turnip so large that the earth could hardly bear it, seem more akin to the humor of the frontiersman Davy Crockett than to the New England Yankee. Because the humor is so closely linked to the Yankee's character, it is difficult to isolate examples, but certainly one of the most entertaining is Ebenezer's account of how his trunk came to be covered with horse hide. Beginning with the trunk on the floor in front of him, the Yankee spins an increasingly incongruous yarn about the horse that the hide came from:

> *Ebeneezer.* I thought likely—it's covered with horse hide; perhaps you don't know what hoss that are skin come off—he was the darndest slickest, fastest hoss you ever did see, I tell you now; he could outrun and outjump anything this side of creation, I don't care where tother was, but he died one day—he got old and thin and weak, so darned weak, that he had'nt strength to lay down, no how—he used to have to lean against the barn, when he wanted to sleep, and dad used to pull his eyelids down, because he had'nt strength to shut 'em himself. Well, he was sleepin' so one day beside the barn, dad had just left him, when a big hoss fly—you've seen a hoss fly—well, a tarnal big hoss fly, see him takin' a nap and perhaps dreaming of happier days and future bliss, and he stung him right under

the eye and the pain caused him to expire without a groan. It was a kinder horrible thing to think on—but I believe after all, it was a blessin'.

Emma. A blessing?

Ebenezer. Yes, a blessin'; he wouldn't never die.

Emma. Never die?

Ebenezer. No, he was tu weak, tu far gone, tu die—he couldn't stood it out; we'd give him up, it was the opinion of the minister he hadn't strength enough to die. I used to tell dad he'd better borrow another horse to help him draw his last breath.

Emma. He was certainly a most singular animal.

Ebenezer. Guess he was. Dad had him skinned, and put his carcase in the cornfield to scare the crows off.

Emma. To scare the crows off?

Ebenezer. Yes, I guess so; none on 'em wouldn't come near the cornfield arter that; they were taken by surprise. Wall, that are's his hide upon my trunk.

Such circumlocution was, as we will see, a convention in New England humor—and would, like the gravely put exaggerations, become a central part of native humor in general—but in this case, Emma's "straight-man" questions literally dramatize the convention and extend the story until it has come full circle, back to the hide on the trunk in front of them.

As Yankee comedy, *Ebenezer Venture* entertains the reader today because it relies less on the individual talents of the actor who played the Yankee role than do most scripts, again usually little more than flexible frameworks for those talents, which included singing comic songs, dancing, and telling stories. However, while the Yankee was the star attraction of a given production, the character was seldom an integral part of the conventional melodramatic plot of the play. Cooper faced a similar problem in his Leatherstocking tales. As Henry Nash Smith writes in *Virgin Land*, Natty Bumpo, "symbol of forest freedom and virtue," adequately embodied the indigenous American experience, but at the same time, this "most vital character occupied a technically inferior position both in the social system and in the form of the sentimental novel" that Cooper used.[31] The Yankee was the "most vital character" in New

England comedy in that he was a readily identifiable American type—*the American archetype*—but as a rustic he was socially inferior and incompatible with Old World standards of literary propriety, standards that prevailed even among those who strove to create a native American drama.

The literary consequences of the dilemma can best be seen in the way romance was dealt with. As did the sentimental novel, the domestic comedy-melodrama conventions called for a love interest, but when the rustic Yankee courts, he does so comically and with a social equal; the "true" love interest, the conventional plot, must be left to Jonathan's social betters. In *The Vermont Wool Dealer*, Deuteronomy Dutiful tries to romance the refined Amanda, but she puts such pretensions in their comic place by promising to elope and then disguising her black maid in her stead. In *A Trip to Niagara*, Jonathan Doolittle wins the hand of the young English woman, Amelia, but Doolittle is, in reality, a suitably genteel Englishman who had assumed the Yankee disguise. Only in *Ebenezer Venture* does the Yankee court successfully a woman who is herself not a rustic. Ebenezer is, in fact, the central character, and unlike most other plays in the Yankee repertoire, the play could not be performed without him.

Humorous Theater Stories

Old World literary conventions may have inhibited the Yankee from being integrated into the dramatic whole, but the flexible structure of the typical New England comedy provided actors who played the role the opportunity to perform individual comic songs, dances, and stories that need have little to do with the story line. (See fig. 12.) So popular were the Yankee stories that they deserve consideration here in their own right, as a subgenre of Yankee theater. Playbills and advertisements featured them as additional attractions to the plays themselves, they were published in book form, and in the work of Dr. Valentine and George Handel Hill, they would seem to anticipate the comic lectures made popular by later humorists such as Josh Billings, Artemus Ward, and Mark Twain.

Humorous recitations and stories, like comic songs and dances, had been an important part of Yankee theater since Mathews's *Trip to America* in 1824. In addition to the "Negro" song "Possum Up a Gum Tree," which Mathews sang, one of the most popular pieces was the story he told in the character of Jonathan

Doubikins about Uncle Ben. Jonathan opens the story with a brief account of his difficulties in New York where he meets his Uncle Ben. Before he gets to the jist of his story about his uncle, though, he gives a brief but incongruously detailed account of his aunt, a "shockin nice woman," he says, who swore only once in her life—when a cat bit her and she said, "Darn the varmin, how sharp her teeth are—that's all she said. But I was telling you about Uncle Ben," he says, and returns to the point. Jonathan and Ben were hunting and shot a squirrel that fell only half way down a tree and hung on a bough. Promised nine pence to get it down, Jonathan does, but his uncle puts off paying him, saying he will do so next time. "Next time, and every time, I met Uncle Ben, he'd always—sartain next time—lied like old Satan, you see," Jonathan complains. "And now, when do you suppose Uncle Ben paid me that are trifle! Well, I swan to man, he's never paid me darn the cent on it, nor have I ever seen Uncle Ben from that day to this." Certainly the story has no comic point or "hit"; the fun is in the telling and in the detailed descriptions that are inconsequential, though Jonathan treats them seriously. The story is, in other words, a classic example of the deadpan, loquacious circumlocution that was conventional in New England humor and illustrates well Mark Twain's observation in "How to Tell a Story" (1895) that American humor differed from European humor by emphasizing the manner rather than the matter of a story. As for the story of Uncle Ben, James Hackett, who said he had told the story to Mathews in the first place, included it in his performance of *Sylvester Daggerwood* in 1826, and Hill reprinted it in his *Little Hill's Yankee Story Book* in 1836.[32]

Although usually the stories were told by the Yankee actor as a character in the play, they had little to do with the plot. As we have seen, Dan Marble's version of *Yankee Land* contains the direction "Yankee story," but no stories are given. Apparently Marble would choose his material according to what was popular or fresh.[33] Another actor, Dr. William Valentine (see fig. 15), connected stories into a single comic monologue. Valentine's name appears on collections of humorous stories and lectures, but biographical information about the man is elusive. In his *Records of the New York Stage* (1866-67), Joseph Ireland describes him as a "well-known mimic and comic lecturer," but he was also "a man of great eccentricity and finally died in the Lunatic Asylum, 1865-6."[34] His "American Character and Characteristics," published as "Extracts from Dr. Valentine's Entertainment Delivered in London," illustrates how stories could be put together for a one-man show.[35] Valentine begins in his own person to introduce a topic he knew to be a favorite of English audiences: "The peculiarities of the American character" and how the American experience had modified the original "English principle." Like so many American apologists for the American experience, however, Valentine argues that given the common heritage of history, language, and knowledge, there is little difference "*nationally*." "But individually and severally," he goes on to say, "there is as much difference as between the unsophisticated rustic of the Provinces and the polished gentleman of the Metropolis." The printed version of the lecture is only an extract, but stories that illustrate the "peculiarities of the American character" include a brief sketch of a black man trying to render Shakespeare, two tales of rustic Yankee courtship, an illustration of New England peddling, and an example of Yankee independence—stories, in other words, of characters from the American "Provinces." That *he* is no provincial, Valentine establishes clearly to his English audience when, in introducing his subject, he entertains them with a wit so sophisticated, so urbane, as to include Latin puns. Also, he appears throughout the lecture speaking standard English, introducing the stories and tying them together within the framework of a formal lecture on American character.

The Yankee storyteller par excellence was probably George Hill. He published a collection of stories, his name appears with Valentine's on another collection, and theater advertisements in newspapers often promised "Several Yankee Stories by Mr. G. H. Hill" in addition to his roles in plays. With "The People and Antiquities of New England, Yankeeologically Speaking" and "Antiquities and Products Ginerally," however, Hill went beyond merely telling stories, or a series of stories, and created a full-fledged comic lecture.[36] In these works, Hill pokes some fun at the tradition of New England learned societies and the growing popularity in the 1840s of the public lecture as a means of bringing erudition to the masses. Hill's mid-nineteenth century biographer puts it this way:

New England is studded with learned societies. The people of the Eastern States seem to be as curious in matters of science as they are in prying into each other's affairs. Boston alone, every year, brings out more new isms and ologies, than all the other cities in the Union put together. I most sincerely believe, that if some vast scientific discovery were to be made today among some newly found people, whose language was different from anything ever thought or conceived before, that in a week, some Yankee or other would advertise a lecture upon the subject, and maybe deliver it in the new tongue.[37]

In both works, a rustic speaker narrates a rambling, disjointed collection of extraordinary facts and absurd theories about New England history. In "Antiquities and Products Ginerally," the Yankee rustic meanders through a variety of subjects, including a comic account of how the ancient Pilgrims brought corn to its perfection by inventing johnnycakes and then whiskey to wash them down with. "This diskivery, undoubtedly, pinted many intu very crooked ways, and gin rise tew the expression that—'This is a great country,'" the speaker soberly concludes. The major part of this lecture is a comic skit that the speaker introduces as part of the subject, and what follows would seem to illustrate what Hill's biographer had said about Yankee curiosity. The local historical society, says the speaker, once investigated a strange "stun" (stone) that bore the inscription "ITIS APU NKIN ITIS." The group "sot tew work on the inscription, thinkin' that as it was antique, it would tell the origin of the plant, or gin us a peep intew some matter of airly history." After heated debate among the members, they merged their sundry opinions to conclude that the inscription is made up of Latin, Greek, and Chinese words that mean "thou goest from Nankin, thou goest." Thus "it is plain as the nose on a face, tew the eye of science ginerally, and tew this society in particular," the speaker concludes triumphantly, "that this stun was once a Chinese fruit, sent eout to this country, to see ef it would *fructify*, and here the darn thing has taken a notion instead to *petrify*!" Not yet heard from, however, is one Zachariah Stanhope, a "consarned dirty little rascal," says the speaker, who swept out the historical room and built the fire. To his unrefined mind, the inscription should read "IT-IS-A-PUNKIN-IT-IS." "And so it was," admits the narrator, "a consarned dried up, petrified punkin, that had dried up more one way than t'other." What Hill has created here is a true comic lecture, not a series of stories much like the kind that appeared in print. In doing so, he opened up a new subject for Yankee humor, the New England penchant for knowledge so recondite that it loses all sense of reality and becomes absurd.

Again, in "The People and Antiquities of New England Yankeeologically Speaking," Hill posed as a rustic speaker who, with awed earnestness, struggles to render the kind of erudition that was to be expected of the formal lecture. The result is comic nonsense. "It is a pooty ginerally conceded fact, that man is a queer critter, and that when he aint movin' abeout, he's doin' suthin' else," the speaker begins. "This pint bein' conceded, we pass on tew remark, that the first race which sot deown in New England, were of this movin' reound kind of critters, and I rekon they hev fixed a leetle mite of their stirrin' reound propensities upon the ginerations that followed a'ter." Eventually he gets to the real "pint" of his lecture, rocks, and he begins with a discussion of that most famous of New England stones, Plymouth Rock:

> Nigh ontew all on you hev heerd abeout the *Rock of Plymouth,* and if you hev'nt, it's a darned shame, for it's often enough talked about. The ancient inhabitants of New England, beyond dispute, landed on this rock, and they found it a pooty solid, *steady* kind of footin'. From this fact grew eout the common sayin' that New England is the land of *steady habits.* Heow could they be otherwise, when they commenced on so solid a foundation? Without runnin' this rock intew the ground, I'd like tew say suthin' abeout its *antiquity.* It is pooty ginerally conceded that afore it was diskivered, it had staid in the same place a pooty long spell—mabbe anterior to Adam! Who knows? I'll be durned if I dew. All I know, and all it's necessary for me tew find eout is, that it is *there,* and I ruther guess, a'ter I hev handled it a leetle mite *there,* I'll leave it.

In the same lecture on famous New England rocks, the speaker proposes a bizarre theory of how the Bunker Hill Monument was built: "The great distinguishin' featur' about this stupendous mountain of stun is the fact, that they begun tew fix it *up* from the top *down,*" a feat achieved with mesmerism. The lecture ends with the description of a rustic courtship scene around a hearth stone. Virtually all of the courtship story is typically comic and told in the rustic dialect of the Yankee speaker; however, in the last paragraph, Hill abruptly steps out of that character to deliver a brief, sentimental paean to the virtues of the New England hearth stone. "The heart of every true New Englander reveres this *hearth-stun*, for around it, no matter whether it be of brick or marble, gathers the loved associations of hum," it begins. Except for the words "stun" and "hum," the language and the style Hill uses at the end of "The People and Antiquities of New England Yankeeologically Speaking" are the same as he uses throughout another lecture, "Lecture on New England," an entertaining but not a comic piece in which Hill extols at length the virtues of New England, concluding with its women.[38] The shift in language and style suggests that when Hill wanted to speak "seriously," that is to say "sentimentally," he found the rustic voice inadequate, too often itself the butt of humor. (As we will see, James Russell Lowell would face much the same problem with the rustic voice of Hosea Biglow.) Thus in his "The People and Antiquities of New England, Yankeeologically Speaking," Hill takes care that although we might smile with his speaker, we will not laugh at him or at what he has to say because of how he says it.

As for Hill's comic lectures, the plays on words, rambling incongruities, and above all the deadpan earnestness of the speaker in the face of such nonsense—these all became identifying features of the next generation of American humorists, "literary comedians," as they are called. Hill's humor is not so exaggerated, however, especially in its orthography, perhaps because he is in the New England humor tradition and sustains a stronger sense of a regional character than did most literary comedians. Henry Wheeler Shaw and Charles Farrar Browne, for example, were both New England born, and although they used conventions from the New England tradition of native American humor, the characters they created and became identified with, Josh Billings and Artemus Ward, are not Yankees.

An indication of changes in the tradition of New England humor can be read in the history of New England theater in the 1850s. In 1849, with the deaths of Hill and Marble, Yankee comedy lost its two leading players. Hackett still lived, but he had given up Yankee roles years before. Joshua Silsbee, who ranks just below these three, died in 1855. A skilled actor, he developed no original roles. Nor did G. E. ("Yankee") Locke, who made his debut in 1851. New England theater drew its life from its performers' talents, but although their loss may have hastened its decline, there were other reasons for the change. The English, for one, had had their fill of Yankee caricature. Of Silsbee's

London performance in 1851, a reviewer in *The Spectator* (27 Sept. 1851) rather archly concluded, "In the first place, what can be regarded as more unattractive than the announcement of a drama constructed for the purpose of showing 'Yankee eccentricities'? Some ten or twelve years ago, we were liberally dosed with Yankeeisms," but "the 'fun' of the first year became the 'bore' of the second."[39] Americans too may have had enough of the stage Yankee. In any case, the attempt by actress Mrs. Maria Williams to bring a female rustic Yankee to the stage about 1850 did not enjoy lasting success. Joseph Ireland thought her a skilled actress, but he did not approve of "that curiously constructed stage monstrosity yclept the 'Yankee gal.'"[40] One reason for these apparent changes in literary taste may be that after the middle of the century, the nation seemed less inclined to embody its identity in the rustic common man, and certainly not in the New England Jonathan. As we shall see in subsequent chapters, New England humor in other media begins to wane at this time, and the rustic Yankee undergoes changes. On stage, there is Joseph Jefferson's portrayal of Asa Trenchard in *Our American Cousin* in the late 1850s; John Edward Owens first performed his version of an older Solon Shingle in *The People's Lawyer* in 1864 (see fig. 16) and played the part for nearly twenty years; and Denman Thompson made his career with Joshua Whitcomb in *The Old Homestead* in the last quarter of the century (see fig. 17).

For more than thirty years, though, New England humor in the style of Jonathan Ploughboy, Hiram Dodge, and Lot Sap Sago made the rustic Yankee the leading native characterization on stages at home and abroad. A survey of histories of the major theaters in New York, Philadelphia, and Boston shows that the role appeared every season from 1830 to 1850, and many actors played the part for many years in theaters large and small throughout the nation. Aesthetically the plays leave much to be desired: they seldom seem written with care, the plots are hackneyed, and the characterizations often appear mere caricatures. But they did what theater should do above all else, they entertained, and although Yankee theater produced no plays of lasting significance, its actors gave body and voice to New England humor.

Chapter 4
New England Humor in Print: Stories, Letters, and Poems

At the same time that Yankee actors brought New England humor to life on the theater stages of cities and towns throughout the nation, printed accounts of the comic New Englander began to appear anywhere magazines, newspapers, comic almanacs, and books could be carried and there were people to read the humorous letters, stories, songs, and poems sometimes "by" but always "about" the rustic Yankee. With a few exceptions—Johnny Beedle, Enoch Timbertoes, and Jonathan Slick, and, above all, the cracker-barrel philosophers to be dealt with in a following chapter—the Yankee characterizations in print were the work of anonymous writers and editors who tried their hand at the popular conventions of New England humor. Various and profuse, New England humor in print provides the most complete catalog of those conventions and thus the most thorough examination of the complex meanings inherent in the Yankee's role as the representative American common man and the touchstone for testing an authentic American experience.

Those meanings and conventions had their origins in the Revolutionary War and the early years of the new nation, as indicated in chapter 2, but no lasting literary tradition was established—no readily identifiable Yankee characterization and no consistent use of the conventions of a literary dialect.[1] Soon after the War of 1812 ended in 1815, though, New England humor began to appear increasingly in print, as it did on stage, and in forms that have much more in common with subsequent developments in humor than had appeared previously.[2] Several factors encouraged that growth, not only the heightening of national self-consciousness and its identity in the broad democratization of American society but also the creation of less expensive, popular media, made possible by technological improvements in printing and publishing, that could serve that democratization. By the end of the 1820s, the requisites of a "tradition" of New England humor in the truest sense had been firmly established in the national popular press.

A good sense of the growth of that tradition can be found in the pages of the *New England Galaxy*. Founded in 1817, the *Galaxy* originated and reprinted New England humor of many kinds, and what with its reviews of Charles Mathews's and James Hackett's stage Yankees and its general commentaries on Yankee character and speech, the *Galaxy* of the 1820s provides an early anthology of the New England comic tradition. Also in the early 1820s, New England humor began to receive wide coverage in newspapers and journals in all parts of the country. The best example is a series of "Jonathan's Visit" poems, a rustic Yankee's account of his first visit to or experience with a steamboat, cotton factory, theater, commencement, and bowling alley. In 1823 "Jonathan's Visit to the Steamboat" appeared in the Cincinnati *National Republican and Ohio Political Register* and in the Washington, D.C., *National Journal*, which had reprinted it from the Providence, Rhode Island, *Journal*. Like the Cincinnati editor, the Washington editor apparently had a particular fondness for Jonathan's reports, for he reprinted several of the poems, taking them from Baltimore, New York, and Portland papers, among others. This borrowing was accepted journalistic practice as part of the "exchange" system, but editors complained when they did not get credit for first publication. An editor's notice in the Portland *Independent Statesman* (30 July 1824) argued that "Jonathan's Visit to the Museum," which a writer in the *Boston Statesman* had tried to "palm off as *original*," had in fact appeared earlier in the Portland paper and subsequently "went the rounds with most papers and is deservedly considered one of the most humorous and pithy of all Jonathan's productions."[3] Because of the exchange system, multiple appearances of stories and poems are so common that it is virtually impossible to determine where or when a given piece first appeared and where and how often subsequently. Given the reprintings that can be documented, however, it is reasonable to assume that any humorous piece, whatever its literary or comic merits might be, "went the rounds" many times over the years.[4] By the mid-1820s, New England humor already had come a long way since 1811, when the editor of *The Chaplet of Comus* tried vainly to answer the charge that "no good thing of a humorous kind can come out of New England."

Also in the 1820s, the first popular serialized Yankee character appeared in print, George Arnold's Joe Strickland, whose first letter in the New York

National Advocate (15 July 1825) puffed Arnold's lottery.[5] Joe went on to give his cracker-barrel opinions on city life and politics in letters soon reprinted in papers and magazines all over the country, letters that inspired so many imitators that editors could speak with knowing good humor of the far-flung Strickland clan. The popularity of the Strickland letters in the 1820s doubtless led to Asa Greene's Enoch Timbertoes letters in Greene's New York *Constellation* beginning in 1830 and certainly to Seba Smith's Jack Downing letters in Smith's Portland *Daily Courier* in the same year. And Jack Downing—the original and the many imitations—would give much the same impetus to the popularity of New England humor in the next ten to twenty years that Davy Crockett gave to backwoods humor in the same period.

All of this is to say that by 1830 a tradition of New England humor was firmly established in the popular press of the nation, and through the 1830s and 1840s, New England humor in print reached a flood tide, as did Yankee theater, that began to ebb in the 1850s. A New York weekly, the *Spirit of the Times,* would feature backwoods humor in the 1840s, but in the 1830s it favored native humor in the New England tradition. (William T. Porter, its editor, had worked on Asa Greene's *Constellation,* and he was, after all, Vermont born and reared.) Fashionable magazines such as *Burton's* and *Godey's* occasionally published a tastefully comic rustic Yankee narrative, and the prestigious *Knickerbocker* saw fit to print Yankee humor in Gaylord Lewis Clark's column, "The Editor's Table," in the 1840s. So popular had New England humor become in the 1840s that it provided much of the content for such aptly titled magazines as *Yankee Blade, Yankee Doodle, The Yankee, Brother Jonathan,* and, in the 1850s, *Yankee Notions* (see fig. 3). Because so little of the humor in the public press was copyrighted, it found its way into the many anthologies of native humor published at home and abroad over the years, including *Georgia Scenes* (1835) and *The Big Bear of Arkansas* (1845), today considered solely as classic collections of backwoods humor. Song books and comic almanacs provided rather different outlets for humor. The comic songs were probably taken from theater performances and featured caricatures of many national and ethnic types, and lyrics and burlesques of then-popular songs. Humorist and character actor W. E. Burton's *Burton's Comic Songster* went through four editions, the first in 1837; someone capitalized on the selling power of Jack Downing's name in 1835 and published *Jack Downing's Song*

Book, which went through five editions by 1839. Beginning with Charles Ellms's *The American Comic Almanac* in 1831, comic almanacs usually featured crudely done illustrations and originated some original humor that newspapers borrowed, but typically they reprinted material from other sources. Despite printing of poor quality, slipshod production in general, and sometimes bad taste, these almanacs had an enormous circulation up to the Civil War, with more than thirty varieties in Massachusetts alone.[6]

Reprinted as often as it was over the years, and appearing as it does in so many forms by so many anonymous writers, printed New England humor does not lend itself to the kind of roughly chronological consideration that can be given to Yankee theater and to cracker-barrel humor. A more meaningful approach is to look at those subjects that are most often dealt with in various ways in print: (1) Yankee speaking, (2) Yankee peddling, (3) Yankee tricks, (4) Yankee courtship, and (5) the Yankee in an urban or industrial setting.[7] These appeared in Yankee theater, of course, but whereas a stage characterization combined them in various ways, printed humor—usually brief, nearly always less than a page, and usually less than a column—typically made one of these situations or character traits the comic core of a piece. Theater stories that followed these conventions often appeared in print.

Of course, these types are more functional than real, and some consideration needs to be given to things not considered here as part of the tradition of New England humor, if only to make clearer how the term *tradition* is being used. For example, just as Dan Marble's stage Yankee sometimes became a frontier hybrid, as did the cracker-barrel philosopher Sam Slick, a handful of stories features the Yankee trying to outdo the frontiersman in backwoods brag. This kind of story, however, would seem to be a response to the sudden popularity of Davy Crockett in backwoods humor in the 1830s, as the titles "Crockett Outdone" and "Georgia vs. Down East" in the *Galaxy of Comicalities* (23 Oct. 1833) and the Camden, South Carolina, *Camden Journal* (31 Aug. 1833) suggest.[8] There are also some early stories, songs, and cartoons about a comic Yankee militia muster. Mathews and then Hackett played it out on stage, an "image of the flounderings and confusions of democratic society," Hodge says, and artist David Claypoole Johnston, illustrator of Seba Smith's first collection of Downing letters, had drawn the muster scene with much the same intent in the late 1820s and 1830s (see fig. 7).[9] So popular had such foolishness become by mid-decade that Poe, commenting on

"The Company Drill" in Augustus Baldwin Longstreet's *Georgia Scenes* (1835), saw it as one "among the innumerable descriptions of militia musters which are so rife in the land."[10] Yankee theater may have kept the comic muster alive on stage beyond the 1830s, but it faded from print soon after Poe's observation. The subject was perhaps too dated and too local to be enjoyed by the national audience that New England humor now attracted. The same can be said of stories such as "Zephaniah and the Sea Serpent" (*Boston Morning Post*, 16 July 1833), a Yankee's rustic account of a phenomenon of some kind that was widely reported in New England newspapers in the early 1830s.[11]

Other stories, although they include a characteristic feature of New England humor, are not essentially humorous. Seba Smith's "The Tough Yarn," from *'Way Down East* (1854), is initially about someone trying to get a rustic Yankee to give a direct answer, but Jack Robinson comes off not so much as an evasive Yankee as a true raconteur, whose circumlocutory tall tales are imbued with local color. Like other stories in Smith's collection, which he subtitled *Portraitures of Yankee Life*, "A Tough Yarn" (another phrase for tall tale) is a worthy precursor of the local color tradition of writers such as Harriet Beecher Stowe, Sarah Orne Jewett, and Mary Wilkins Freeman.[12]

The title character of "The Yankee Engineer in Love," in *Graham's Magazine* (Mar. 1840), narrates what first appears to be a typical, funny story of rustic Yankee courtship, but the tale ends melodramatically with the death of the girl, and the Yankee, years later, still mourning her. The story is, in other words, an example of the sentimental literature that high-toned magazines such as *Graham's* encouraged as respectable native letters.[13] On the other hand, a story such as William Burton's "A Cape Codder Among the Mermaids" in *Burton's Gentleman's Magazine* (Dec. 1840) is humorous enough. A Cape Cod sailor, filled with the chaplain's liquor, dreams he is under the sea sporting with "marmen and marmaids," but except for an entertainingly rustic Yankee dialect, the story makes no use of traits usually attributed to the Yankee, traits pertinent to his role as a national archetype—nor did it initiate any trait that would be.[14]

Much the same is true of Samuel Kettell's "The Rime of the Ancient Pedlar," in the *New Yorker* (27 Jan. 1838), a bizarre story of a slippery Yankee narrated in vernacular but a tale that makes no use of the Yankee's legendary peddling skills. What humor it has to offer is as a burlesque of Coleridge's classic poem. Works such as these often fell under copyright restrictions that tended to keep them out of the exchange network, and in any case they were too long to fit the format or serve the needs of much of the popular press. Take the example of another of Seba Smith's stories from 'Way Down East, "John Wadleigh's Trial." The Yankee Blade (25 Mar. 1847) printed it in full as "a droll story of the old Puritan times" that was going the rounds. On the other hand, the leading humor journal of the time, the Spirit of the Times, printed (10 July 1847) only the short court scene, which featured a popular peculiarity of Yankee speaking.

New England humor in print was typically brief and used a single character trait or situation as the humorous raison d'être of the given piece. Those traits and situations were certainly not uniquely American as sources of humor, but the exigencies of the national experience between the Revolutionary War and the Civil War charged them with the uniquely American meaning that had something to do with their popularity.

Yankee Speaking

No trait was so important to the tradition of New England humor, of native American humor of all kinds, as vernacular speech. Over the years a distinctive vocabulary, spellings that reflected speech, and types of expressions evolved that were not accurate transcriptions of New England vernacular but that gave the characterization a sense of rustic New England authenticity and were humorous in themselves.[15] Jonathan Slick's account of going to a theater for the first time has it all: "Gloves pressed down on each knee, and staring like a stuck pig with my mouth a leetle open, a lot of folks dressed off in short jackets and trousers cut off at the knees, come a dancing out of the house, and begun tu talk all at once, and chatter and laugh together as chipper as a flock of birds. They seemed as happy as clams in high water."[16] Although not consistently an authentic New England vernacular, this kind of language served well enough in print and entertained as well. Yet humorous as Jonathan's lingo might be, the situation—the incongruity of his being there in the theater at all—makes it so and gives it its meaning. "Yankee Salutation and Reply," from the Boston Evening Transcript (8 Apr. 1833), is very different:

In a neighboring town in our county of Essex, where the parish parson is reverenced as a "right *down steady* man," the following salutation and reply is quite common. "Good morning, neighbor A——, how d'ye today?" "Why, I'm pretty much *arter the old sort—'tween three and one*—how's your woman this morning?"

"Well she's pretty *much what for her* considerin—how's yourn?"
"*So's to be crawling*, I thank you—good morning."

Nothing humorous about the situation here, nor about the characterizations, other than what they say, and the italicized words emphasize that *they*, odd ways of speaking, are the source of humor. This "quarantining of the vernacular," as Richard Bridgman calls it, "resembles the humorist's frequent use of a frame of standard English to enclose vernacular stories." Federalist writers of mock pastorals did so consistently, and the practice continued in the nineteenth century for much the same purpose. "The presence of a literate narrator to introduce the vernacular speaker," Bridgman continues, "permitted the reader to enjoy colorful informality, yet be assured that the hierarchy of social values still stood, that the vulgar were still under control."[17]

Typically, stories found something humorously distinctive in the *manner* of Yankee speaking. Royall Tyler made exactly that distinction in an anecdote in his novel *The Yankey in London* (1809). The narrator, trying to find "some *shibboleth* to distinguish an Old from a New England man," found it not "in pronunciation, nor yet in expression or accent—not in words but in mode," a distinction he illustrated with the following: "What time of day is it by your watch?" an Englishman asks a New England man. "Why, I can't say, what o'clock is it by yours?" is the reply. Then, trying to preclude such a response, the Englishman asks another Yankee, "What is the reason you New Englanders always reply to a question by asking another?" "Why, is that the case, sir?" replies the Yankee. The story, reprinted as one of the few examples of New England humor in *The Chaplet of Comus* (1811), well illustrates the evasiveness that the Portland *Eastern Argus* (19 Nov. 1807) called giving "a Yankee answer." Some forty years later, the *Spirit of the Times* (1 Dec. 1849) picked up from the Chicago *Journal* another version of Tyler's anecdote that added dialect and titled the story "A Yankee Answer."

In Tyler's brief anecdote, the Yankee spoke no dialect, but when later humorous stories elaborated on this peculiarity of Yankee speaking, vernacular speech added to the fun. The ultimate story on the evasive Yankee, "Cross Questions and Crooked Answers" from *The American Joe Miller* (1853), features two Yankees in something of a contest. The long dialogue ends as follows:

"Do you look to be making great dealings in produce up the country?"

"Why that, I expect, is difficult to know."

"I calculate you'll find the markets changeable these times?"

"No markets beant very often without changing."

"Why, that's right down true. What may be your biggest article of produce?"

"I calculate, generally, that's the biggest as I makes most by."

"You may say that. But what do you chiefly call your most particular branch?"

"Why, that's what I can't justly say."

A classic example of giving "a Yankee answer," the story also illustrates another peculiarity of New England speaking that had become a conventional source of humor. According to the preface to this story, "Nothing, in fact, can equal their [the Yankees's] skill in evading a question excepting that with which they set about asking one." English travelers often charged New Englanders, and by extension Americans in general, with compulsive inquisitiveness,[18] but Cooper, in *Notions of the Americans* (1828), his answer to English travel books, argued that "this putative inquisitiveness, if ever true, is now a gross caricature." Certainly it became so in New England humor. In a widely circulated story—it appeared as late as 1880—entitled "An Inquisitive Yankee On a Train" (also titled "Yankee Inquisitiveness"), in the *Yankee Blade* (13 Mar. 1852), "a lean, slab-sided Yankee, every feature of whose face seemed to ask a question," cornered a widow on a train. With a series of pointed questions he learns that her husband has just died, then slyly asks, *"Was you cal'lating to git married agin?"* Indignant, the widow seeks another seat. "She needn't be mad—I didn't want to hurt her feelins," says the Yankee, and unshaken by the rebuff he turns to the passenger behind him to begin again: "What did they make you pay for that umberel you got in your hand? It's a real pooty one!"

Despite the Yankee's obnoxious intrusiveness in such stories, readers surely enjoyed the discomforting effect, and in those stories in which someone presumed to thwart the Yankee's persistent prying, the comic triumph seems certain. George Hill, in a widely reprinted story, got so irritated by a Yankee's incessant attempts to learn where he was born that he gave him enough information to satisfy even the most curious: "I was born in Boston, in the year 1809, in the 8th day of October, at six o'clock in the morning." "At six o'clock eh?" asks the Yankee. "At six o'clock precisely, down in Water Street," Hill adds. But he stumps the Yankee only momentarily. "Dew tell," he says, "but stranger, *dew you remember the number of the house?*"[19] One of the best stories on that topic appeared in the *Carpet Bag* (30 Aug. 1851) with the apt title, "Horrors of a Yankee Inquisition." Virtually an essay on the subject, the story begins with the supercilious, learned observation by the apparent author, "Peter Snooks, Esquire," that there is indeed an "inquisitorial penchant which operates on the general mind of almost every item in these diggins—male and female—that has not been born dumb—and with whom I have come, or been dragged, into confabulative contact." Snooks prides himself on having already outwitted two such Yankees, but this encounter with a third is not so successful. Finding Snooks fishing, the curious Yankee asks him what his fishing pole is made of, and Snooks answers with information ad absurdum, including the measurements of the pole, where he bought it and for how much, the contents of his pockets and how much each item cost, where he lives and for how long. For a moment, Snooks is smugly pleased, "Happy in having furnished one individual, at least, with a *quantum sufficit* of information." Scarcely has he put his line back into the brook, though, when the undaunted Yankee asks, "Say, stranger, *where d'ye dig yer bait?*" The learned Snooks has to admit that the rustic Yankee has "completely flummoxed" him.

Seldom could the Yankee be foiled, but it did happen in "Yankee Curiosity" in the *Pittsburgh Gazette* (5 June 1818), which took it from "an Eastern paper." (Another version appeared in the *Spirit of the Times*, 30 June 1832.) Stopping at a New England inn, a one-armed sailor finds the Yankee landlord curious indeed about the missing limb. "I'll tell you," he says to the landlord, "if you won't ask me another question." Agreed. "Then," says the sailor, "'twas bit off." The Yankee keeps his word, "but at length in an ague of impatient curiosity, but too mindful of his promise to ask the question direct, he burst forth with this ejaculation—'I wish I knew what bit it off!'"

Private about his own business, but compulsively curious about the business of others, the rustic Yankee could also be simply garrulous, readily spoken if not well spoken. Take the case of the Yankee called "An Original Character" in the *Exeter News Letter* (15 June 1841). A stranger traveling through rural New England reported coming upon a Yankee rustic, "a tall raw boned, overgrown, lantern jawed boy . . . one of the roughest specimens of domestic manufacture that ever mortal beheld." Asked how far it is to the next house, Jonathan answers at inconsequential length:

> The fust house you come to though, is a barn, and the next is a hay stack; but old Hobsin's house is on beyeant. You'll be sure to meet his gals long afore you get there; tarnal rompin' critters, they plague our folks more'n little. His sheep git in our pasture every day, and his gals in our orchard. Dad sets the dog arter the sheep and me arter the gals—and the way we makes the wool and the petticoats fly, is a sin to snakes.

Other responses are not so long, but they would seem just as inconsequential. Asked, for example, why one leg is shorter than the other, he says it makes it easier for him to plow, especially on hillsides; asked "How do your potatoes come off this year?" he replies, "They don't come at all; I digs 'em out and there's everlastin' snarl of 'em in each hill." These kinds of ready responses, much like the evasions and persistent questions of other Yankees, suggest a defensive caution on the part of the rustic New Englander, particularly in dealing with a stranger who was also a social and cultural superior, which was usually the case in such stories. As the narrator of this story assured his readers, the rustic he met was "a Jonathan of the first water."[20]

Just as often in New England humor, the Yankee was loquacious for the sake of humorous loquaciousness itself. Like other attributes of Yankee speaking, it was well suited for live representation on stage, as the popular story of "Uncle Ben" attests, but printed stories usually attributed the trait to Yankee widows, who stereotypically gossiped and prattled, as in the story "The Garrulous Yankee Widow" in *Yankee Notions* (Oct. 1857) and in the serialized characterizations of Mrs. Scruggins, by "Ned" in the *Spirit of the Times* in the late 1840s, and Mehitable Ross in *Vanity Fair* in the early 1860s. Benjamin Shillaber's highly popular characterization of Mrs. Partington is often cited as an example of the type, but although Mrs. Partington speaks inconsequentially enough, she sounds more like an American Malaprop, or an early literary comedian (perhaps "literary comedienne") than she does a New Englander.

A more satisfying character of this kind is Frances Whitcher's Widow Bedott. Although she has all of the unpleasant features of the stereotype, her monologue about her husband, "Hezekiah Bedott," is a masterpiece of circumlocutory inconsequentiality and a true classic of New England humor. "He was a wonderful hand to moralize, husband was, 'specially after he begun to enjoy poor health. He made an observation once when he was in one of his poor turns, that I never shall forget the longest day I live." Thus the widow begins, and takes the reader with her in a digression that has something of stream of consciousness to it and that delays with fine comic effect the memorable moralism until the very end of the story. Heightening that effect are her solemn assurances of the import of "what husband said," her promises to get back to what he said, and her impatience with people who do not get to the point. "Now there's Miss Jinkins, she that was Polly Bingham afore she was married, she is the tejusest individooal to tell a story that ever I see in all my born days. But I was a gwine to tell you what husband said." And what *did* husband say that the widow could not forget? The story ends thusly: "Says he to me, says he, 'Silly.' I says to him, says I, 'What?' He says to me, says he, '*We're all poor critters!*'"[21] Stories of Yankee speaking such as this are early examples of what Mark Twain would call in "How to Tell a Story" (1895) the "humorous," or "American," story that "depends for its effect upon the *manner* of the telling" rather than "upon the *matter*." With "Hezekiah Bedott," Yankee speaking becomes true literary art because the author's telling is significant, not just the character's. That is, the reader laughs at the ending, but then goes back to look at what came before, just as one does with Twain's classic of the same kind, "The Story of the Old Ram" in *Roughing It* (1872). The reader has been "sold," ultimately, by the writer, not by the character.

Most stories of Yankee speaking are essentially jokes the Yankee plays on someone in the story who is neither a Yankee nor a rustic, jokes that are based in a traditional source of humor generally but have a particular significance in the American experience: that of the historical inferior—the colonist/former colonist—whose manner of speaking in the story comically confounds by putting off, often by "putting on," those who represent the values of the historical superior—the colonialist/former colonialist. However, the stories of Yankee speaking—as stories—capture the Yankee only for that moment triumphant. His implicit inferiority does not change, and readers laughed at the triumph because they saw it—only *if* they saw it—as comically incongruous. In the long run, for themselves and for the nation that Jonathan represented, most of them aspired to something better. To paraphrase Richard Bridgman, readers enjoyed the "colorful informality" of the vernacular character but needed to know that higher cultural values prevailed, "that the vulgar were still under control."

Yankee Peddling and Tricks

The Yankee triumphed as well in stories of peddling and tricks, but nineteenth-century readers could find something more to celebrate in their countryman's ingenuity, a *'cuteness* that seemed to have deep native roots, although one fraught with ambivalent import. According to Perry Miller, a synod called at Boston in 1679 to determine the causes of increasing godlessness found, among other things, that "New Englanders were betraying a marked disposition to tell lies, especially when selling anything."[22] Thus Edward Ward's observation twenty years later cannot be taken merely as an early calumny that malcontent visitors in the nineteenth century leveled against the Yankee, and by extension, the American character. In *A Trip to New England with a Character of the Country and People* (1699), he wrote that although the Saints of New England "wear in their faces the Innocence of Doves, you will find them in their dealings . . . as Subtile as Serpents. . . . And it is a proverb with those that know them, Whomsoever believes a New England Saint shall be sure to be cheated; And he that knows how to deal with their Traders, may Deal with the Devil and fear no Craft."[23] Much later visitors would tell about Yankees peddling wooden nutmegs and gun flints made of horn, but although such scams were the stuff of myth, they were too commonplace for printed stories. In one of these, Joseph Beachnut peddled ten gross of tooth powder, but the little boxes were nothing more than solid blocks of wood with labels;

in another, a peddler took the sandbags from a Texas fort, painted them to look like hams, and sold them. According to the Yankee, they made the merchant who bought them "*grit* his teeth."[24] In "A Yankee in Court in the Lower Regions," in the *Comic Monthly* (Sept. 1859), we find what happens to Yankees of that ilk. Even as a boy, Virgil Hoskins had shown promise at the age of six in making a counterfeit dollar of pewter and cheating his father with it. "My parent seemed to be real glad when he found it eout," the unrepentant Yankee tells the devil. "He said it showed I had a genus." Among his other "sells" was stealing an old grindstone, covering it with cotton cloth, smearing it with butter, and selling it as a cheese. The devil, out of patience with New Englanders, sentences Virgil to have the grindstone tied to his neck and be thrown into a lake of molasses, where nearly all of his countrymen already are.

Usually, though, stories about Yankee peddling featured not outright frauds but the Yankee's ingenuity in making a deal while leaving himself essentially blameless. Such stories not only offered more literary and comic opportunities for the writer but also reflected better on the American character. An early poem in the *New England Galaxy* (15 Jan. 1819), from the *Pittsburgh Gazette,* gives an indication of what would become the basic features of what may well be the most popular type of story in printed New England humor. According to the preface:

Yankee Puns—No. 1

Not Walnut, *alias* Knot Walnut; *alias* Poplar Wood

> By foreigners 'tis often said,
> That Yankees, in the way of trade,
> With all their moral, pious preaching,
> Are very fond of over-reaching;
> Nay, some can give the world a beating
> In most ingenious, downright cheating;
> And, rather than to lose the knack,
> E'en their own nation they'll attack;
> Will over-reach and cheat each other;
> A parent, sister, or a brother.

In the tale that follows, a "Cit" asks a peddler what he calls the wood he has for sale: "*Not* walnut, sir," replies the Yankee truthfully enough, but knowing that the "Cit" will hear "knot" walnut and buy it as good firewood.[25] Later stories would better develop the character and comic ingenuity of the Yankee than this account, which relies exclusively on the pun vaunted in the subtitle, but the preface quoted gives some insight into the comic and cultural context in which such stories were read. It speaks not only to the belief among foreigners in the New Englander's compulsion for gain so inveterate that he would cheat his own kin but also points out the incongruity, made comic here, between Puritan piety and Yankee "over-reaching," which Edward Ward had warned of. That incongruity gives an unmistakably American cast to the traditional stories of the trickster and an additional comic dimension to these stories, as the Yankee balances his nineteenth-century yen for the main chance with the piety of his Puritan ancestors. In the story "The Devonshire Bull," from the *Constellation* (15 Oct. 1831), a peddler named Joshua Peabody boasted that he had never cheated anyone, "told no lies, and never travelled a road which he was afraid to travel again." Having accepted a sickly calf as partial payment for a clock, Joshua took the animal to the farm of a squire, an old acquaintance noted for his interest in fine stock, who somehow gets into his head that the calf is a genuine Devonshire bull imported from England and insists on buying it. Joshua warns him more than once against the purchase but gives in at the end, although still protesting the deal. "If the 'squire has a mind to cheat *himself*, it's nobody's business. *I* can't be to blame," he had rationalized on the way to the squire's farm.

Many stories of peddling and trading show the variety of ways the Yankee could thus manage a victim and leave himself blameless. In "The Cutest Yankee Trick Yet," reprinted in the *Yankee Blade* (Jan. 1852), a Connecticut peddler with too many brooms cannot find a buyer willing to pay the cash he needs for them. When a Providence storekeeper offers the Yankee any stock of his choice at wholesale in exchange, the peddler finally agrees to accepting half in stock and half in cash. The merchant pays the cash, takes the brooms, and then tells the peddler to select his merchandise. The Yankee paces the floor, scratches his head—then loads up the brooms. "I know them like a book, and can swear jest what you paid for 'em," he tells the merchant. "And, so saying, the pedlar commenced re-loading his brooms, and having snugly deposited half of his former load, jumped on his cart with a regular Connecticut grin, and leaving the merchant cursing his impudence, and his own stupidity, drove off in search of another customer."

A particularly ingenious peddler could even get money from a merchant who refused to deal. In one often reprinted story, "A Yankee Trick," in the *Rutland* (Vermont) *Herald* (16 Nov. 1843), a storekeeper tries to run off a peddler who wants two dollars for his razor straps. Undaunted, the Yankee bets five dollars that he will take anything offered for them. Depositing their wager with a bystander, the merchant offers the peddler a picayune, a small coin, for the straps. "They are yourn," says the Yankee, who pockets the bet, having sold the strops for more than he had hoped. Actor Dan Marble had a version of the story, printed in *Yankee Notions* (June 1852), that carried the Yankee's cuteness one step further. Pretending it has all been a joke, the Yankee offers to trade back. The storekeeper agrees, hands back the straps, and gets the picayune in return. However contrary such practices might be to the spiritual conscience of earlier New Englanders, they do capture and implicitly celebrate the spirit of capitalism that most nineteenth-century Americans valued and that so many English travelers deplored.

Much the same was true of stories of what were called *Yankee tricks,* a phrase that conveyed "to the mind of the hearer an idea of a depravity peculiar to the people of New England," Matthew Carey wrote in the December 1809 *Port Folio*—the same year that Washington Irving wrote at some length and with some glee in *A History of New York* of New York Dutch frustrations with Yankee sharpers. Much like peddling, tricks required ingenuity and usually left the Yankee richer, but the stories typically found something especially meaningful and humorous in the rustic New Englander's victim. In "A Yankee Farmer's Double Sell" from *The Book of 1000 Comicalities* (1859), a group of "consequential young college students" in a tavern outside Boston thought they would have some fun with the old Yankee who enters accompanied by his dog:

> "Do you belong to the church?" asked one of the wags.
> "Well, I don't belong to nothin' else, except Betsey," said the farmer.
> "I suppose you would not tell a lie," said the student.
> "Not for the price of that air cur, an' Betsey's weddin' gown, an' all the fixin's belongin' to it, to boot," said the farmer.

"Now, what will you take for that dog?" pointing to the farmer's cur, who was not worth his weight in Jersey mud.

"I won't take twenty dollars for that dog."

"Twenty dollars! why he is not worth twenty cents."

"He's worth twenty dollars to me. He perfects the house and keeps the plaguey Shanghaes from roostin' on Betsey's clothes-line."

"Come, my friend," said the student, who, with his companions, was bent upon having some capital fun with the old man, "now you say you won't tell a lie—let me see if you will not do it for twenty dollars. I'll give you twenty dollars for the dog."

"I'll not take it."

"You will not? Here, let me see if this won't tempt you to lie," added the student, producing a small bag of half dollars from which he commenced counting in numerous small piles upon the table. The farmer sat near, with his hat between his knees, apparently unconcerned. "There," added the student, "There are twenty dollars, all in silver; I will give you that for your dog."

The old farmer quietly raised his hat to the table, and then, as quick as thought, scraped all the money into it except one half dollar and exclaimed:

"I won't take twenty dollars!—nineteen and a half is as much as the dog is worth—considerin' he's got one broken leg from Betsey's brumstick—he's your property."

Although smart-alecky city types were popular and appropriate victims of Yankee trickery, American Dutchmen and Southerners appeared frequently as the comic gull. The Dutchman had long been a popular comic caricature on stage and in print, his thick, exaggerated accent identifying him as a foreigner and thus in stories of Yankee tricks, appropriate game for the native ingenuity of the rustic Yankee. "A Yankee Trick" appeared twice in the *Constellation* (5 Feb. 1831 and 29 Sept. 1832), each time crediting a different source, and gives an American twist to an old story. Jonathan contracted with Michael Van Higgenbeck to farm "by halves," the Yankee to get the bottoms of all he planted, the Dutchman the tops. The first year's crop being potatoes,

Van Higgenbeck demanded the bottoms the next year; but then the Yankee planted wheat. The Dutchman persisted, though, and the third year demanded both tops and bottoms. Arriving to get his due at harvest, he finds that Jonathan had left him both the tops and bottoms of the corn he had planted.

Another popular victim was the Southerner, naturally enough, given the historical antipathy that existed between North and South. One of the most widely reprinted Yankee stories—in all parts of the country—was Asa Greene's "The Tin Pedlar and Sleepy David," which first appeared in Greene's *Constellation* (23 Feb. 1833, and again 24 Aug. 1833) and then in his book *A Yankee Among the Nullifiers* (1833). No one at the South Carolina race track could believe the Yankee was serious in offering to pit his horse, Sleepy David, against the finest Southern horse flesh, for Sleepy David "was a lean, slab-sided, crooked-legged, rough-haired, milk-and-molasses-colored son of a gun as ever went on four legs" and who "stood all the time as if he was asleep." The Yankee loses the first race, but then offers a bet of a thousand dollars against the local favorite, Southron. Needless to say, the Yankee knows what he is about, as Sleepy David wins the race and takes the purse as well as the bets that the Southerners had so eagerly made. The story of a wretched-looking animal winning a contest is certainly common enough in the literature and folklore of many cultures, but this story of a motley Yankee peddler's deception of proud Carolina gentlemen in a horse race and on their own turf had a very special meaning, appearing as it ultimately did in a book that satirized South Carolina's attempt in November 1832 to nullify federal law.[26]

Another comic dimension could be added to stories of tricks if the victim had the audacity to try to beat the Yankee at his own game. The Dutchman in "A Yankee Trick" had made it "his chief boast that he had never been cheated," which makes the Yankee's triumph all the more comic. Others, knowing the Yankee's legendary propensity for tricks, wanted to learn one, only to be tricked themselves for the asking. In one popular story from the *Oxford* (Maine) *Observer* (24 Aug. 1826), taking it from the Winchester (Virginia) *Republican*, a Virginia tavern keeper and his wife should have known better than to put aside their antipathy to New England peddlers on the condition that a Yankee wanting a room show them a trick before he leaves. Rising before dawn and gathering together the articles in the room into the coverlet from the bed, the New Englander urges the landlady to buy them, which she does, remarking that the coverlet would match one of her own exactly. As the peddler prepares to leave, his hosts remind him of the trick he had agreed to teach them. "O, never-mind," he replies cooly, as tricksters so often do, "you'll find it out soon enough."

Given the Yankee's legendary ingenuity in peddling and tricks, still another comic incongruity lay in the New Englander's being taken at his own game. In "A New-York Trick" (the *Constellation*, 4 June 1831, crediting the *Yeoman's Gazette*), a Dutchman tempts a Yankee's penchant for speculation by offering up to a dollar each for cats suitably trained, which meant they had to be well fed, kept in an upper room with only one small window, and whipped severely every third day. Buying up cats at nine pence, the Yankee puts them in his attic as requested. The caterwauling is bad enough, but when he begins to administer the required whipping on the third day, the cats revolt, attacking the shaken Yankee as they flee the room. According to the Dutchman, "It was merely a slight offset for the wooden nutmegs, horn gun flints and oakleaf and skunk cabbage cigars, which he had purchased of the puritanical tin pedlars." Another version of the type is "The Ill Looking Horse: a Pun that was No Joke" in the *Yankee Blade* (2 Aug. 1852), in which a French Canadian answers all of the Vermonter's questions positively but often adds in his broken English, "He's not look ver good." The horse looks fine to the Yankee, though, and he buys him, only to return a few days later, outraged that he has been cheated—that the horse is blind as a bat. "I vas tell you he was not *look* ver good," the Canadian tells him; "I don't know if he *look at all*."[27] A small return in kind, perhaps, for wood that was "knot walnut." Yet even in apparent defeat, the Yankee could triumph. The Green Mountain Yankee in "The Yankee Horse-Jockey and the Auctioneer" in *Dr. Valentine's Comic Lectures* had wanted fifteen dollars for his horse at an auction, but accepts a dollar and a half—and then learns that the money must go for auction fees. The Yankee decides, though, that he had not done too badly after all: "I couldn't give him away last Tewsday," he admits.

For the most part, though, taken together, the stories of Yankee peddling and tricks celebrate the ingenuity and material success that so many of the stories resulted in—a celebration of a rustic triumph over anyone conventionally seen as culturally superior or who presumed to triumph over that legendary, native ingenuity. That ingenuity is crucial to the stories. For one thing, it made for literary and comic variety, but more important was its significance to the broader meaning that the Yankee represented in the American experience. In the earliest stories, such as "Yankee Puns #1," it rationalized a regional, Puritan religious conscience; in later stories—in most stories of peddling and tricks—the Yankee's apparently indigenous ingenuity comically undercut the material gain it resulted in. In doing so, it answered English observers who deplored New World materialism personified by the Yankee and calmed the apprehensions of Americans who celebrated economic growth at the same time they feared its changes on what they wanted us to see as a pastoral society. Embodied as it was in the rustic Brother Jonathan, that apparently indigenous ingenuity had its origins *in* pastoral society, in pastoral values, and thus made that materialism acceptable. At the heart of the legendary tricks and peddling triumphs in nineteenth-century American popular literature lies an appetite for the material gain promised by the New World experience combined with a native ingenuity that could rationalize that appetite. However closely, then, such stories may parallel folk motifs and literary examples of other cultures or even hearken back to earlier New England origins of such ingenuity, they comment directly on the American identity Jonathan had come to represent in the nineteenth century.

Yankee Courtship

Comic accounts of rustic Yankee courtship are in origin and meaning very different from stories of Yankee speaking, peddling, and tricks. American writers found convenient examples in the eighteenth-century English novels and comedies of manners, but as we have seen in the early American examples of *The Contrast* and the Federalists' mock pastorals, the cultural-political history of the new nation gave a different import to the traditional humor of rustic courtship. The stories and poems in print after 1815 do not have the narrow political intent of those earlier works, as the nation as a whole struggled with the profound implications of the vernacular, democratic identity that the rustic Yankee had come to represent. True, the basis of the humor in these later versions is the same as in the earlier ones—the incongruity between the tender sentiments and genteel comportment that the reader expects from romantic experience contrasted with the bucolic barbarisms and foolish ineptitude of the rustic Yankee; however, the judgment inherent in that incongruity is more cultural than political, more covert than overt.[28]

The manner of rustic Yankee speaking was important in these stories as a source of humor, but the situation of courting made it so. "Courting," in *Elton's Comic Almanac for 1834* and widely reprinted, did it this way:

A Kitchen.—Sally, the house maid, paring apples in the corner. Enter Obadiah, who seated himself in the corner opposite to Sally, without saying a word for fifteen minutes, but finally, scratching his head, breaks silence with—

There's considerable imperceptible alterin of the weather since last week.

Sally.—Taint so injudicious and so indubitable cold as twas; the thenomicon has lowered up to four hundryd degrees higher than zenith.

Obadiah.—I think's likely, for birds of that species fly a great quantity higher in warmer days than in cold ones.

Both parties assume a grave and knowing look, and a long pause ensues. Finally Obadiah gives his pate another harrowing scratch and again breaks silence.

Well, Sally we chaps are going to raise a sleigh-ride, its such inimical good sleddin to morrow.

Sally.—You are? Our folks are suspectin company all day to-morrow.

Obadiah.—I spoze they'll hav insatiate times on't. I should be undefinitely happy if you would disgrace me with your company; I should take it as a deropitary honer; besides, we're calculating to treat the gals copious well with rasons and black strap.

Sally.—I should be supernatural glad to disgrace you, but our folks suspect company; I cant go.

Obadiah sits scratching his head a while, and at length starts up as though a new idea had come upon him.

Well, now I know what I'll do; I'll go home and thrash them are beens, what have been lyin in the barn a darnd while.

(*Exit Obadiah.*)

More coarse and just plain silly than most stories, perhaps (it may have appeared first in a comic almanac), but it was often reprinted, and it represented "The Way They Court Down East," according to the title given by the *New York Mirror* (9 Mar. 1839). More typical would be "My First and Last Courtship" in the *Camden* (South Carolina) *Journal* (29 Mar. 1834). Egged on by his father, Obadiah Bashful rubs two tallow candles in his hair and goes to court Deb, "a rotten nice gal." At her place he sits on her bonnet, overturns a chair, and splits his pants; asked if he had ever heard a "serenade," he says he knows no "Sarah Nade." When he knocks her into someone's lap, her wig falls off, and he offers to make her a new one next shearing time. Back home, he tells his father that *he* can court Deb if he wants to.

With its action and modest plot, "My First and Last Courtship" has more to offer than "The Way They Court Down East," but the comic possibilities of Yankee courtship were limited to the single situation and succumbed easily to the exaggerated and the ludicrous. Most of the letters in the "Yankee Letter" column of *The Yankee* in the late 1840s were ostensibly the work of men and women who shared empty-headed, repetitive accounts of courtship in rural New England. Consider "A Letter from a Lady" (3 Apr. 1847), one Sublime Butts. She likes her "boo" well enough, for although not handsome, "he is as clevver as suckin dove, and has gut sumthin to ecspect from his ant wen she is ded," and he "can't liv without me no how at all: speshally since he seen me to wurk on a caff that i wos skinnin won day." Blind to her ignorance and vulgarity, blithely assuming that her writing is the stuff of conventional romance, Sublime Butts's letter, like so many in the series in *The Yankee,* seems a callous caricature of rustic character, as are those in the "Dutch Lecture" column by a German American.

The lovers in the stories in *Jonathan Jaw-Stretcher's All-My-Nack* (1851?) are not so grotesquely unpleasant, but the humor is limited to outlandish names and extravagant expressions. Love struck Quizzikiah Cranequill says he "felt the delirium screamens all over my entire circulatin' medium," and Pete Progress declares that Comfort Honeysuckle is "handsome enough just in one of her lips to turn a hull tub o' apples into apple-sass, an' to make crab-apples perspire sweet cider." In a different effort to add something new to an otherwise conventional story of rustic Yankee courtship, "A Tale of a Bag of Beans" in the *New England Galaxy* (23 Oct. 1829) included a picture of Joe Bunker, mounted on his horse, Posset, on his way to court Hannah. The graphic suggests that Joe, "a genuine unsophisticated Yankee clodhopper," literally looked the horse's ass that he acted in the story (see fig. 8).

Most courting rustic Yankees acted much like Joe, but such behavior did not have to appear so ludicrous. Among the best and maybe most popular of the courting stories were those about Johnny Beedle's sleigh ride, courtship, and marriage, by W. J. McClintock. These appeared first in the *"Portland Courier"* in the 1830s and "passed with great rapidity through almost every public journal in the country," according to *Bicknell's Register,* quoted in one of the several book collections.[29] The stories have most of the conventions of rustic courtship—Johnny courts fearfully and awkwardly and he is "given the bag" more than once—but they never appear to satirize or caricature as most stories of the type do. Although as bucolic as any Yankee lover, Johnny has an ebullient good nature and high spiritedness, but above all, perhaps, an awareness of himself that causes the reader to laugh with him as much as at him. In turning down his marriage proposal, the school marm Hulday Hossam tells him "'I've great respect and esteem for you, Mr. Beedle, but—' and so forth." As Johnny willingly admits, "Nothing will cool a man down quicker than 'respect and esteem,' unless it is a wet blanket." Minor characters too are drawn deftly and with good humor. Dr. Dingley, for example, tells Johnny he can do nothing to help him and advises Mrs. Dingley not to interfere either: "Let every body skin their own eels," he counsels. But she will not hear it. "Hold your tongue, you fool," she retorts, "did ye ever hear of me burning my fingers?" More conscientiously than other writers of such stories, McClintock used rhythms of speech and expressions that are humorous but that appear natural, not contrived for comic effect. Thus Johnny describes an interfering mother as "a stump that is neither to be got round nor moved out of the way," and a rival suitor as carrying "a straight back and a stiff neck, as a man ought to when he has his best clothes on; and every time he spit, he sprung his body forward, like a jack-knife, in order to shoot clear of the ruffles." With such descriptions, Johnny convinces us he is right, not merely spiteful.

In much the same spirit as the Johnny Beedle stories is one of the classics of nineteenth-century New England humor, one collected in American litera-

ture anthologies today, James Russell Lowell's "The Courtin'." The first version of six stanzas Lowell wrote quickly to fill a blank page in the first series of
the *Biglow Papers* in 1848, but it proved popular enough to be set to music in
1850 as "Zeekel and Huldy, or a Natural Courtship." Importuned to "finish"
it, he added six stanzas in 1857 and then twelve more in 1864 to make the
"standard" version printed in *The Biglow Papers, Second Series* in 1867. This
version, as do the Johnny Beedle stories, treats rustic Yankee courtship with
touches of authentic local color and good-natured amusement. Almost a short
play, the poem has a detailed setting and depth of characterization that belie
its brevity, as in two lines summarizing the feelings of the Yankee girl and boy
just on the verge of meeting: "His heart kep' goin' pity-pat, / But hern went
pity Zekle." Lowell consistently treats the characters sympathetically, not
satirically, and his vernacular in poetry permeates the subject with homespun
quaintness, as in the following description of Hilda:

> The very room, coz she was in,
>   Seemed warm f'om floor to ceilin',
> An' she looked full ez rosy agin
>   Ez the apples she was peelin'.
> 'T was kin' o' kingdom-come to look
>   On sech a blessed cretur,
> A dogrose blushin' to a brook
>   Ain't modester nor sweeter.

In the evolution of Lowell's "The Courtin'" over time and from six stanzas to
twenty-four, we see the lowly conventions of Yankee courtship turned into art,
much as Frances Whitcher's "Hezekiah Bedott" did with loquacious Yankee
speaking. Lowell surely knew the earlier tradition of comic Yankee courtship
(Fessenden's "The Country Lovers" and Samuel Kettell's "Josh Beanpole's
Courtship," among them), as Arthur Voss says, and the first six-stanza version
is much closer "in tone and meaning" to those pieces. In the later version,
however, he "took the somewhat crude and broadly comic story of the rustic
of the rustic courtship and refined it and idealized it into a poem of homely
sentiment and romance."[30] As Lowell himself said in *The Biglow Papers, Sec-*

ond Series, in writing the final version he had "infused a little more sentiment in a homely way."[31] He felt it likely that he had thus spoiled it, but he did make the poem consistent with the tone of the second series of *Biglow Papers,* which features the old-fashioned morality and political values of Hosea Biglow, however anachronistic, and thus impractical, they are. What Voss calls the "crude and broadly comic" earliest version, however, is consistent with the first series of *Biglow Papers* in which it initially appeared, dominated as that series is by ironic personae, in particular that of crudely vernacular, politically pernicious Birdofredom Sawin, Lowell's bitter embodiment of contemporary democratic politics.

The Yankee and Modernization

Despite the limited comic opportunities that rustic courtship had to offer, it was a popular source of humor in print as well as on stage and appeared too in backwoods humor of the time, most memorably in William Tappan Thompson's *Major Jones's Courtship* (1844).[32] More popular, though, and certainly more varied, were stories of the Yankee's experiences in an urban, industrialized society, stories that have much the same literary origins as stories of courtship. The source of the humor is much the same as well: the comic incongruity between the rural innocence of the Yankee and a modern—that is to say, industrial, urban, and sophisticated—society. Royall Tyler had used that incongruity skillfully in *The Contrast,* and in the nineteenth century, other vernacular types, such as the Irishman and the black, sometimes appeared in that comic role. In more recent times a family of Tennessee hillbillies has entertained television audiences for years with their persistent inability to understand much about the modern world as represented by Beverly Hills.

In the nineteenth-century tradition of New England humor, the variations on this comic theme are well illustrated in the "Jonathan's Visit" poems (mentioned earlier in this chapter) recounting the Yankee's first reaction to a variety of new experiences. Two stanzas from "Jonathan's Visit to the Cotton Factories" from the *Cincinnati National Republican* (26 Sept. 1823) give a good idea of the form and substance of these widely reprinted poems:

Our Fac'try: I vow, 'tis a smasher!
  'Tis pretty near flat on the top.
  You might put our house here right on it
  An' Uncle Sam's saw-mill an' shop!
I walked round awhile, and went in it,
  Then, whew! what a terrible buzz!
  I swagger! 'twas more than a minute,
Before I could tell where I was!

Despite the disorienting noise of the place and the fact that Jonathan is clearly not of this new industrial order of things, he describes the factory with naïvely rustic exuberance punctuated by exclamation marks and gives it his approval in deeming it a "smasher." Although a colloquially appropriate term of approbation, the word *smasher,* like the word *terrible,* has an ominously covert meaning that becomes overt in stories that show the Yankee the victim of the machine. From the St. Louis *Reveille,* the *Harbinger* (Nov. 1846) picked up "A Yankee in a Coal Screen," in which a rural New Englander finds himself trapped in a machine that screens coal, much to the delight of those who run the contraption. Another Yankee backed into the string carding machine of a cotton factory when a worker frightened him with the story of a student who had been caught in the machinery and manufactured into No. 16, super extra, cotton warp yarn. (The grieved mother bought five skeins of it for herself "as melancholy relics," and his fellow students even bought one "to be set in lockets, and worn in remembrance of departed worth.") Titled "A Yankee in a Cotton Factory," and originating in the *Yankee Blade* (2 Oct. 1847), the story was widely reprinted and predates by twenty-five years the episode in Mark Twain's "The Story of the Old Ram," in *Roughing It* (1872), of a man manufactured into fourteen yards of carpet, rolled up and buried with some difficulty.

As Twain's still later novel *A Connecticut Yankee in King Arthur's Court* (1889) would indicate, stories such as these had a meaningful place in a nation that struggled to define itself in terms of a pastoral ideal in the face of inexorable modernization. Twentieth-century cultural historians have analyzed and documented widely and well the often covert ambivalence in that struggle.[33]

but surely no more cogently than did the anonymous, nineteenth-century author of "Jonathan Jolter's Journal" in the *New England Magazine* (Nov. 1834). Feeling confined by his life in rural Vermont, young Jonathan sets out, eager to learn something of the world at large. Steam power, he finds, runs that world, and its many manifestations first mystify the farmer. "Says I to my friend, 'Is n't this all a dream?' / "'No,' says he, 'all such matters are done here by steam,'" even Harvard College. This does not calm Jonathan's fears, though, and on seeing a train for the first time, he describes it in threatening terms: "This must be the sea-snake, from an overland tour / Returning, pell mell, his own ocean to find, / And dragging a horrible earthquake behind." Although threatening, the references to the sea-snake and the earthquake have their origins in nature, and for the moment Jonathan's traditional Yankee courage would seem to be enough: "No Yankee knows fear, that e'er grew on the soil." But when he comes to Boston, his rural experience becomes inadequate to describe what he sees, and his vision turns apocalyptic when he fears that the day of judgment is at hand. Truly shaken by his experiences and finally convinced that the ubiquitous steam "must rise from the bottomless pit itself," Jonathan Jolter hurries home to Vermont, ending the account of his ventures with the following vow:

> Give me peace and quiet among the green mountains,
> Beneath shady groves, and beside the pure fountains;
> No more will I lavish in traveling expenses,
> Hereabouts, till the people recover their senses.

Although his descriptions of what he does not understand are funny, Jonathan Jolter is no mere comic victim of the machine here. On the other hand, his retreat to his rural paradise and the affirmation of the values he voices offer no meaningful response to industrialization, based as that affirmation is on a condition that will go unfulfilled.

Stories of the rustic Yankee's first venture into a city have a similar cultural/humorous basis, but the experience made for more variations. Unique is the poem "Jonathan's Description of Joseph Bonfanti's Fancy Store," in the *New England Galaxy* (17 Jan. 1823). According to the third stanza,

There we saw a walking-stick,
Bonfanti kind of blow'd it,
And made it play a tune so sleek;
Fags! how I wish I know'd it.
There were glasses made to show
How the pulse is beating;
I wish I'd one for uncle Jo,
The doctor's always cheating.
Yankee doodle—what's the odds,
Spectacles are handy,
So are canes and fishing rods,
Yankee doodle dandy.

The poem is unusual because Jonathan's exuberant, awed account of what he sees (the humorous riddles and the poetic form hearken back to "A Yankee's Visit to a Camp") becomes one with the typical list of merchandise that storekeepers used as advertisements in newspapers of the time. Originally a clever ad for Bonfanti's store, reprinting and imitation made the poem a part of the tradition of New England humor that had inspired it.[34] The rustic Yankee's first visit to a city could also initiate and then sustain a serialized New England characterization. Joe Strickland first went to New York to buy and thus to advertise the lottery tickets sold by his creator, George Arnold; Jack Downing hauled a cartload of notions into Portland to sell and stayed on to report on the doings of the legislature. (These characterizations will be discussed in the chapter on cracker-barrel philosophers.) Ann Stephens's popular character Jonathan Slick took his produce from Weathersfield, Connecticut, to New York on Captain Doolittle's sloop.

Some accounts found the rustic comically ignorant of urban ways and thus an easy mark for city slickers. In London, Jonathan Homebread was nearly cheated by a cab man and then inveigled into paying for a donkey ride at Hampstead with the threat of a fine from the "Duke of Hampstead."[35] In "Nehemiah Flufkins's Visit to the City of Notions" in the *Yankee Blade* (12 Apr. 1851), the verdant Yankee gets charged admission to the commons, taxed for being in the city for the first time, and then fined for not taking his hat off at the mayor's house and for smoking in the street. Out of cash and running to catch the next train out of town, he gets stopped by someone merely asking for directions, but the harried Flufkins misunderstands by this time: "'Can't help it if 'tis a fine to run; I haven't got no money.' And he dashed on like mad towards the railroad station." Enoch Timbertoes played it smarter than most and had some good advice for his country brethren in the city: "A man don't know who's who or what's what without he keeps a sharp look-out—no tricks on travelers, is my motto, but they try plagy hard here to poke 'em to you I tell you."

As often as not, though, the rustic Yankee needed no help in getting into comic straits; his rural ignorance was enough. One Jonathan thought a recruiting station was a Boston clothing store and nearly enlisted inadvertently; another, in a Boston restaurant, objected heatedly when he thought the menu was his bill for food he had not yet eaten.[36] In a millinery shop, Ann Stephens's Jonathan Slick mistook a French corset for a fancy sidesaddle, which he decided to buy for his mother (see fig. 19). Asked to throw in the other riding tack, the salesclerk is puzzled to say the least, although Jonathan's attempt to explain himself would seem to fit both corsets and riding gear. "I mean the straps that come down in front to throw the chest out, and give the neck a harnsome bend, and the things to girt up in the middle with. Marm wont know how to use this new-fashioned thing if I don't send all the tackle with it." Stephens satirizes women's fashions with this, which assumes that the reader knows something, however stereotypically, about them, but she has us laugh too at Jonathan's ignorance of such things, just as we laugh at his rustically gauche behavior at a formal dinner or at his prudish urge to drape a nude statue with calico.

Despite his laughable lack of sophistication, though, Jonathan Slick emerges as an essentially decent, sometimes endearing characterization, in large part because Ann Stephens lets him speak for himself. Other authors framed their stories of the rustic in the city in their own voice, making their Jonathans more ludicrous and thus their judgment of that character more emphatic. The urbane narrator of "Doughnuts," in *Yankee Notions* (Jan. 1852), described his Yankee as "one of the *genus* verdant—a regular, no mistake, Jonathan—with eyes and mouth wide open at the novelties that he met at every turn," who stayed at a fashionable Boston hotel with his new bride, "a strapping, flaxen-haired lass, bedecked with a profusion of ribbons and cheap jew-elry." On the first morning, Jonathan demanded to know where the washbowl and towel were. "'Here are the conveniences for washing, sir,' said the land-lord, stepping to a mahogany wash-sink and raising the lid. 'Gosh all Potomac!' exclaimed our Yankee, *who'd ever thought of that 'ere table's openin' on top that way?*'" Then, at breakfast, "having burnt his throat by drinking coffee too hot, and attempting to eat an omelette with his fingers," the Yankee spotted some fish balls, "which are, as everyone knows," says the narrator, "fish and potatoes minced together, rolled into balls about as large as an ordinary sized apple, and cooked brown." Jonathan does not know, however, and "opening his capacious jaws, took a huge bite from his, when suddenly he disgorged the morsel with an expression of much disappointment, and turning to his bride, exclaimed, 'I swow, Patience, *these doughnuts are nothin' but codfish and 'taters!*'" With the italicizing of Jonathan's gaffes and with his arch "as everyone knows," the author clearly separates himself—and the reader—from such bucolic comic ignorance.

The title of another story in this vein, "The Public Tooth-Brush" in the *Yankee Blade* (18 Oct. 1851), would be enough to put off most readers. The gentlemanly narrator on "the splendid steamer Connecticut" found himself in the washroom with "a tall and verdant specimen of the incipient Yankee traveller." He explained to the rustic how to use the marble sink, and then missing his toothbrush, "was astonished to perceive the Yankee applying it vigorously to his tobacco-stained ivories." Told of this breach of decorum—and offered the brush to keep as his own—"the Yankee looked puzzled at first, as if he suspected a trick, but at length he exclaimed: 'Here, yeou, take your confounded thingumbob! But I should like to know what in thunder has become of the *tooth-bresh that belongs to the boat!*'" As in "Doughnuts," the author identifies the rustic Yankee as a type and uses italics to emphasize Jonathan's hopelessly crude ignorance of the niceties of modern, civilized life.

The italics also emphasize that such stories are often essentially jokes, relying as they do on a single ludicrous incident and ending as they do with a punch line. The rustic Yankee's account of attending, often inadvertently, a city theater or cultural event of some kind, on the other hand, usually made for a more elaborate, more humorous story, as Royall Tyler had early proved with his Jonathan's account of visiting the theater. Invited by his cousin to attend the Park Theater, Jonathan Slick recalls that his Puritan upbringing in rural Connecticut had warned against theaters, "filled with sinful devices and picters of the devil's own painting," and "nothing more nor less than scraps of the infarnal regions sot up here on arth tu delude away poor mortals." But he goes anyway, and observing the highly decorated ceiling of the theater decides that if it is indeed one of the devices of the devil, "Old Nick is no slouch at putting the shine on the ruff of his house, anyhow." He cannot honestly believe, however, that the theater is such a den of wickedness after all, although the costume of the ballerina does unsettle his Puritan sensibilities. "It was enough to make a feller cuss his mother because she was a woman," he admits, but when he covers his eyes with his hands, he finds that his fingers keep slipping, "so that I couldn't help but look through them at that plaguey, darned harnsome, undecent critter." In the end he is smitten by the lovely Madam Celeste.[37]

The episode shows Jonathan Slick's rural, Puritan teachings as anachronistic, but it does so without making the Yankee the consummate fool Tyler's Jonathan reveals himself to be. Slick goes to the theater knowing what it is and reveals a humorous but rather human ambivalence about what he sees there. In much the same spirit, the Yankee in "One of the 'Audience'" (*Spirit of the Times*, 23 Oct. 1847), mistakenly enters a theater in which the acrobatic Ravel Family is performing, thinking it a meetinghouse. Stunned by the goings-on, he admits it must be "the devil, sartain," but concludes, "Wal, blister me ef I don't come to town, and 'tend *this* meetin' three times a week, *sure*."

Other stories of this kind judge unequivocally the superiority of vernacular values to city fad and fashion, particularly when they represented a strayed-from traditional religion or were identified with foreign origins, as in Zachariah Strickland's denunciation of the opera (chapter 1). In a letter in the *Lantern* (1851), Miles Whittling reported from Boston to the folks back home in Whittlingwood how far people in the city had fallen from good old-time religion. "Strikes me they think its kind o' flatterin to the Almighty to put on their new coats and gownds when they go to worship. This is one of the Boston notions. Besides, goin tu meetin here is somehow turned into a kind o' buzness transaction, purty generally," he writes, using an appropriate country way to put the problem: "I'm sorry to say that there aint much of the raal old ginewine piety—the right down milk o' human kindness, that haint been skimmed, and watered, and chocked, and turned sour—in this setty."

Where Miles Whittling blames the materialism of his citified countrymen for the decline of old fashioned virtues, Asa Greene's Enoch Timbertoes, writing letters in the New York *Constellation* in 1830–31, placed the blame farther from home, making the issue pugnaciously nationalistic. In his letter published 31 March 1831, he argues that right-thinking Yankees "endeavor to keep up the old primitive manners, handed down to them with so much care by their forefathers," but he feels that "this mixing in of foreigners and our own countrymen will come to no good bimeby. Already they are undermining some of our good orthodox principles." City folks, he observes, "don't make no more account of sabbath day than any other day, and read novels or stroll about the streets without once thinking of going to meeting." Among the "outlandish customs" being introduced, Enoch gives particular attention to waltzing:

> You stand up in the middle of the room with your partner, and you begin scraping round her and round her, just like a hen scratching gravel for her chickens, the music all the while playing as slow as Saul's dead march or the tune the old cow died of—then you put your arm round her waist, and she her's round you—mighty affectionate it looks I tell you—and you commence poking your foot here and your foot there, and swinging and whirling in little semicircles round the room, till you get fagged out.

The very thought, Enoch says, "is enough to make an honest Yankee redden with indignation." Enoch himself tries the waltz after practicing with a three-legged chair, but his comic ineptitude satirizes the dance, not the dancer. Equally pernicious, according to Enoch, is the fad of playing the piano, which he describes in a letter in the *Constellation* (16 Apr. 1831) as a "sort of machine made of mahogany and is about as big as a meal-chest, inside of it there are wires so that by thumpin with the fingers on some little blocks outside, it makes a kind of music." The focus of the story, though, is not the comic description of an object the rustic is unfamiliar with but Enoch's judgments of the "kind of music" it makes: "To my ears the music of a spinnin wheel is vastly more agreeable . . . I shouldn't care about marryin one of these pianer girls, cause why? all the pianers in the world wont learn a woman how to darn a coat or make a pudding and whats the use of a wife that dont know how to do that?" he asks.

As unsophisticated and even reprehensible as such judgments might seem to many readers today—and to some, surely, in the 1830s—they were intended to represent superior vernacular values because religion, the indigenous purity of American womanhood, and pretensions to Old World culture were at stake. Jonathan Slick, although the comic bumpkin when he fails to understand that the people at a masquerade are in costume, stands for rustic good sense that has the force of down-to-earth American virtue when he scolds American young women for taking up with foreign fops and condemns Yankees such as his citified cousin Jason who go "a hankerin arter the big bug lords that come over here, on'y jest because they's got a long tail to their names." On that topic, Enoch Timbertoes concluded in one of his letters in the *Constellation* (8 Jan. 1831) that "this sort of tagragandbobtail nobility wont take in the publican country." However righteous Miles, Jonathan, and Enoch might be on such matters, though, their tone reflects an unhappy sense of irreversible declension from the rustic morality and national character these Yankees stood for. That troubled tone seems particularly clear in Ann Stephens's delineation of Jonathan Slick, besides Jack Downing the most extensive serialized Yankee characterization in the popular press.

Jonathan Slick's letters, appearing first in the *New York Express* late in 1839 and in *Brother Jonathan* beginning in 1842, were reprinted in other papers around the country and published in 1843 as *High Life in New York*. More letters appeared in over six subsequent editions of *High Life in New York*, one of them in German and the last printed in 1893. And although not a stock character on stage, Jonathan did appear in "A Grand Yankee Melange" at Barnum's American Museum in 1848. Ann Stephens, who originated the characterization, grew up in rural Connecticut, had begun her literary career in Portland in the mid-1830s, and in New York in the 1840s was an editor, popular author, and bona fide member of the literati. Over the several years she wrote them, her Jonathan Slick letters covered a wide range of topics. In the early ones he is alternately awed, horrified, and comically naïve about urban fashions and manners. He does not know a soirée from a staute or a corset from a saddle and he bullies black servants for laughing at him, but others treat him as an eccentric celebrity and with a hearty condescension that takes some of the comic sting out of his many gaucheries and faux pas. Over time, though, Stephens seems uncertain how to use the rustic voice. As an ironic persona to condemn urban sweatshops, he does not convince, and although he delivers a spirited and meaningful speech about sham nobility, he is unwittingly drunk when he does so. Twice feeling "deginerated" by city life and drawn by the sylvan simplicity of rural Connecticut, he goes "tu hum," but each time he returns enthusiastically to New York. The second time he meets with President Tyler, but nothing comes of it, then falls for a coquette who charms him into ignoring his provincial convictions against drinking and gambling. As the book ends, Jonathan, mortified by his gullibility, is on his way back to his rural home, for good, it would seem. And yet in the preface (in reality, the last of this series) to the 1854 edition of the book, he admits that he finds farm chores dull and that "onion tops and garden sars genereally ain't considred the sort of greens that a literary chap wants put round his head."

In her study of Jonathan Slick's letters in *High Life in New York*, Linda Ann Finton Morris concludes that they ultimately reflect Ann Stephens's ambivalence about the attractions of urban life, an awareness of its shallowness, and her "sense that the agrarian way of life was rapidly becoming outmoded." The book makes no overt value judgments but tries rather to "exploit the contrasts between the two ways of life and to reconcile them." As Morris says, though, they are "finally irreconcilable," and Jonathan Slick's letters ultimately express "a profound sense of loss that we can only believe is Mrs. Stephens's own."[38]

But the loss was not, of course, Ann Stephens's own. Her Jonathan was the nation's Jonathan, and the tradition of native American humor in which she wrote was humorous to the extent that it too exploited the contrasts between the values of an older, pastoral America and those of a modern, urban America. The New England tradition of native humor thus dealt with the ambiguities inherent in the issue that dominated the nation in the early decades of the nineteenth century: the dilemma of national identity on rustic terms in the face of change. New England humor in print reflected the many dimensions of that change and attempted to reconcile the dilemma in two judgments of the archetypal common man.

With the inferior Yankee—the one who spoke a grotesque vernacular, the laughable lover, the boorish rube in the city, the hopelessly inept bumpkin in the factory—the judgment seems clear enough. Such stories calmed fears about cultural change and modernization because they judged rustic values and experience as hopelessly, because laughably, out-of-date. As the urbane narrator of "A Yankee in a Coal Screen" says as a kind of moral for all such types, the New Englander was "more verdant than a Yankee ought to be." In his final version of "The Courtin'," Lowell avoided that judgment by using a dialect that was close to real speech and by placing the situation in a sentimental literary and cultural context (as did McClintock, to a lesser degree, with Johnny Beedle). Frances Whitcher's "Hezekiah Bedott" also avoids the dilemma, by making the manner of speaking and the speech itself seem natural, and although they are laughable, we laugh at the particular character and situation Whitcher created, not the type.

The superior Yankee was perhaps more common in print—it is impossible to make accurate quantitative conclusions—but in any case, the judgment is ambiguous. In giving a Yankee answer and asking persistent questions, the Yankee usually outsmarts his social and cultural betters easily enough, but these are evasive reactions to an implicit, felt threat from those people who represent what is, in fact, the dominant culture. The rustic's triumph is humorous only because the reader understands that it is, truly, incongruous. In stories of peddling and tricks, on the other hand, the Yankee possessed an apparently native genius compatible with both seventeenth-century Puritan spiritual values and the modern, materialistic order of things. True, serious thinkers such as Henry David Thoreau believed that the issue was not so easily put to rest by humor (although his own New England humor has been underappreciated.) The rhetorical stance in *Walden* scolds his "neighbors" for their frenzied materialism, but the parable at the end of that book, like the imagery of dawn throughout, shows that he had some hope that "John or Jonathan" could reform.[39]

The Yankee could not so readily outsmart city slickers or foreigners when they represented modernization or urbanity. And even when the Yankee stood for a morally superior point of view about such newfangled changes, as he does in "Jonathan Jolter's Journal" and in many of the letters of Enoch Timbertoes and Jonathan Slick, the character is still comical in much of what he does and says, and his triumphant tone sounds sometimes strident, often plaintive. In either case, it is the tone of frustration, the tone of loss.

Chapter 5

New England Humor Illustrated

The same technological advances in printing that made New England humor so widely popular made it a visual humor as well. Beginning in the 1830s, for example, commercial lithography made possible the many cartoon broadsides featuring Jack Downing, illustrations that isolated and thus simplified still further the political complexities of Jack's cracker-barrel letters. The late 1840s and early 1850s, in turn, saw the beginning of illustrated humor magazines, such as *Yankee Doodle* and *Yankee Notions*, in which visual fun prevailed, with pictures not only adding something to humorous stories but increasingly being comic in themselves.

For Yankee actors, engravings (and later, photographs) played a rather different role. They promoted the actors' careers, certainly, but as the careful detail given to facial expressions and costuming reveals, they also gave—and still give—something lasting to performances that were by necessity transitory. Illustrations in books, magazines, and newspapers provided a society without mass electronic media a sense of reality to the characterizations that had become so widely popular in words—characterizations that everybody "knew" but had never seen because they did not in fact exist. Readers then as now can readily identify the visual cues that mirror those in print.

More clearly even than nineteenth-century readers could, however, we can literally see, for example, how Brother Jonathan in the 1860s became identified with the North in the Civil War. And, looking at the delineations of Brother Jonathan and Jack Downing over the years, we understand the crucial place of the pictorial arts in the evolution of Uncle Sam, a figure now recognized almost exclusively by his visual attributes.

Figures 1 through 6. The evolution of Brother Jonathan, the rustic Yankee as the representative American into Uncle Sam, can be seen in these diverse pictures covering fifty years.

Figure 1. "Brother Jonathan's Administering a Salutary Cordial to John Bull" (1813) celebrates Commander Oliver Hazard Perry's 1813 naval victory in the War of 1812. Although already the archetypal American, Brother Jonathan does not yet wear the striped trousers, top hat, and swallow-tail coat that would become the identifying visual features of the rustic Yankee characterization and in time Uncle Sam. The artist, Amos Doolittle, often signed his work "Yankee Doodle Scratcher." Reproduced by permission of the American Antiquarian Society.

Figure 2. "Uncle Sam Sick with La Grippe," (1837?), printed and published by H. R. Robinson, New York, is an early pictorial delineation of Uncle Sam as the personification of the nation, here suffering the effects of President Andrew Jackson's removing the government's deposits from the Bank of the United States. Administering to him from left to right are President Jackson ("Old Hickory"), Speaker of the House Thomas Hart Benton, and Vice-President Martin Van Buren. Uncle Sam responds, "How the deuce Dr. Hickory can I have been overeating when I am half starved? and as for your *Mint* drops and Gold pills, Apothecary Benton, they have tied up my bowels and given me this infernal Grippe. Over issues you say Aunt Matty—if you all go on at this rate, I shall have nothing left to issue. You are to nurse me now, Aunt Matty, but I tell you I was once as hearty an old cock as ever lived till the Doctor and the rest of you took me in hand, and if you don't leave off ruining my *Constitution*, with your quack nostrums, I'll soon give you your walking ticket, Aunt Matty, and call in Doctor Biddle [former president of the Bank of the United States] to prescribe for me." Outside the window, Brother Jonathan (here the Whig voice of the "people") tells Nicholas Biddle, "Oh Doc Biddle I'm so glad you're come. Uncle Sam's in a darned bad way I guess, he's in kinder dwam like, I hope you'll ease him," to which Biddle responds, "I'll try what I can do Brother Jonathan . . ." Library of Congress.

Figure 3. One of several magazines to capitalize on the popularity of the Yankee as the American archetype, the New York monthly *Yankee Doodle* promised "to embody and reproduce in permanent form, that free spirit, that exuberant life, that creative energy, and refining enthusiasms which so eminently characterize us and distinguish the New World from the Old." Library of Congress.

Figure 4. "Jonathan to John," words by "Hosea Bigelow [*sic*]," music composed by F. Boott (1862), was inspired by one of James Russell Lowell's second series of *Biglow Papers*. Brother Jonathan proudly represents the North in this encounter with his British counterpart, John Bull, over England's support of the Confederacy. Reproduced by permission of the American Antiquarian Society.

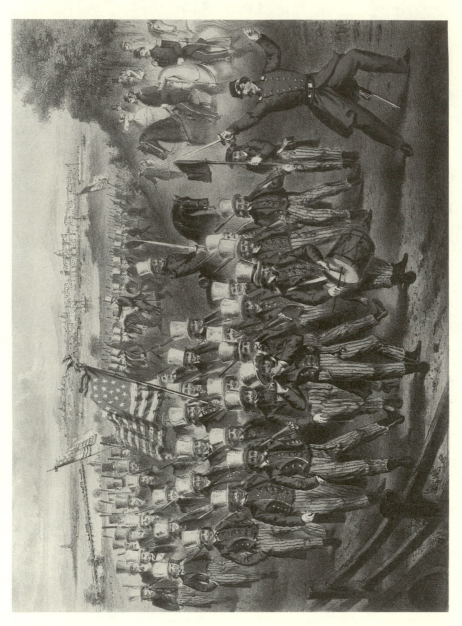

Figure 5. Featuring literally platoons of Brother Jonathans marching off to war, the 1862 lithograph published by J. H. Bufford, Boston, titled "Yankee Volunteers Marching into Dixie" illustrates vividly how the figure was identified with the Union cause. Library of Congress.

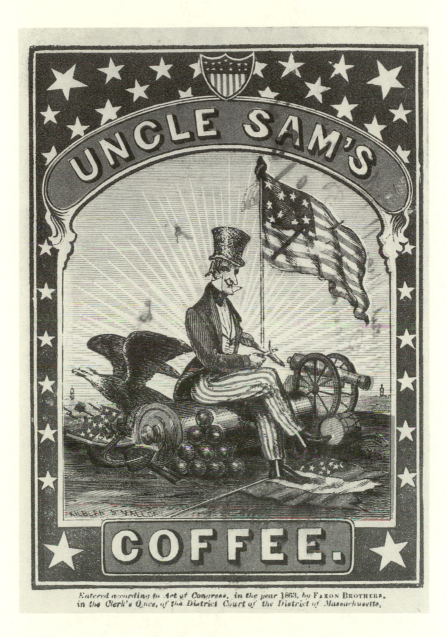

Figure 6. The 1863 label for "Uncle Sam's Coffee" (originally in red, white, and blue), is unusual not only as an early commercial use of Uncle Sam but also because it identifies him with the North. The whittling is something of a throwback to earlier years, when it was portrayed as a typically American past-time, particularly by foreign travelers. Library of Congress.

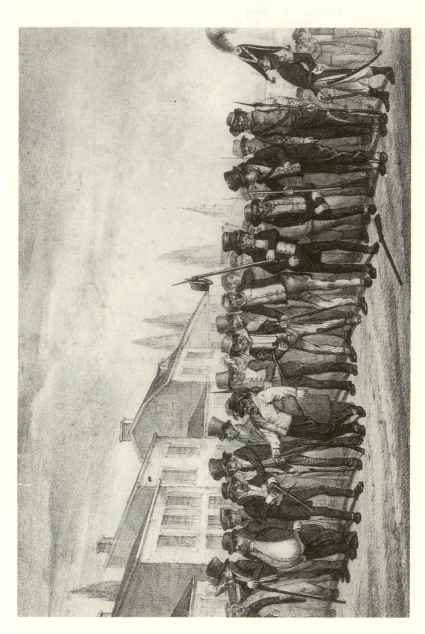

Figure 7. David Claypoole Johnston's "A Militia Muster" (1828), one of several he did over the years, illustrates a popular source of humor for a time in stories and on stage. Johnston himself is the third figure from the left. His watercolor version was exhibited in the Boston Athenaeum in 1829 along with works by leading American artists of the period. Reproduced by permission of the American Antiquarian Society.

Figure 8. Illustrations were also used to add comic dimension to a story in print, as in this picture of Joe Bunker on his way to court Hannah, from "A Tale of a Bag of Beans" in the *New England Galaxy* (Oct. 23 1829). Courtesy of the American Antiquarian Society.

Figures 9 through 17. The rustic Yankee was the most popular American type on stage in the first half of the nineteenth century, and the character was played throughout the country as well as in England. Nearly all of the material is now lost, but there are many graphic reminders here of the popularity of Yankee stage comedy.

Figure 9. "The Mathew-Orama for 1824 or Pretty considerable d . . . d particular *Tit Bits* from *America* being all well at Natchitoches," from *The London Mathews: Containing an Account of This Celebrated Comedian's Trip to America* (1824.) English actor Charles Mathews' "Jonathan W. Doubikins (a real Yankee)," according to the caption, is third from the left. Harvard Theatre Collection.

Figures 10 and 11. Displaying prominently the names of Marble and Hill, these theater playbills illustrate graphically the importance of the actors themselves to the popularity of the stage Yankee.

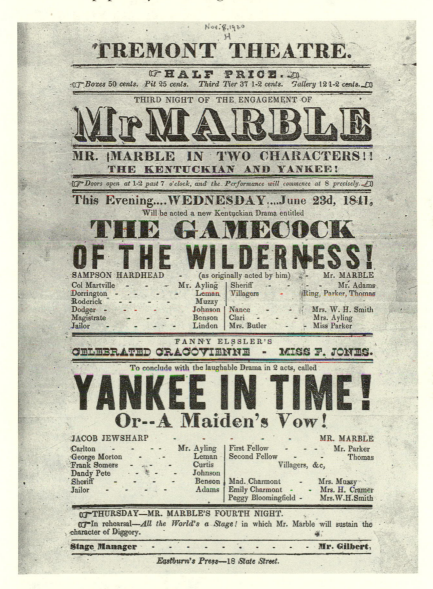

Figure 10. This 1841 playbill suggests the origins of what would become actor Danforth Marble's hybrid Yankee, part New Englander, part backwoodsman. Reproduced by courtesy of the Trustees of the Boston Public Library.

Figure 11. London engagements were an important drawing card for Yankee actors, as this 1837 playbill for George Hill shows. *Old Times in Virginia*, it promises, will be played for the first time in America, featuring Hill in the role of Hiram Dodge "as performed by him at Drury Lane Theatre, London." The actor would play the part with great success throughout the country for the rest of the year. Harvard Theatre Collection.

Figure 12. "Corn Cobs" (1836) sheet music cover. As part of their roles in comedies, Yankee actors also performed comic stories and songs on stage, often in a separate olio. This was one of George Hill's most popular songs and would seem in part to celebrate the technology represented by the machine, "Hooker's improved patented Corn Shucker, warranted." Reproduced by permission of the American Antiquarian Society.

Figure 13. Joshua Silsbee as Sam Slick, the Clockmaker (1840s). Although Sam Slick was not as popular as Jack Downing on stage, Silsbee opened the role in New York in 1844. Harvard Theatre Collection.

Figure 14. Silsbee as Jonathan Ploughboy in Samuel Woodworth's 1825 *The Forest Rose*, an 1825 comedy that many Yankee actors adapted to their individual talents. In 1851 in London, Silsbee played his version for one hundred twenty-three consecutive performances, the longest run of any Yankee comedy. Harvard Theatre Collection.

Figure 15. Like Joshua Silsbee "Dr. (William) Valentine" originated little Yankee theater material, but he was a popular character actor and humorous lecturer. Harvard Theatre Collection.

Figures 16 and 17. These illustrate the evolution of the older stage Yankee after the 1850s.

Figure 16. (1879?). John Owens, as Solon Shingle, adapted the role from Hill's earlier version of *The People's Lawyer*. Harvard Theatre Collection.

Figure 17. (1889). Denman Thompson made his career playing Joshua Whitcomb in *The Old Homestead* in the last quarter of the century and was influential in Cal Stewart's turn-of-the-century characterization of Uncle Josh Weathersby. Harvard Theatre Collection.

Figures 18 and 19. Inspired by the popularity of cracker-barrel philosopher Jack Downing, Nova Scotian judge Thomas Chandler Haliburton in 1835 created the Connecticut clockmaker and peddler Sam Slick, whose books were particularly successful with British readers. The characterization of Jonathan Slick, initiated by Ann Stephens in the early 1840s, traded on the popularity of his Yankee "cousin" Sam as well as Jack Downing.

Figure 18. From the first series of Thomas Chandler Haliburton's *The Clockmaker* books (1836), in his original role as clock peddler, Sam Slick demonstrates his keen knowledge of "soft sawder and human natur,'" as the caption says, in selling his wares.

Figure 19. Although dressed well himself, Jonathan Slick reveals a comically rustic misunderstanding of women's fashions. "Come now, s'posing we strike up a trade," he says in the caption. "I've took a sort of a sneaking notion to that are new-fashioned side-saddle. So, if you'll throw in the tackling, I'll give you ten dollars for it, cash on the nail." From Anne Stephens's *High Life in New York* (1854).

Figures 20 through 26. Jack Downing may well have been the most popular literary figure in nineteenth-century America. He first appeared in the early 1830s in letters reprinted throughout the country as the confidante of Andrew Jackson, at times ironically, as the embodiment of the nation's conscience, and for that reason, perhaps (as in figures 21, 22, and 23), often dressed much like the more general archetypal American, Brother Jonathan.

Figure 20. David Claypoole Johnston's frontispiece illustration of Jack for Seba Smith's 1833 *The Life and Writings of Major Jack Downing of Downingville.* Overseeing Johnston's work, Smith worried that Jack appeared "too knowing," although in fact the artist had captured accurately the satiric intent of the letters.

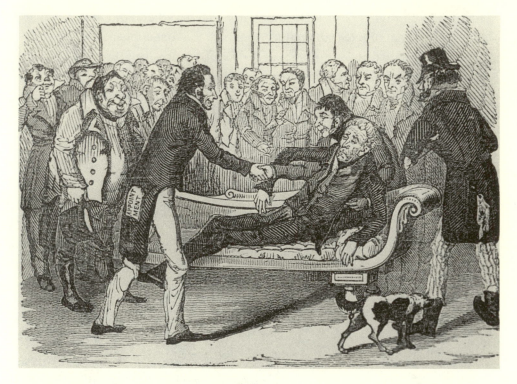

Figure 21. Also from Seba Smith's *The Life and Writings* (1833), by Johnston. Jack's solicitude for a weary President Jackson during his widely reported tour to the Northeast illustrates one of the more popular Downing letters.

Figure 22. "Downfall of Mother Bank, Draw'd off from Natur by Zek Downing, Neffu to Major Jack Downing." Published by H. R. Robinson, New York, 1833. One of many ostensibly by "Zek Downing," although in fact by different artists, but one of the few in which Downing champions Jackson's bank policy. Jack, on the right, cheers Jackson on: "Hurrah! General! if this don't beat skunkin, I'm a nigger, only see that varmint Nick how spry he is, he runs along like a Weatherfield Hog with an onion in his mouth." President Jackson says, "Major Jack Downing, I must act in this case with energy and decision, you see the downfall of the party engine and corrupt monopoly." On the left, friends of the bank flee the destruction. Daniel Webster says, "There is a tide in the affairs of men, as Shakespeare says, so my dear Clay, look out for yourself." Clay replies, "Help me up! Webster! or I shall lose my stakes." Director of the bank Nicholas Biddle, portrayed here as a Devil, says "It is time for me to resign my presidency." Library of Congress.

Figure 23. Based on a Jack Downing letter by Charles Augustus Davis, the bottom caption of "Political Firmament" (1836) reads "As seen through Martin van Buren's newly invented Patent Magic High Pressure Cabinet Spectacles." Attributed at the bottom: "From a big picter painted for the Nation by Zek Downing Historical Painter to Uncle Jack and Jineral Jackson." Reading a copy of his bank veto wearing the "glorification spectacles," the president sees only glory in the firmament representing his political career. Jack tells him, "Jineral, when that last ring of glory was made, it was a smasher. But I gess you had better been along with me in Downingville woods smoking out skunks." Reproduced by permission of the American Antiquarian Society.

Figure 24. This Bromley and Co. broadside (1864) promoted the publication of *Letters of Major Jack Downing*, the Civil War series of letters that had appeared in the New York *Day-Book* (also titled the *Caucasian*.) The "political caricatures" illustrated could also be purchased for twenty-five cents a copy, sixteen dollars for a hundred. Library of Congress.

Figures 25 and 26. Jack Downing also appeared in a wide variety of forms in popular culture that had no apparent political significance.

Figure 25. "Major Jack Downing's March" (1834?). One of at least two examples of sheet music inspired by the popular Yankee, this illustrates how occasionally Jack would be drawn in full-dress military regalia rather than clothes more like Brother Jonathan's—appropriate, perhaps, for this non-political delineation. Reproduced by permission of the American Antiquarian Society.

Figure 26. Originally over 4 by 6 feet, this poster (1835?) shows "Major Jack Downing" third from the left, as one of the figures in a traveling wax museum, along with President Jackson, George Washington, Queen Caroline, Chief Black Hawk, and Washington Irving, among others. This touring attraction was apparently a separate part of the "Zoological Institute's" traveling menageries, one of them featuring a pony-riding monkey named Major Jack Downing. Circus World Museum, Baraboo, Wisconsin.

Chapter 6

The New England Cracker-barrel Philosophers

In the twentieth century, both *crackerbox philosopher* and *cracker-barrel philosopher* have been used to designate the American version of a character with roots deep in the folklore and literature of many cultures, that of the wise fool—in this country, the unsophisticated, unschooled person who has wise things to say, although often ironically, on matters of political and social significance. Jennette Tandy used the term *crackerbox* in her 1925 study, *Crackerbox Philosophers in American Humor and Satire,* but a *Time* film reviewer in 1938, identifying the work of now-forgotten columnist and actor Robin Burns as in the tradition of Will Rogers, preferred *cracker-barrel,* the first use of that adjective, according to the *Dictionary of Americanisms* (which does not cite *crackerbox* at all). Norris Yates used both terms interchangeably in his 1964 book, *The American Humorist, Conscience of the Twentieth Century.* Daniel Royot, among others, used *crackerbox,* a deferential nod to Tandy's pioneering work, perhaps, but because recent dictionaries sanction only *cracker-barrel* as an adjective, that will be used here. No reason to belabor the point, really: both terms denote the central feature of a country store where local folks gather to talk over the issues of the day. (The pot-bellied stove would be an appropriate and more familiar feature, but it makes a rather inelegant adjective.) That setting in turn is suggestive of the town meeting, a potent symbol of political power in American democracy in the popular mind today, however anachronistic the town meeting might be to modern political practice—or the cracker barrel to modern grocery buying, for that matter.

Over the years, cracker-barrel humor has appeared in various vernacular characterizations that reflect the nation's persistent faith in a dynamic, democratic pluralism. The first popular cracker-barrel philosophers were male, white rustics: the Yankee, Jack Downing, and the frontiersman, Davy Crockett, in the 1830s, and those who followed their example: the Yankees Sam Slick and Hosea Biglow, and then Artemus Ward and the Civil War commentators he inspired. By the end of the century, the most popular cracker-barrel philosophers were an upstate New York rural woman, Marietta Holley's Samantha, and a Chicago Irish barkeep, Peter Finley Dunne's Mr. Dooley. The cracker-barrel figure reached its peak of national popularity—on radio and stage, in newspapers and movies—in the person and persona of Will Rogers in the 1920s, but the tradition did not die with him in 1935. In the 1940s Langston Hughes's "Simple" gave a black vernacular voice to the cracker-barrel tradition of native American humor, a tradition that still has a place in the columns of local newspapers in many parts of the country.[1]

As a tradition, cracker-barrel humor began in the late 1820s and flourished in the 1830s, when the language so long used to define the contrast between Old World and New World became one with a political rhetoric that celebrated, or made its appeal to, the common man. That took place in the figure—in the symbolic figure—of Andrew Jackson, whose victory at New Orleans in 1815, however meaningless to the outcome of that second war of independence, identified him with both the new nationalism that the war engendered and the democratic political rhetoric that would in large part define that nationalism.[2] That is, the language of victory that contrasted the triumph of untrained frontiersmen over the mannered professional soldiers of England in 1815 became politicized in the 1820s and 1830s with the persuasive, combative language of Jackson's candidacy and presidency, which argued principle and justified practice with appeals to the people, the masses, the common man. The conjoining of national identity and democratic politics was nevertheless fraught with some apprehension. Speaking and writing publicly on "The Poet" in the 1840s, Emerson included "our log-rolling, our stumps and their politics" in a catalog of appropriate subjects for an American poem yet unsung, but his private thoughts recorded in a journal entry for 18 June 1834 were more ambivalent:

> We all lean on England, scarce a verse, a page, a newspaper but is writ in imitation of English forms, our very manners & conversation are traditional and sometimes the life seems dying out of all literature, & this enormous paper currency of Words is accepted instead. I suppose the evil may be cured by this rank rabble party, the Jacksonism of the country, heedless of English & of all literature—a stone cut out of the ground without hands—they may root out the hollow dilettantism of our cultivation in the coarsest way & the newborn may begin again to frame their own world with greater advantage.[3]

Historians still argue hotly about how much "real" democratic reform took place in these years,[4] but certainly there were changes that at the very least gave the appearance of democracy: among them, presidential electors were elected by voters rather than by state legislators, statewide voting procedures were adopted, and more people could vote. These innovations in turn led to significant changes in the character and structure of political parties and campaign strategies that sought power by appealing and catering to the people as a new, national constituency. Citing too "the revolution" taking place in communication and transportation and its relevance to political change, Richard McCormick sums up the effects on what he calls (accurately, given the inclusive sense of the word) the political "environment" after 1830: "The sum effect of new conditions was to give an increasingly popular tone to politics. Campaigns and elections assumed the aspect of folk festivals. Candidates and voters indulged themselves in a moving, engrossing, and satisfying experience."[5] That "tone" was necessary because politics had become more national, with the campaigns of presidential candidates playing a new role in determining political strategies that increasingly became the business of professionals at work in more highly organized political parties.

That all of this has something to do with the political environment as we know it today goes without saying, but the innovation most indicative of the changes in the political environment of the time, one that would effect still more change, took place in 1832. In that year both major parties held for the first time national nominating conventions for presidential candidates, which, as Douglas Miller says, "satisfied the idea that a party's candidates and positions represented the will of their members."[6] Throughout the 1830s and culminating in the "Log Cabin Campaign" of 1840, both Democrats and Whigs fought their political wars on that principle. In the name of the people, President Jackson used the veto power, invoked the spoils system, and waged war on the bank; in doing so, the Whigs fired back, he had usurped the rights of Congress, the true representative of the popular will.

Party newspapers provided the battleground for this war of words to win the hearts, minds, and votes of the people. "Indeed," says Gerald Baldasty, "party and press were so intertwined that both are best understood in relation to each other," with editors themselves serving to organize these "new political machines" that nurtured party papers as a means of "converting and mobilizing the voters. The new political parties that grew out of the election of 1824 needed new mechanisms for creating bonds with the electorate, and the party press was ideally suited to the task."[7] In the years after his defeat by Adams in 1824, Jackson and his party had developed a highly effective network of party newspapers throughout the nation, with the Washington, D.C,. *National Telegraph* at its center, and as president he doled out patronage to editors in the form of appointments and government printing contracts.[8] As for the anti-Jacksonians, various factions had coalesced into the Whig party by 1834. Mott says the Whigs enjoyed "a substantial leadership over the Democrats in the number of newspapers,"[9] but Andrew Jackson—or rather the Jacksonian personality and political style as they were portrayed in the press of both parties—dominated and defined the rhetorical war, and would continue to do so for many years beyond his presidency.

The Whigs had no candidate, no personality that could do battle with the charismatic figure of Jackson (that would change with their media version of General William Henry Harrison in 1840), but the cracker-barrel philosophers Jack Downing and Davy Crockett served the Whig cause well in the 1830s. Much as the political personality of Jackson had been, they were created for and popularized by the press, and in that sense they would rival the popularity of the president himself, with Whig editors promoting both as apolitical "people's" candidates for the presidency.[10] As we have seen, rustic character, above all that of the Yankee, had a meaningful place in the cultural environment as the archetypal American; in the political environment, his "low" cracker-barrel vernacular seemed "above" the pompously empty, often vitriolic, and patently opinionated journalistic style of the typical Jacksonian—even the typical Whig—newspaper. Also, commenting on the political scene with humor reinforced the sense that the cracker-barrel philosopher was free of party constraints.

In reality, of course, the cracker-barrel philosopher served the highly political interests of writers who had little political sympathy for the common man and none for the policies of the Democratic party. That incongruity is interesting in itself, but profoundly so given the larger place of the rustic Yankee in the national identity. Jack Downing, for example, served timely political purposes as the Whig representative of the people, but like Brother Jonathan—both often decked out in the iconographic garb of striped pants, swallow-tail coat, and top hat—played a crucial role in the evolution of the apolitical, because neither rustic nor Yankee, figure of Uncle Sam as the archetypal American. Jennette Tandy went further still in concluding that the cracker-barrel figures in American literature usually could be seen as "successive incarnations of Uncle Sam, the unlettered philosopher."[11] Her conclusion has been often quoted because there is something fundamentally satisfying about it, for in the broadest—and that is to say, often sentimental—sense in which American humor and democracy are often understood, these cracker-barrel folks, with their vernacular way of speaking, do speak as, and apparently for, the common man, who ostensibly has ultimate power in a democratic society: although he does not carry out policy, he determines it by electing those who do.

However, looking at Jack Downing and the other New England cracker-barrel philosophers within the contexts of their time, as we will here, we find complexities that belie the comfortable assumptions that reflect the ideological needs of a later era. Each of these cracker-barrel personae evolved over many years and played widely different roles, as the writers who created them struggled to adapt them to diverse, even conflicting, ongoing opportunities and constraints. Because these personae *were* so popular for so many years, the writers had not only to accommodate them to changing events—that was the fairly easy part—but also deal with the popularity itself and the implications of that on their own literary careers and expectations. Above all there was the dilemma of using for specific political purposes a figure, the rustic Yankee, that had taken on larger cultural meaning that was often in conflict with those specific purposes. Putting simply the issue that is the crux of this chapter, each New England cracker-barrel philosopher would play an ironic role and speak as the satiric embodiment of the common man and all that he had come to stand for in politics.

Although coined in the twentieth century, the term *cracker-barrel philosopher* itself raises compelling questions about that character in American popular literature. Whether *cracker-barrel* or *crackerbox*, each combines a recent American coinage that some dictionaries still judge as colloquial with *philosopher*, a word derived from ancient Greek connoting traditional, intellectual learning. Together the two become an oxymoron that reflects two very different attitudes about the common man and the political and cultural values he embodies. Does the adjective affirm New World experience, a democratic identity that "modifies" centuries of formal, Old World values in a way that some like to call "typically American"? Or does the second word, the noun, attempt to give Old World respectability to New World experience? That the term does both is consistent with the epigrammatic ambiguity of the oxymoronic phrase, an appropriate rhetorical figure for expressing the fundamental dilemma about the common man elaborated in the first chapter. To return, then, to the origins of the term: in the 1938 movie review of Bob Burns's persona, *Time* brought up the actor-writer's $400,000 income and concluded by drawing attention to the ironies inherent in the term it had coined: "In real life Cracker Barrel Burns has an $85,00 house, amuses himself with amateur astronomy, and maintains the common touch by driving about in a Ford."

Joe Strickland

Seba Smith would put the cracker-barrel philosopher permanently in the national consciousness with his Jack Downing letters beginning in 1830, but he would acknowledge his debt to the character of Joe Strickland, the earlier creation of George Arnold. Joe Strickland was not only the first in the New England cracker-barrel tradition, but also the first serialized, widely reprinted, and imitated rustic comic Yankee.[12] Looking for gimmicks to attract buyers to his New York city lottery in 1825, George W. Arnold tried a couple: he put a simulated perpetual motion machine in his window and published in the New York *National Advocate* (later in the *Enquirer*) the letters of Joe Strickland, a barely literate rustic Vermonter whose early adventures in the city included winning big at Arnold's "lotry." Joe's first letter (15 July 1825), addressed to his Uncle Ben and reprinted from the fictitious *Vermont Recorder*, puffed Arnold's lottery, but it did much more. References to folks back home such as Betty Webster, who had "given him the bag," and expressions such as "thick as toads arter a rain" and "all to smash" give the characterization a lively sense of rural New England authenticity. True, the misspellings are too often simply inane: "horse spittle" for "hospital" is an all-too-typical, strained attempt at humor. Occasionally, though, Joe's misspellings represent some effort to indicate real colloquial speech, as in "jist," "heerd," and "sumbody." Also, Joe's ungrammatical syntax is not merely the facile signature of the semiliterate but frequently captures the natural mode of a person who communicates best orally, as in Joe's description of the perpetual-motion machine: "I stood and see it go about 2 ours, nothen under, heven turns it, oney, large balls, about as big as your fist that go round, chuck, chuck, one arter tother, thinks I thats perpeteral moshin by gum." Already, in this first letter, Arnold had created the most complete Yankee character to appear in print. If not that, then one that became widely reprinted and imitated, an unmistakable precursor of Jack Downing, the most popular Yankee characterization in the nineteenth century and the precursor in turn of Enoch Timbertoes, Sam Slick, Jonathan Slick, and other serialized rustic New Englanders as well as the backwoods characterizations of Davy Crockett and Major Jones.

George Arnold must have had literary ambitions, because within a year, references to the lottery became perfunctory, as he further developed the characterization of Joe by elaborating on the fictitious homeplace and people back home in Vermont and by giving the rustic Yankee an occasional voice in the news of the day. Early on Joe had run for "korryner" in New York (he lost despite giving out large quantities of rum), and in 1827 he took on fully the role of cracker-barrel philosopher with a commonsense speech to the New York legislature against a bill curtailing lotteries. When he told them that trying to stop the selling of lottery tickets would be "jist like tryen tu hold a live eal by the tale," it "maid them stair like stuk pigges."[13] By the time of Arnold's last Strickland letter, in 1830, Joe had touched on national politics in writing about the disappearance and alleged murder of an anti-Mason. When newspapers reported that the man was hiding out in Smyrna, Joe wrote about it all in a letter from "Konstanty Nople" itself.

Arnold had given markedly new dimension to the Yankee character in popular literature and initiated a form of native humor that quickly caught on. Despite the personal and parochial purpose of the letters, other papers in other states reprinted them, and in less than a year letters appeared by writers claiming to be members of the far-flung Strickland clan, including Zachariah, Sam, Bob, Ike, Jerry, and even two crudely illiterate blacks—the creations of a business rival—who claimed to be fourteenth cousins and wrote to complain that they drew only blanks at Arnold's lottery.[14] A week after brother Sam Strickland's first epistle about his adventures in Boston appeared in the *New England Galaxy* (9 June 1826), the Strickland parents put in their "adverteyesmeant," discussed in chapter 1, for the two runaway boys. Joe's subsequent denial of it added to the fun, as did editorial prefaces that spoke knowingly, if condescendingly, of "this intellectual family." Some of these letters are more in the cracker-barrel vein than the originals, but none have the good humor or artfulness of those by Arnold. Sam Strickland wrote a couple of letters from Washington as a newly elected member of the 1828 "Kong Grease," but his unabashed self-interest and his barely readable prose show that the author was more interested in satirizing the burgeoning Jacksonian form of democracy than he was in contributing to a literary tradition. On 11 January 1828, Sam writes that although he has not made up his mind whom to vote for, he will go for Jackson if he can get an appointment that pays well. He has little hope for his chances, though, because, the "jaxon phoux theive more pigs now than kan find tits & i reckn when jaxon gits in therle be sum darnd lowd squeel in a mung um." The *Galaxy* had promoted the Strickland vogue early on, prefacing two letters of 9 November 1827 with the ironic but good-humored conclusion that the letters "are universally read and are as likely to become the admiration of posterity, as those of Dean Swift." In the heat of Jackson's first months as president in 1828, though, editor Joseph Buckingham found country character an appropriately ironic, satiric embodiment of the newly democratic political style. The *Galaxy* for 20 June 1828 featured a group of four letters by rustic writers, one from "that worthy family, the Stricklands" (signed "jozef Bunker," who had earlier claimed kinship), and called each an "attempt to ridicule the Jackson manner of arguing," according to the editorial preface.

By 1833, the New York *Daily Evening Transcript* (2 Feb.) still referred to "the numerous Stricklands from 'Varmont'" in a sketch about Ike, but in fact Strickland characterizations appeared only occasionally, although widely, in the 1830s: Asa Greene included his version of Joe in *Travels in America by George Fibbleton, Esq.* (1833) and letters by Joe Strickland, Jr., found their way into the *Greenville* (South Carolina) *Mountaineer* (21 July 1832) and the Chicago *Democrat* (7 May 1834).[15]

Jack Downing

By the early 1830s, the Strickland letters had been eclipsed in popularity by those of another Yankee cracker-barrel philosopher, Jack Downing, from "away Down East in the state of Maine," the creation of Seba Smith. Born in Buckfield, Maine, in 1792, a graduate of Bowdoin College in 1818, and a newspaper editor in Portland in the mid-1820s, Smith knew the cracker-barrel humor of the Stricklands, a fact he acknowledged early by making Jack Downing Joe Strickland's nephew.[16] Like Joe, Jack was a Yankee country boy in the city for the first time who wrote about it to his uncle back home, and Jack too lost his girl for staying away too long. Seba Smith, though, drew his cracker-barrel Yankee with a far defter hand than George Arnold had: the Downing vernacular is less contrived, the personality more true-to-life, the cracker-barrel humor more at the heart of it all.

Jack's first letter appeared in January 1830 in Smith's Portland *Daily Courier,* the first daily newspaper north and east of Boston, which Smith had started late in 1829, and in his *Family Reader,* a weekly. At first Jack reported on the doings of the Maine legislature, then ran for office himself, and his letters were eagerly reprinted, not only in Maine newspapers but also in Boston and other Massachusetts papers. Then, in 1831, Smith made Jack the friend and advisor of President Jackson, giving the letters a national audience and inspiring imitations that in time threatened to overwhelm the popularity of the original. In part to protect the integrity of his original creation, Seba Smith late in 1833 published many of his letters in book form as *The Life and Writings of Major Jack Downing of Downingville, Away Down East in the State of Maine, Written by Himself.*[17]

Already, though, Jack Downing had passed out of Seba Smith's control to take on mythic proportion in the popular mind. John Neal observed that Jack Downing was "the subject of conversation in all the steamboats, stages, and taverns along the road," and Emerson could not convince Ezra Ripley that Jack Downing was not a real Yankee.[18] Editors knew better, but they gave their own kind of verisimilitude to Jack. One paper reported that Jack's signature had appeared on a ten dollar bill issued by a Connecticut bank, another that he was running for office, and in typically bad taste, a comic almanac told about a child born to Mrs. Zebedee Doolittle who had features amazingly similar to Jack's.[19] As happened with the Strickland letters, imitators claiming to be part of the Downing clan or even Jack himself wrote letters widely reprinted along with Smith's own—in the East, south to Kentucky and Georgia, west to Michigan and Indiana—and in 1833 and 1834, the letters of "J. Downing," by New Yorker Charles Augustus Davis, challenged the popularity of the original. Book-length collections by both Smith and Davis were published in England, and reviewers there, and some in America, touted them as the first fruits of an indigenous literature.

The character of Jack Downing took on other forms as well: in political cartoons, broadsides, and paintings, on stage, as the author of a biography of Jackson, and as editor of a songbook (see figs. 20 through 26). For a time it seemed as if Jack Downing might replace Brother Jonathan and even Uncle Sam as the national sobriquet, Alton Ketchum writes in his book on Uncle Sam.[20] All of this was in the 1830s, but in one or several of his many and various manifestations, Jack Downing appeared before the American public each year between 1830 and the mid-1860s. His popularity led to the New England cracker-barrel philosophers Sam Slick and Hosea Biglow, probably had something to do with the cracker-barrel Crockett, and surely had much to do with popularizing New England humor of many types. Jack Downing may well have been the most popular literary characterization of nineteenth-century America.

Seba Smith began it all that January in 1830 when Jack Downing, a farm boy from Downingville, Maine, took off for Portland to sell a cartload of notions and then stayed on to write letters back home about the goings-on in the legislature there. Smith, perhaps still smarting from the political brouhaha he had stirred up a few years earlier as a Portland editor, which led to his being challenged to a duel,[21] vowed to stay aloof from party politics in the *Courier,* a pious promise he often repeated. The *Courier,* in other words, would be conducted with "character and dignity," virtues reflected in tasteful advertising as well: "If someone wants to advertise his ability to swallow a two-edged sword a foot and a half long, his notice will not appear in the *Daily Courier,*" he promised smugly in the first issue. The letters of Jack Downing, then, provided Seba Smith with the political voice he needed, a cracker-barrel character whose rustic letters back home separated him from the learned editor, a spokesman who represented, initially, at least, the only "party" that the *Courier* acknowledged, the "party of the people."

For Smith, that phrase meant "*no* party," a sincere, if conventional, affirmation of the *Courier* and his own political neutrality. In the early letters Jack *is* of that party, one of the people; he is the idealized common man, whose rural innocence of what he sees and his homespun way of saying it Smith used to mock gently and widely the political bickering and dickering of the factions in the Maine legislature in 1830, the Democratic Republicans and the National Republicans (roughly Jacksonites and anti-Jacksonites, respectively.) In the first letter, for example, Jack puzzled over the refusal to "seat" a Mr. Roberts, whose credentials were contested. "And I thought it a needless piece of cruelty, " Jack wrote, "for they want crowded, and there was a number of seats empty."[22] As innocent as he is kind, this early Jack does not understand the political machinations of the evenly divided legislature. In another letter he reported that the president of the state senate could not "table" a document because the constitution required a quorum for such an action. "But I believe he finally *let it drop* on the table; and I spose there was nothin in the constitution against that." Here, Jack's innocence of the basic usages of formal parliamentary procedures pokes gentle fun at the realities of political practice, but that fun, the satire, is unconscious on Jack's part, as it is with his use of rustic analogy, a cracker-barrel technique that Smith used skillfully and to good effect. For example, the battle between the National Republicans and the Democratic Republicans was so even, Jack reported, that it was "jest like two boys playin see-saw on a rail. First one goes up, and then 'tother; but I reckon one of the boys is rather heaviest, for once in a while he comes down chuck, and throws the other up into the air as though he would pitch him head over heels." For Jack, the analogy clarifies political practice in a way that he and his Uncle Joshua, the recipient of the letter, can understand, but at the same time it also gently satirizes both parties by treating them as boys at play; yet it does not satirize Jack or the "party of the people" Smith wants him to represent. References to and letters from Downingville folk—Uncle Joshua, Cousins Ephraim and Nabby, and Jack's mother—soften the satiric edge and add touches of local color that affirm Jack's pastoral innocence.

However, although at first the naïve cracker-barrel observer, by March of 1830 Jack sees politics for what it is: becoming a candidate for office "means the same that it does at a shooting match to set up a goose or a turkey to be fired at," he says in a letter dated 30 March. Although still the apolitical common man and representative of the party of the people, he now consciously chooses the rustic analogy, making the satiric intent conscious as well. Within a short time, though, he pays no attention to his own shrewd insight nor to the admonitions of his mother and Cousin Nabby, who can see no good in his dallying in Portland (he has already lost his sweetheart to the schoolmaster), and he becomes a candidate for governor.

In making Jack an office seeker, Smith radically altered the satirical role of the cracker-barrel philosopher and the reader's judgment of the rustic values he had stood for. Smith espoused no particular party in the *Courier*, but he had spoken out vehemently against office seeking: "The causes of their [politicians'] divisions and contentions *very seldom have any connection with the public interest*. The whole scramble is for *office, office, office*," he had written in the *Courier* (27 Jan. 1833). As an office seeker himself, then, Jack speaks as an *ironic* cracker-barrel persona and becomes the satirical embodiment of Seba Smith's growing concern with what he saw as the sundry evils of unprincipled, democratic politics—specifically, Andrew Jackson's corrupt version of the "party of the people." That Jack Downing, the rustic Yankee and archetypal common man, could be corrupted reveals how insidious democratic politics could be. And corrupt Jack is, for he accepts without question the strategy for office seeking laid down by his Uncle Joshua and the nominating caucus at Downingville. In a letter to Jack setting up that strategy, Joshua Downing offers no positive action that would reform the ills of the state. The only goal is to win, and the high-minded announcements he proposes for the public press (a parody of those that typically appeared) contrast hypocritically with the self-interest of his private postscript that ends the letter: "If you get in, I shall expect my son Ephraim to have the office of Sheriff in this County. . . . The other offices we'll distribute at our leisure." With the bald callousness of that last sentence, Uncle Joshua drops any semblance of pastoral innocence, for he knowingly adopts a political practice that Jackson's critics called "the spoils of office." And in accepting that practice, Jack also loses his rural innocence, but the loss is worth it, because as Joshua had told him earlier in the same letter, running for governor "will be worth more to you than the best farm in this County," because even if he loses, "it will be the means of getting you into some good office."

The earlier Jack Downing would have had something pertinent, however innocent, to say about such doings. A month or so before, for example, hearing about "polls," a politically naïve Jack had urged his Cousin Ephraim to haul some "poles" to Portland to peddle. Now, as an ironic cracker-barrel persona, Jack eagerly adopts unprincipled electioneering. Renting a horse and cart he hauled loafers to the polls to vote for him, then became self-righteously indignant when they failed to do so. Downingville remained true, however, casting all of its eighty-seven votes in its own interest and for its favorite son. By the end of 1830, although "dished in the governor business," Jack decides his political and financial fortunes might be found in Washington, and in December 1830 he tells his uncle to "set me up for member of Congress up there, and get me elected as soon as you can." Nothing comes of it, though, nor of Jack's brief comments on international affairs and national politics. Seba Smith had some things to say about what was happening beyond the borders of Maine, but he needed a new role, an appropriate entrée for the cracker-barrel character who would say them. That opportunity came with the breakup of President Jackson's cabinet reported in the *Daily Courier* on 26 April 1831; the next day, Jack writes that he is off for Washington to get an appointment and the six-thousand-dollar salary that goes with it.

In Washington, Jack found the cabinet vacancies filled, but he did become Jackson's closest friend and advisor, closer even than the president's famous Kitchen Cabinet. The relationship seems a natural one, for Jack's rustic speech and bluff, informal manner are more appropriate to a President Jackson than to an Adams or a Monroe. He is not a crassly ironic persona, nor is he critical of Jackson himself, for to do so would undercut the relationship he enjoyed. Neither is he politically innocent, for he reveals in his letters the divisive jealousies and selfishness of Jackson's Kitchen Cabinet, the circle of advisors who were more vulnerable to censure by the opposition press than the charismatic president. As Jack becomes a part of that inner sanctum, there are increasingly fewer letters from his Downingville kin and less mention of them; more often, he addresses his letters to the editor of the *Courier*, legitimizing his role as political correspondent.

Smith studiously avoided serious, specific political issues, though. He burlesqued the snubbing of Secretary of War John Eaton's wife, Peggy, for example, with Cousin Ephraim's report of the shabby treatment of Mrs. No-tea by some of the "topping-folks" in Downingville. The widely reported Eaton affair certainly had political implications, leading to the cabinet resignations that had sent Jack to Washington in the first place, but the Downingville allegory had more to do with social foolishness than political ideology. Jack's first important duties sent him back to Maine, commissioned as a captain in the United States Army to deal with the Madawaska boundary dispute there. Again the issue was politically "safe," and Jack's mock heroic reports to the president are all the more entertaining because of Jack's good humor and vernacular way of speaking.

Jack's foray into serious national politics came with South Carolina's attempt to nullify federal law at the end of 1832. Although a critical constitutional issue that foreshadowed the Civil War, the Nullification Crisis did not encompass the ills of Jacksonian politics. In the North, at least, Jackson's firm and formal proclamation against the threat by South Carolina on 10 December 1832 was not an arrogant assertion of executive power and thus met with wide approval, as Uncle Joshua's letter about the "tussle" they had in Downingville to keep the Federalists from praising it is intended to show. When the president asks Jack's opinion about what to do, Jack offers up a lucidly rustic allegory of how Bill Johnson back home cut the lashings on a raft some of the boys had made and tried to paddle his log alone and then had to beg the others to let him join the raft. The moral is clear: "If you let South Carolina cut the lashings you'll see such a log-rolling in this country as you never see yet." Jackson agrees, of course, and appoints Jack to lead the redoubtable Downingville militia against the rebellious state. When he climbs to the top of the Capitol to listen for shooting, though, the only firing he hears is inside the Congress itself, "where the members were shooting their speeches at each other." For his efforts in the crisis, Jack gets promoted, and it is as "Major" Jack Downing that he—the original as well as the imitators—was known thereafter.

To capitalize on the popularity of his stand against nullification and to celebrate his second inauguration, Jackson made a tour of the northeastern states in the spring of 1833. The occasion provided Seba Smith an excellent opportunity to exploit the intimate relationship between Jack and Jackson, and he did so by combining the widely reported facts of the tour with the fiction of that relationship. In Alexandria, Virginia, for example, Jack became the one who defended the president from an attack by Lieutenant Randolph, and Jack came to the rescue in New York when a bridge collapsed at Castle Garden. In Philadelphia, Jack tells about shaking hands for a seriously ill president. "Then I kind of stood behind him and reached my arm round under his, and shook for him for about a half an hour as tight as I could spring," Jack reports (see fig. 21). Editors from all parts of the country enjoyed reprinting this bit of solicitude, and apparently President Jackson did too. Abed in the Tremont House in Boston with a "severe cold and bleeding of the lungs," the president enjoyed a reading of the most recent letters of Jack Downing, "the most widely reprinted and plagiarized newspaper humor of the day," according to historian Marquis James.[23]

Probably the most popular letter of the tour, though—the most widely reprinted and imitated—was Jack's account of Jackson's receiving an honorary doctorate of laws degree from Harvard.[24] The actual event aroused all of the fundamental antagonisms between those who lionized Jackson's unschooled genius and natural ability and those who stood for formal learning and proven experience. John Quincy Adams, Harvard graduate and Jackson's opponent in the 1828 presidential election, refused to witness the college's "disgrace in conferring her highest literary honors upon a barbarian" who could hardly spell his own name.[25] Seba Smith, although no Jackson partisan, treated the occasion with better humor. According to Jack's letter, neither he nor the president know what a doctor of laws is, but it seemed just the thing Jackson deserved. "I have had to doctor the Laws considerable ever since I been to Washington," he tells Jack. "And I made out so well about it, that these Cambridge folks think I better be made into a regular Doctor at once, and then there'll be no grumbling about my practice." The admission substantiated Whig charges that Jackson exceeded constitutional limitations on the presidency, but Smith's play on the word "doctor" is more humorous than critical. Smith also passed up the chance to burlesque Jackson's conduct during the ceremony. Considerable speculation had arisen about Jackson's reception of the speech given in Latin and his response in accepting the degree—also in Latin, as protocol required. Jack, who had advised the president to "act knowing," merely reports that the president was a little puzzled "but stood it out like a hero and got through it very well." Others were not so kind. The *Salem* (Maine) *Register* (10 July 1833) reported the following toast at a Fourth of July dinner: "Andrew Jackson—In War a Hero—in Politics a Statesman; in literature an LL.D. and an A.S.S."

That in turn lead to a commemorative coin featuring the representation of an ass labeled "LL.D.," although an anonymous imitator tastefully rendered it as "Amazin' Smart Skoller."[26]

Downing Imitators: Charles Augustus Davis

With the president's tour of the northeastern states, Seba Smith's Jack Downing reached its peak of popularity, but the cracker-barrel character Smith had created took on a life of its own. Newspaper editors contributed to the Downing mystique with stories that he was married and that the city of Boston had spent too much for liquor in entertaining the presidential party during the tour, laying the blame to the major's extraordinary thirst.[27] Above all, though, there were the imitators themselves. "Roused by the Major's account of their 'coming full chisel,' and of his shaking hands for the president at Philadelphia, everybody betook themselves to writing Jack Downing, till the letters almost overshadowed the land," according to the *National Gazette*.[28] Seba Smith was hardly flattered by the flood of imitations, for he could profit little from the celebrity of the character he had created. Jack had his own say about the "rascally counterfeiters": "He that steals my munny-puss steals trash, but he that steals my name ought to have his head broke," he complained with a rustic rendition of a Shakespearian aphorism in a letter dated 25 June 1833. Smith could not know it was the same date of the first letter of his most serious rival, Charles Augustus Davis.

Davis was an urbane, Whiggish New York iron merchant at home with bluestocking aristocrats and Knickerbocker writers. His letters, signed "J. Downing," originated in the New York *Daily Advertiser* and were eagerly reprinted in newspapers throughout the country, often on the same page with the letters of the original Jack Downing. Despite the clear differences in the styles and signatures, readers were often confused by the two cracker-barrel philosophers, and Davis enjoyed twitting Smith about that confusion. Both would publish their letters in a book—Smith's *Life and Writings* late in 1833 and Davis's *Letters of J. Downing* in early 1834—but an enterprising publisher in Cincinnati had already taken advantage of the Downing mania and published a collection of six of Davis's, six of Smith's, and nine imitators' as *Letters Written During the President's Tour* in the fall of 1833.[29]

Like Seba Smith, Charles A. Davis made Jack the president's most trusted confidante whose letters would represent the apparent truth of the inner workings of the Kitchen Cabinet. As the editor of the *Daily Advertiser* wrote, "If it were not for the Major, the public would know nothing of what is going on inside the cabinet. His communications are invaluable because they may be implicitly relied upon. Everybody will believe the man who sleeps in the same bed with *'the Gineral.'"*[30] Unlike Smith, though, Davis had a political ax to grind, using the cracker-barrel voice of J. Downing almost exclusively to turn public sentiment against Jackson's latest battle in his war to destroy the Bank of the United States. Long opposed to the bank on constitutional grounds and for the paper currency it encouraged, Jackson in July 1832 had vetoed Congress's bill to recharter it. His attack on the bank was controversial even within his own party (he would dismiss Secretary of the Treasury William Duane for refusing to remove the government deposits), but Jackson had interpreted his election in November of 1832 as a mandate from the people to continue his assault against the "monster bank," and by June 1833 plans were underway to slay it by removing the government deposits. Davis's single-minded purpose required ingenuity in writing Jack's letters because he had to react to events as they unfolded, and at the same time he was uncertain how the issue would ultimately be resolved. Thus there is not a consistent sense of the cracker-barrel role Jack should play.

Early in the series, the president appoints Jack as a special investigator of the bank, because, as Jackson admits to him, "I'm stump'd about that Bank of U.S., and I want you to help me figure it out." As a Yankee rustic with down-home good sense, Jack makes a favorable contrast to more "official" advisors such as Amos Kendall and Martin Van Buren. Jack's letters reveal that their reports on the bank had been politically motivated, self-interested—reports that Jackson confesses to Jack, early on, at least, that he does not understand nor is certain he believes. Jack, of course, vows to be rigorously fair—"to give Mr. Biddle and his money-bags a stirring up"—and in the Yankee's report, Biddle appears courteous and forthrightly honest—"a rale friend of ourn"— and the bank sound. Although the early letters represent Jackson as accepting Jack's version of things, Old Hickory was in fact unshakable in his intention to destroy the bank by removing the deposits, which he announced in a procla- mation in mid-September. Davis, searching for the right strategy for Jack, discussed it with Nicholas Biddle himself, who rewarded the author with a place on the board of directors of the New York branch of the bank.[31]

At first Davis made Jack an ironic persona, and his own proclamation, dated 26 September, is a willfully venal catalog of self-interested motives that parodies Jackson's report. Subsequent letters, though, indicate that Davis was not satisfied with an ironic cracker-barrel philosopher, and so he made Jack's pro-bank principles appear as common sense for the good of the nation in contrast to the patent self-interest of a Democratic administration that had no concern for the public welfare. As Jack's homely exempla become more doctrinaire—as Davis's cause becomes more desperate—they also become more elaborate and contrived. Because of a hole in his pocket, for example, the president loses his spectacles, then finds them "broke to flinders" in his boots, which leads Jack to a "curious notion" that he shares with the president: "If you had kept your spectacles in your side breast-pocket, they would be on your nose now," as he tells him, "but that ain't the worst on't, I'm afeard . . . Gineral, we've got too many pockets for our money, and when we want it we shall all come to our shirts and boots before we find it." The moral does not sit well with Jackson, however, "and so we stomped about a spell, cussin and discussin most things, till we got cool agin—but it was a considerable of a storm, I tell you," Jack concludes. Then, when Jack tries to fix the spectacles, he discovers they are "glorification spectacles," ingeniously made by Vice-President Martin Van Buren so that the president cannot see the true effects of his policies but only scenes that reflect glory on him and those policies (see fig. 23). As contrived as this seems today, it was highly entertaining, given the charged atmosphere of the time, and the spectacles became an icon of the anti-Jackson press, as did an ax sent to Jack for "subtracting every superfluous wheel from the government."

Davis leveled his sharpest satire at Jackson's cabinet, which complains heatedly, according to the letters, about the good major, who nonetheless argues steadfastly the case for the bank. In a meeting to thrash it all out, one of the hangers-on argues that there "are things in all Governments, and in this in particular, that require cookin up before the people should be sarved with it; but the Major hands the dishes over to the people, raw and uncook'd; this is not right." Davis saved Jack's reply for the next letter, one of the longest and one of the last before book publication, the climax of Davis's efforts on behalf of the bank. Surveying the whole history of the bank, the Yankee exposes the errors of Jackson and his party, then answers the charges against the bank one by one: that it has too much power, that it has no right to recharter, that a bank is not needed, and that it should not pay interest to foreign investors. At the end, in a dramatic gesture that verges on bathos, he holds up a list of its "owners," a list that includes "old widows, and old men, trustees of children, who hain't no parents livin, and all our own people" who put money in the bank for safekeeping. In the letter, Jack speaks as and for the common man of common sense who has been betrayed by the democratic rhetoric of the Jackson party, a desperate diatribe against a cause already lost.

Davis and Smith

Published in a book in February 1834 in response, perhaps, to Smith's collection (in its second edition by February) and to take advantage of the still lingering effects of the bank war, Davis's *Letters of J. Downing* went through at least eight editions before the year was out, with letters added at each printing.[32] Davis's Downing letters, in fact, were probably more popular at the time than Smith's because they spoke to the most topical issue of the day. The bank war was over, but Jackson's presidential tactics provoked political, even constitutional, battles that would rage for years. Smith's Jack Downing had little to say about the bank. In a letter dated 30 September 1833, even as the bank war reached its climax as the removal of the deposits neared, Jack made Amos Kendall responsible for the decision, and concluded too lamely, given the crisis, that "this storm about the bank begins to blow over." More kindly than had Davis, Smith portrayed Jackson as usually reasonable but somewhat confused, honest but wrong-headed, a weak leader who confessed to Jack in their private conversations to many of the charges aimed at his administration. Smith blamed others: members of the Kitchen Cabinet and the divisive, self-interested influence of that coterie. Alone with Jack, the president admits, "There are so many cooks, the broth must always come out rather bad. If I have to write a message, one must put in a sentence, and another, til it gits so at last I can't hardly tell whether I've written any of it myself or not. . . . And then there was such a pulling and hauling for offices along in the outset, it seemed as though they would pull me to pieces." With this admission, Smith has

Jackson himself give credence to charges against his administration, but he deflects those charges from Jackson himself.

Vice-President Martin Van Buren fares less well, with Smith characterizing him as vain and jealous of Jack's popularity with the public and the president. Although less a Whig ideologue than Davis, Smith had come to distrust the Jacksonian style and political practice, and expressed it openly in one of Jack's last letters in the book. Here Jack reports, of all things, that President Jackson had urged him to become the running mate of Daniel Webster, the leading opposition candidate; only those two can save the country from the storm portended by nullification, according to the president. "But Daniel is a Federalist," Jack protests with true party spirit, "and I should like to know which is worse, the jaws of nullification or the jaws of Federalism." In labeling the opposition as "Federalist," Jack invokes the anachronistic caviling of Jackson's own press, but according to Smith, the president will have no such foolishness: "The jaws of fiddlesticks," he retorts, and goes on to prove that Webster is as sound a republican as anyone. Jackson's argument is patently absurd, for Van Buren was heir apparent, as the president had earlier and more than once made clear to Jack himself. It is also dramatically inconsistent with Smith's delineation of the president in all of the other letters and severely strains the credibility of that delineation. (Tellingly, it takes Smith two letters to get this out.) Smith had become disenchanted with Jackson, and he would soon alter Jack's relationship with the president and establish a different, forthrightly political forum for his opinions. As 1833 drew to a close, though, he needed to get the book published in order to capitalize on the popularity the imitators had contributed to as well as to assert the integrity of the characterization he had originated. To that end, he included an appendix with six of the "best specimens" of the imitations.

He included as well an important addition of his own making, an introductory sketch of some six thousand words titled "My Life"—important because it reveals much about Smith's conception of the cracker-barrel philosopher he had originated and evolved. In it Smith evoked a highly idyllic vision of the New England village of Downingville—its history, its customs, its pastoral virtues. (Jack's grand-father's account of the battle at "Burgwine" is particularly touching and at the same time amusing.) In this version, self-consciously, even self-righteously, apolitical, the town had once voted to evict a lawyer who had put up a sign with his name and the word "office," for "it was unanimously agreed if the man wanted an office he should go somewhere else for it, for as having an office seeker in Downingville, they never would." Unlike Charles Augustus Davis, Seba Smith had strong personal ties to New England, and in delineating the Downingville milieu and the Downings who live there, he had drawn upon members of his own family. In particular, Samuel Andrews, of Bridgeton, Maine, was clearly the prototype for Uncle Joshua, Jack's mentor and political advisor.[33] Yet in the early letters, Smith had satirized Downingville and its inhabitants as the embodiment of unprincipled political practices and its favorite son as a caricature of the selfish, hypocritical office seeker. In May 1830, on the road to Washington to curry favor with the president, Jack had fantasized about his triumphant return to his hometown in a spirit very different from that of the introduction to the book: "You'll see me coming dressed up like a lawyer," he bragged.

The discrepancy between the satirical intent of the original letters and Smith's purpose in adding the "My Life" piece to his collection of those letters can be seen in his difficulties with the illustrator for the book, David Claypoole Johnston, difficulties that delayed its publication. Johnston did not like the introductory sketch, reported Smith, who in turn was not pleased with Johnston's illustrations. He "can hardly touch any thing without running into caricature. I have to watch him, and sometimes get him to alter," he wrote to his wife.[34] Smith, although certainly no Jacksonite, wanted the illustrations to capture the intent of the sketch and redeem the lost virtues of the letters; Johnston, a less sentimental anti-Jacksonite, wanted them to reflect the ironic political satire of the newspaper letters.[35] (See fig. 20.)

Copyrighted as it was, and as the *Courier* letters were not, the introductory "My Life" gave Smith's own stamp to his original letters, but the New England cracker-barrel philosopher he had created took off in many directions in 1834, and for many years to come, Smith would rail at those who denied him his due as the originator of Jack Downing. His book and Davis's were published in good season to take advantage of the highly charged political events of 1834, and both books would go through several editions, including ones in England. (Bad luck plagued Smith with the failure of his publisher in the fall of 1834.) It was not merely Jackson's defeat of the bank that coalesced anti-Jackson sentiment but also his assertion of presidential power in that attack, claiming that his power came from the people by virtue of his election as president. By the spring of 1834, those who opposed Jackson had formed a new political party, the Whigs, "adopting this name to designate their opposition to concentrated power in the hands of the chief executive,"[36] and thus the Whig press raged against the man they dubbed "King Andrew."

As for Seba Smith and Charles Augustus Davis, they followed up on Jack's break with the president and stepped up their attack with new, highly political formats. *Major Downing's Advocate* began publication in New York 12 March 1834. A triweekly newspaper begun as an inexpensive way to get the letters circulated, according to the *Advocate* (12 Mar. 1834), it accompanied them with "such news of this very peculiar time as will prove most interesting." Most of the news had to do with New York city and state political struggles related to the bank, whereas most of the Downing material consisted of earlier letters, when he was the president's confidante, making for confusing reading. In July 1834 the *Advocate* merged its title with the *Mechanics' Journal,* and although it featured new letters by Davis's J. Downing, it seems to have been short lived.[37] Accused by Jackson of changing his politics, Jack here admits, "It may be so, for a man may as well change his teeth, says I, if by keepin his old set he can git nothing to bite with 'em." The paper itself took a hard-nosed Whig stand on the issues, above all the bank, and featured New York state and city political personalities and their battles on those issues, but although Jack has clearly broken with the president, he claims no party affiliation. "It wont do no good to be botherin' yet about who is to be the next president—its time enuff to select a miller when we've got the harvest home and all thrash'd out; it will be enuff to see that we get a good honest miller then" (9 July 1834). Jack takes the political high road as spokesman for and of the party of the people against one-man rule, a convenient stance for reiterating Whig castigations against King Andrew.

Much more enduring—perhaps because of its broader political appeal and its literary diversity—was Seba Smith's *Downing Gazette,* published weekly in Portland from 4 July 1834 to 15 January 1836. In the first issue, Jack announces his break from the president with a "Second Declaration of Independence," and as a former partisan he seems all the more credible as the spokesman of the people, whom Jackson apparently has forsaken. Jack is no mere letter writer for his *Gazette,* but a down-home editor who gives a cracker-barrel presence to the paper as a whole. As Uncle Joshua reports, Downingville "has got to be a real whig town" (19 Sept. 1834), and in that spirit, Aunt Nabby takes the "Gineral" to task for breaking up cabinets: "There'd be no keeping furniture of any kind in the house any time at all." With Jack running the paper, his Cousin Joel becomes the correspondent from Washington, taking on Jack's old role as the president's confidante full of rustic good sense and advice. Not all the news was political, though. Sarah Downing, the local schoolteacher, offers a history of the Downings that has all the conventions of sentimental literature, and letters from a Timothy Jones report local color from a place called Wortleberry.

The *Downing Gazette,* in other words, had features of a real newspaper and for that reason, perhaps, was widely popular—"spread all over creation," Jack says, then adds with sarcastically parenthetical apology "(I mean the Gineral's creation)"—and the many letters from correspondents, including a Captain Shadrach Downing, a forty-ninth cousin from Georgia, lend credence to that claim. Smith's reasons for starting up the *Gazette* certainly reflected his repugnance for Jacksonian politics, but the tone is not so strident, the ideology not so Whiggish, the subjects not so geographically parochial as those in the New York *Major Downing's Advocate and Mechanics' Journal.* As in the earlier series, Jackson's heir apparent, Martin Van Buren, provided a common target for ridicule of the party, as did members of the cabinet. Letters from former Jacksonians who, like Jack, had seen the wisdom of Whig opposition to Jackson's high-handed political style have a prominent place. A common feature of opposition newspapers, they seem particularly fitting in one edited by the most famous and most intimate of the president's former partisans.

Then, in February 1835, with a keen insight into the political scene and the role of the news media in it, Seba Smith had editor Downing ask Davy Crockett to contribute his cracker-barrel opinions to the *Gazette.* Crockett, of course, had once been elected to Congress as a Jackson man, but he too had parted ways with the president, and in 1835 the figure of "Davy Crockett" was largely the creation of Whig writers who turned him into a cracker-barrel spokesman for their cause—inspired in part by the example of Jack Downing.[38] Davy seems curiously reluctant to respond to Jack's invitation, but with more prodding from Jack, he would do so over the next several months. Thus "did the careers of two of America's most important comic figures converge for a brief moment," says John William Ward,[39] but that convergence is plagued with confusion of several kinds. Davy's letters are strictly political and lack the cracker-barrel conventions and comicality of much of the other Crockett material. The letters were almost certainly not the work of Crockett himself, but of a Whig ghost writer who for some reason addressed Smith's *Jack* Downing as if he were Davis's *J.* Downing.[40] That confusion is compounded by a modern-day Crockett scholar, James Shackford, who says that when Crockett told of sitting down with "the rale Major Jack Downing" in New York in 1835, "it is entirely possible that David and Seba Smith may indeed have sat down 'to cold turkey' on April 30, 1834, in New York City."[41] More likely, of course, it was the sociable Whig and New York cracker-barrel humorist Charles A. Davis whom Crockett had dinner with, not Seba Smith, busy editing two newspapers in Portland, Maine.

Crockett's last, lackluster letter appeared in September 1835, and very soon thereafter the Downing cracker-barrel material itself began to decline. Seba Smith may have been preoccupied with the land speculation frenzy set off by Jackson's defeat of the bank, which, ironically, would bankrupt the Maine publisher. But he may, or may also, have become uncertain about what to do with the cracker-barrel philosopher, given his ambivalence toward the values that figure represented. Smith was no Whig ideologue and thus not motivated by specific issues to exploit Jack as that party's avatar of the common man, as Davis had done and as Whig writers had done with Crockett. In creating and then sustaining Jack Downing, Seba Smith, as the Rickels say in their biography and as that introductory sketch to *Life and Writings* suggests, was often beguiled by "the pastoral innocence and purity of his literary figure," but he could find no political faith in the common man, "who, for all his worth, is a creature of low intellectual and moral development."[42] Smith's reservations are evident in the first issue of the *Downing Gazette*, when Jack writes of stumbling over a stack of Uncle Joshua's books. Finding a copy of "Ferguson's Essays," he quotes the learned words at length to clarify his political philosophy, language more appropriate to Seba Smith. (James Russell Lowell would also find the cracker-barrel persona difficult to sustain as a spokesman for issues the writer felt deeply about.) In subsequent issues of the *Gazette*, Jack writes less vernacularly and turns political reporting over to his more rustic Cousin Joel, whose letters in time too become less rustic even as they become briefer and, like Jack's, less frequent.

Seba Smith's struggle with the role Jack could play seems evident as events unfold in the pages of the *Gazette* in 1836. In January, Nabby reports that Jack is quite ill, and he remains so for two more months, according to occasional updates, as Smith decided what to do. His decision becomes graphically clear in the *Downing Gazette* of 26 March: a front page bordered in black announces that Jack Downing has died at the age of forty-two. A letter from Uncle Joshua recounts his nephew's cracker-barrel career, pointing to his ability to illustrate complex problems with homey references and down-to-earth allegories. A letter from Nabby, herself in failing health, reports in detail the death-bed scene, including Jack's last words: "Heaven bless my old friend of the Portland Courier and Heaven bless the dear Gineral." Curious words given Jack's "Second Declaration of Independence," which had inaugurated this phase of the original Jack Downing's cracker-barrel career, but they do reflect the persistently conflicting sentiments of the writer who had given him life.

A National Phenomenon

For whatever reasons Seba Smith wanted to lay to rest the Yankee cracker-barrel philosopher he had created, the character of Jack Downing continued to live in many forms. As we have seen, both Davis and Smith started newspapers featuring Jack as the editor and as author of letters that continued to be printed in all parts of the country, as were those by imitators. Eugene Current-Garcia reports their popularity in Georgia newspapers in 1833 and as late as 1854, and Wyman speaks of "western imitators" in 1834, calling "very clever" a series by Joel Downing in the *Detroit Journal and Michigan Advertiser.*[43] One imitator wrote a satiric biography of the president, in 1834, *The Life of Andrew Jackson*; in 1836, another capitalized on the popularity of Jack's name with *Jack Downing's Song Book*, which went through four editions by 1839.[44]

Giving vivid visual dimension to the cracker-barrel characterization of Jack was a series of lithograph cartoons, political broadsides that first appeared in 1833, and by 1838, an English traveler writing in *Bentley's Miscellany* wrote of "hearing of Major Jack Downing of American ubiquity, who is spread abroad and met with as a resident in most of the large towns and many of the quiet villages." Several of the cartoons published over the years bore the signature of "Zek Downing, Neffu to Major Jack Downing," but they were done "in many manners and are probably by several hands," William Murrell says in his study of American graphic humor, which reprints examples.[45] Most of these were highly critical of the Jackson presidency, but not all. "The Downfall of Mother Bank" (see fig. 22) shows a triumphant Jackson holding up his order to remove the deposits, while in another part of the picture the pillars of the bank crumble and fall, burying Whig politicos and editors. Jack appears at the president's side, cheering him on. Here, as in many of these broadsides—both for and against Jackson—the Yankee is dressed in swallow-tail coat, striped trousers, and a top hat, illustrating Jack's place in the early iconographic history of Uncle Sam. According to Murrell, "The Major Downing of the cartoons came very close to a personification of the American people; and he figured in drawings . . . for fully thirty years."[46]

On stage too, actors of the day capitalized on the Downing vogue, giving life to Jack in many forms, and although none of the material is extant, something of its nature can be gleaned from newspapers, playbills, and theater histories. In Boston in July 1833, for example, a Mr. Johnson, "in the character of Jack Downing," recited his "description of the President's reception at Downingville" as part of an olio, reported the *Boston Evening Transcript* (8 July 1833), and a few months later (12 Sept.) reprinted an announcement from the New York *Gazette* that one of that city's "talented writers has nearly finished a play in which Major Jack Downing is the principal character. Among the dramatis personae is one called the Gineral—and most of the old and new cabinet, are likewise introduced. The conversation between the Major and his coadjutors is said to be inimitably ludicrous." The major actors of the day also added the role to their repertoire for a time. James Hackett's *Major Jack Downing, or the Retired Politician,* which opened in New York in May 1834, was "undoubtedly drawn" from "Smith's amusing rustic biography," Francis Hodge says, and suggests that it may have been a companion piece to that actor's earlier hit, *Lion of the West,* which had taken advantage of the popularity of Davy Crockett.[47] Actor Yankee Hill certainly did so with his performance in *Lion of the East; or, Life in New York* in New York in June 1835. Again, none of this material became permanent in the repertoire of Yankee theater, but Jack's popularity on the boards was neither short term nor limited to Eastern theaters. The New York *Daily Express* (20 Sept. 1837) reported "Jack Downing in Louisville [where] Mr. Kelly is playing Jack Downing in the

City Theater," and Dan Marble played Jack in *Life in New York* in St. Louis in 1840, perhaps a "borrowing" of Hill's material, Hodge says.[48] Jack appeared in rather different form on another kind of stage in 1835 as part of a circus side show, one of a group of wax figures that included President Jackson, Mrs. Trollope, and Washington Irving (see fig. 26).

The New York Daily Express

In his original role as cracker-barrel letter writer, Jack appeared most prominently in an intermittent series of letters beginning in August 1837 and continuing for nearly four years in the *New York Daily Express*, a staunchly Whig paper that had merged with the *New York Daily Advertiser* in which Davis's letters had been published. Rumor had it that the editor, James Brooks, a Down Easter who had studied law in Portland, was the author, but Mary Alice Wyman says some were by Brooks and some by Davis.[49] The letters were highly partisan and inconsistent in style, sometimes in the form of conventional editorial reporting under a "Downingville" byline, at other times in Jack's vernacular voice, indicating dual authorship, says Wyman. Such was the drawing power of Jack Downing's name, though, that the early ones brought on extra editions of the newspaper and were reprinted in "the Press in all parts of the country," as the *Express* (27 Aug. 1839) proclaimed and as the many quoted testimonials would seem to confirm. One letter inspired an eleven-by-four-feet painting—"no caricature drawing but a painting"—of Jack's visit to Uncle Sam that was exhibited in the Academy of Fine Arts, where visitors received a handbill copy of the letter that inspired it, according to the *Express* (5 Jan. 1838). Jack also appeared graphically in "Notice to Quit," an 1840 political cartoon touted by Horace Greeley's campaign newspaper, the *Log Cabin*.[50]

Clearly, Jack Downing was an important cog in the machinery of Whig politics in the election of 1840. Although in the late 1830s they were about as badly divided as the Democrats, Whigs had something of a common cause in the continued financial panic that they blamed, with some reason, on Jackson's victory over the bank and the continued hard-currency policy. For the most part, the Downing letters in the *Express* rehashed these issues tirelessly and with little imagination, and Jack's cracker-barrel stance on the issues is not consistent. This Jack Downing hit his cracker-barrel stride in 1840, though, when he headed out for North Bend, Ohio, to visit William Henry Harrison, the Whig presidential nominee, to "measure him cross-ways and length-ways—perpendicular and slantindickelar" to determine if he is a party president or for the whole people (25 Mar. 1840). Sure enough, Jack's letters from the "Log Cabin on the North Bend" confirm that Harrison is indeed the down-home, cider-making, cider-dispensing ploughboy that the Whig press had proclaimed him to be. Once the bedfellow and right-hand man of Andrew Jackson, the "Gineral" and democrat of Democrats, Jack Downing becomes "Gineral" William Henry Harrison's personal secretary, who along with the icons of the log cabin and the cider barrel, gives credibility to the Whig campaign to promote itself as the party of the common man. As if already conceding the November election, the *Democratic Review* of June 1840 acknowledged bitterly the success of the cracker-barrel strategy of what it called the "Log Cabin and Hard Cider" campaign: "We have taught them to conquer us!"

Seba Smith Resurrects Jack

If Seba Smith voted in the 1840 election, he did so in New York city and no doubt for Jack Downing's candidate. Bad luck and bad business judgment had forced him to sell his Portland newspapers, and the family moved to New York, where Smith and his wife, Elizabeth "Oakes Smith," as she began to call herself, struggled over the years to make their living by writing.[51] Smith probably voted for Harrison in 1840—never "the little magician," Martin Van Buren, the Democrat nominee—but he did not enlist his own cracker-barrel talents in "Old Tip's" cause.[52] However, Smith did bring Jack back to life in the New York *New World* with a short series of letters beginning 2 May 1840.[53] Jack's description of how a Doctor Solomon Smiley's marvelous pills slowly fleshed out his skeleton seems unduly lurid, but it confirms that it was the authentic Jack Downing that had come to life, the one created and then killed off by Seba Smith, as the editor of the *New World* made clear in a note. Jack does so too, protesting counterfeiters, particularly the one who printed his letters in the New York *Advertiser* and who "kept 'em up in the New York *Express.*" And although he speaks fondly of "Gineral" Jackson and how they "fit that Bank," he does not enter the political fray. No doubt like many writers who create a popular humorous persona, Smith was torn between that popularity and the need to establish his own identity, particularly a more legitimate literary career.[34] In 1840, for example, in addition to writing tales and poems and looking for editorial duties appropriate to his age and experience, he was busy completing *Powhatan; a Metrical Romance* in seven cantos of two hundred pages, published in 1841. In *Graham's Magazine* (July 1841) Poe dismissed it with derision, and surely knowing the discomfort it would cause, insisted upon referring to the author as "Jack Downing," who "never committed a greater mistake in his life than when he fancied himself a poet." Seba Smith would continue to assert his intellectual autonomy with stories, poems, and essays— even a geometry book—but he would return to Jack several times over the years.

By 1844 Smith had the editorial connection he wanted, with the *Rover*, a minor but respectable literary weekly, and Jack's letters began to appear in January 1844, perhaps to distinguish the *Rover* from the horde of other New York magazines. (The issue for 23 March 1844 featured his picture on the cover.)[35] Jack complains at some length about "Mr. Davis," who "goes round among folks, and tries to get into notice, and into good society, *by calling himself me*" and who had recently been introduced as Jack at a dinner honoring Charles Dickens during an American visit. Jack also puffs a library of "cheap literature" that Smith was apparently an agent for, and reports on some city events, such as a "picter bible" published by James Harper that ministers protested as indecent, which Smith parodied with an account of the protest in Downingville. Jack does write to the retired President Jackson expressing his concern over a badly divided Democratic party (and thus drawing attention to that division), but the early letters have little, certainly no political, focus.

However, Smith did have growing political concerns appropriate to Jack's cracker-barrel style, native Americanism, and beginning 26 July 1844, his letters originated in a forthrightly political weekly, *Bunker Hill*, with Jack Downing as editor.[56] Jack's letters appeared also in the *New York American Republican*, a daily newspaper edited briefly by Smith at this time, the journalistic forum of James Harper, who had been elected mayor of New York on the Native American party ticket.[57] As a political movement, nativism had originated in New York in 1835, and with the tacit support of the Whigs it had its greatest influence there. The movement spread from New York to other Northern cities; in the south, nativists feared the growing power of the Northern antislavery states. Nativist rhetoric played on two principal fears, according to Louis Scisco: foreigners were unfit for citizenship until ties with their country of origin had been fully obliterated, and Roman Catholics were unfit because of their obedience to the Pope.[38] Politically, many Whigs, such as Seba Smith, saw these newly enfranchised voters as easily manipulated by urban political bosses to vote as a Democratic block.

In the *Bunker Hill,* Sergeant Joel Downing writes humorously of events in Europe. Of the birth of a baby to Queen Victoria, he calls it "a Duke of York or a Duke of Kent. . . . I spose when the doctors get time to examine him a little more they'll find out which he is," but nativism dominates. "Straight," conventional news and editorials on that issue feature the impassioned, often shrill message of nativism about the dangers of foreigners, with Jack Downing's editorials and letters by other Downingville folk providing some semblance of a more reasonable, because vernacular, tone. With typical editorial rhetorical flourishes, for example, "Reasons for Native Americanism" in the *Rover* (1844) uses the image of the tree of liberty: it can stand firm against traditional party conflict, "but the foreign population that is flooding the country, and the foreign influence growing up from it, are laying the axe at the root of the tree, and, before we are aware, may prostrate it forever." In the same issue, and with cracker-barrel contrast, Uncle Joshua writes that "this ere business" (the tree of liberty) reminds him of "our red sweet apple tree when your [Jack's] father and I was boys," and he launches into an allegorical reminiscence that brings the elaborate metaphor of the editorial down to earth and does so in a vernacular style that amuses more than harangues—that tempers the shrill tone of a narrow ideology. In a letter reprinted in the *Rover* (17 Aug. 1844), Jack's Aunt Nabby identifies clearly the cracker-barrel appeal that the *Bunker Hill* was intended to have: "Thinks I to myself, now we shall have a paper sich as the folks in Downingville will know how to read. None o' your stupid papers made up of big, hard words, enuf to crack a body's jaw to get them out, and full of stuff such as no body ever heard on, or dreamed on, or thought on, afore; but about things that folks can understand." Despite Nabby's optimism, James Harper failed to be reelected in 1845, and although the Native American party called a national convention in Philadelphia in 1845, its popularity waned and its influence died in 1847, its nativist cause revived a few years later by the Know-Nothings.

Smith's My Thirty Years Out of the Senate

By 1847, though, Seba Smith had a new cause and a new forum for Jack Downing in a series of letters in the Washington, D.C., *National Intelligencer* from July 1847 to January 1856. These letters, along with those from *The Life and Writings* in 1833, were published in 1859 as *My Thirty Years Out of the Senate*.[59] None of the Jack Downing letters from the 1840s, nor any from the earlier *Downing Gazette*, were included. The "missing" letters had been lost in a fire and created the "gap in history," Jack explains in the preface to *My Thirty Years*. James Shackford, however, argues that Smith left them out because he repented the strong Whig stand he had taken in them: "The letters had been 'destroyed' so far as his collected works were concerned because of the 'fire' of passion which had led Smith too far in giving his support to what, in calmer hours of reflection, he decided he did not want to preserve under his final endorsement and name."[60] This ignores not only Smith's dismay over Democratic politics in the first series and his unremittingly Whig positions in the second, but also the fact that the title burlesqued *Thirty Years' View* (1854–56), the autobiography of Missouri senator Thomas Hart Benton, who had led the battle against the bank in the Senate and had supported Polk in the war against Mexico. Shackford also ignores the fact that in publishing the 1833 *Life and Writings,* Smith had omitted nearly a third of the material that had originally appeared in the *Courier* and in turn, omitted several letters from the 1833 collection for *My Thirty Years.*

Although the letters in the *National Intelligencer* were published over nine years, a third of them appeared from June 1847 to December 1848 and deal with the last year and a half of James Polk's presidency and his direction of the Mexican War. As he had done so successfully with Jackson, Smith made Jack the confidante of and unofficial advisor to President Polk, an appropriate figure for that role. A staunch Jacksonian from Tennessee, Polk, as Speaker in the 1830s, had led the final victory in the House of Representatives over the Bank of the United States, and what with Jackson's early endorsement of his dark-horse candidacy for president, Polk tried to pass himself off as "Young Hickory." As the series begins, he is on a tour of the Eastern states, and tells Jack that he seems to be more popular than Jackson had been on his famous tour in 1832. Jack tries to be loyal, but he confesses that the acclaim seems to have "a sort of *mother-in-law show* about it."[61] With Jack's honesty and Polk's persistence, Smith satirized as foolishly vain Young Hickory's attempts to capitalize on the undeniable charisma of the former president.

Smith's major concern in this group of letters was the administration's conduct of the war against Mexico, because he saw it as part of the expansionist philosophy of Manifest Destiny, which guided Democratic party foreign policy in the middle of the nineteenth century.[62] In his conversations with Jack, Polk admitted to all of the self-interested, unprincipled motivations that the opposition press, such as the *National Intelligencer*, accused him of: that he had started the war and continued it to further the Democratic party and his own political career; that he jealously resented the successes of his generals in the field, Zachary Taylor and Winfield Scott, both Whigs; that he therefore failed to give adequate support to the armies; that he temporized in making peace; that he even conspired with the Mexican leader Santa Anna. Jack's confidential relationship with Polk and the intimacy inherent in the epistolary form gave greater credibility to these charges than Whig editorials could. President James Polk became an ironic persona, a self-caricature.

As the *National Intelligencer* noted wryly in a prefatory note to Jack's first letter, Jack Downing offered a view of President Polk "which that distinguished functionary had not thought necessary to confide to his most confidential friends before he met the major." To keep the relationship credible, Jack had to remain loyal, but when Smith felt strongly about an issue, he often turned Jack's acquiescence into bitterly satiric irony that strains that credibility. Jack tells Polk to pay no heed to critics who say his annexation policy would mean the destruction of the country. The man who built the temple of Diana at Ephesus is forgotten, Jack says, but history remembers well the man who burned it down. "So in this great annexin' business of yourn," he advises, "if you should set fire to the great temple that Washington built, and burn it down, don't fear your name will live on the page of history full as long as Washington." Here, the irony, like the learned allusion, is too patently Seba Smith's, not Jack Downing's.

Many in the nation, particularly in the North, opposed the Mexican War, and James Russell Lowell used the tradition of Yankee cracker-barrel satire, which Smith had pioneered, to articulate that opposition. But whereas Lowell's *Biglow Papers,* First Series (1848) attacked the extension of slavery into annexed territories and argued against the morality of the war in general, Smith's Downing letters expressed his fear that the war in Mexico portended a policy of expansionism—"annexin'" is Jack's code word—that would overextend the national strength and leave it open to foreign invasion. According to Jack, Polk planned to carry the war into South America and annex it and then try his hand at annexing Europe and Africa. "And to prevent any quarreling beforehand about it on this side of the water," Jack confides, "he's agoing to agree to run the Missouri Compromise line over there and cut Europe into Free States and Africa into Slave States." The humor in the exaggeration alone would have served to satirize Polk's foreign policy, but it was not enough for Smith. In the tradition of the cracker-barrel philosopher at its homespun best, Jack talks about Bill Johnson's attempt to get honey from a hornet's nest by knocking the hive apart, a homey anecdote to warn the president that a peace is never "conquered," only scattered. In the same letter he reports a dream in which the country turned into a "monstrous great ship of war," captained by Polk, and bound on an ill-fated campaign to annex the world. Smith's message was all too clear: jingoistic visions of Manifest Destiny threatened the security of the nation. This paranoiac fear, originating from Smith's own narrow native Americanism, runs through most of the letters in this series. It was implied, for example, in Jack's letter to the Hungarian leader Kossuth, who toured America in 1851–52 urging support of his country's democratic revolution, and it would dominate Jack's letters to Franklin Pierce, whose election in 1852 again instigated a militant foreign policy.

James Polk had been correct in his concern that the success of Zachary Taylor in Mexico might spell trouble for the Democratic party. Nominated in 1848 by the Whigs, who counted not only on the general's popularity but also on the fact that he professed no principles and would thus offend no voters, Taylor defeated the two candidates nominated by the badly splintered Democrats. Smith could exult in the triumph, but with a Whig president, there was little for Jack Downing, confidante and advisor to Democratic presidents, to do but join others of his party at the head waters of the Salt River, where out-of-office politicians reportedly bided their time between elections. Smith tentatively turned to consideration of the most serious issue facing the nation, the extension of slavery into newly annexed territories, an issue that had splintered both parties and one that Smith, typically, feared would divide the union itself. In a long letter dated 25 October 1849 (the last letter for three years), Uncle Joshua spins a highly elaborate allegory about an "Uncle" Sam West, a farmer who died, leaving the Southern farm to John, the Northern to Jonathan. The two argue about John's growing thistles (slavery) until he gets into a fight with the Silverbuckles (Mexico), whom Jonathan helps to defeat. In reparation, the Silverbuckles deed them a gold-apple field (California), but the two argue about whether to grow thistles there, and Jonathan puts up a sign prohibiting it (the Wilmot Proviso prohibiting slavery in California). John, in response, puts up a fence between the farms (secession), a division that leaves the country vulnerable to take-over by the Silverbuckles, the Goldthreads (South Americans), and the Boheas and Shushons (Europeans). Dividing the union over slavery, in other words, would leave the nation open to incursions by other countries. It was the only time Smith concerned himself with slavery, and typically his concern was not with the morality of the peculiar institution. Even here he blunted the thrust of his position with the elaborately allegorical device.

The ironic cracker-barrel voice better suited Smith's intentions and, perhaps, skills, and an opportunity came for both early in 1852 as the Democrats prepared for another presidential struggle. In the caucus at Downingville, the arguments among the leading citizens there, though agitated by local jealousies within the fictitious community, mirrored the seemingly irreconcilable factions within the Democratic party, each with its own candidate. The always politic Uncle Joshua, however, voices the kind of unprincipled politics that Smith liked to ascribe to the Democrats: the Downingville caucus should choose the nominee who has the best chance of winning—and then they can decide on the principles. "It isn't principles that give us office, but the man; and we must elect the man or git no offices. The Dimocratic principles can be regulated after we agree on our man, for they are all very simple and plain; and the fewer the better." Although writing the letter before the party met in Baltimore, Smith accurately predicted the conditions if not the ultimate result of the convention. As had the Downingville caucus, the delegates in Baltimore agreed to select a candidate before drawing a platform, with Jack comically describing the three days and two nights of interminable balloting in terms of a ploughing contest, with each candidate representing a team and each ballot a "pull."

Neither Seba Smith nor anyone else could have predicted that the contest would be won by Franklin Pierce, a dark-horse candidate whose very obscurity meant he would not offend the various factions. The most genuinely humorous letter in the series (dated 20 July 1852) is Jack's report of the convention to a doubtful Uncle Joshua, who has never heard of Franklin Pierce. "It ain't a fictitious name, is it?" he asks cautiously. "Upon my word and honor, there isn't a particle of joke upon it—it was all done in real arnest," Jack replies. The Whigs had nominated Winfield Scott, the successful general in the war in Mexico, and though he was in reality as colorless and uncommitted as Pierce, Smith poked fun at the Democrats' attempt to sell their candidate as a wounded war hero:

> "Whereabouts was his wound?" [Uncle Joshua asks.]
> "Well, he had several hurts," said I; "I believe in his foot and ancle, and other parts."
> "Rifle balls?" said Uncle Joshua, very earnest.
> "O no, nothing of that kind," says I.
> "What then; sword cuts? Or did the Mexicans stick their bayonets into him?"
> "No, no; nothin' of that kind, nother," says I.
> "Then it must be grape[shot] or bombshells," said Uncle Joshua, "how was it?"
> "No, no, 'twasn't none of them things," says I. "The fact was, when they was skirmishing round, getting ready for the battle, his horse fell down with him and lamed him very bad."

Comic anticlimax has seldom been better used, and it was all the more effective because everything Jack said was true. The final irony, however, turned on Seba Smith and the Whigs, for Franklin Pierce was indeed elected—and by a wide margin.

The election of a Democrat did give Smith the opportunity to use Jack in his most effective cracker-barrel role as advisor to still another president. For the Democrats, the campaign had only temporarily calmed the political storms, and Pierce's appointment to his cabinet of men representing the various factions provided no oil for troubled waters. Although that gave President Pierce little comfort, the factionalism did give Seba Smith the principal domestic issue for Jack's last group of letters. The dominant concern, however, was foreign policy. In his inaugural address, President Pierce had revived the expansionist policy of the Polk administration by announcing that he would not be restrained "by any timid forebodings of evils from expansion." The prize sought in the 1850s was Cuba, and the various attempts to wrest that island from Spain represent a sordid history of pugnacious diplomacy, nationalistic bluster, and illegal filibustering; Jack Downing was in the thick of it. As Pierce's plenipotentiary minister-general and then as president of the Ostend Congress and commander of forces poised to capture Cuba, Jack voiced the rhetoric of belligerent expansionism, and Seba Smith had little need to exaggerate with irony the words and actions of those Americans who stood for that philosophy. As Jack reported, Caleb Cushing (attorney general) did indeed envision an American empire on a Roman model; Jefferson Davis (secretary of war) had in fact clandestinely encouraged John Quitman's formation of a private invasion army; and Minister to Spain Pierre Soulé had really instigated revolt in that country. The Ostend Congress, a meeting of American foreign ministers held in October 1854, was the culmination of such jingoism—a meeting so unpopular in Europe that it had to move from Ostend to Aix-la-Chapelle. The manifesto it produced, a semisecret document that embarrassed the moderate secretary of state, William Marcy, put forth two policies that appeared as an ultimatum: either Spain must sell Cuba or America would take it. Jack uses this as a cue for the name of his flagship, *The Two Pollies,* and enthusiastically quoting the more blatantly belligerent sections of the manifesto, takes it as a commission to invade the island. Then, when Pierce's agent to Cuba, Jefferson Davis, failed to go through with the take-over, Jack lays the blame to the factional division in the cabinet. "Mr. Davis received his secret commission from *one end* of your cabinet, and, somehow or other, accidentally made his report to *t'other end of it,*" he complains to the president.

The public furor over the Ostend Manifesto, the revelation of Quitman's intentions to invade Cuba, and the actual invasion of Nicaragua by Robert Walker's private army forced the Pierce administration to back down from its bellicose foreign policy by the end of 1855. On the domestic front, the Democrats faced a tough election battle, what with the growing power of the newly formed Republican party. Its success in the fall congressional elections gave them enough strength in the House to sustain a six-week effort to get one of its members elected presiding officer. In reporting that struggle in his last letter, dated 21 January 1856, Jack Downing returned to the role that had initiated his career some twenty-five years earlier. In a postscript he wrote that he may contribute to a new magazine, the *Great Republic Monthly,* Seba Smith's last publishing venture, but no further letters from the Yankee have been found.[63]

Downing and the Civil War

With *My Thirty Years Out of the Senate* in 1859, Jack Downing retired from literature and politics as far as Seba Smith was concerned;[64] however, the cracker-barrel Yankee did appear once more, in a series of letters in the *New York Weekly Caucasian,* 8 February 1862 to 6 February 1864, published as *Letters of Major Jack Downing, of the Downingville Militia* in 1864 (see fig. 24). (It would go through at least three editions, and was published in London as *Major Jack Downing to Lincoln* in 1865.) Originally the *Day-Book,* founded in 1848 to promote the pro-slavery cause in the North and during the war a Copperhead paper banned for a time from the U.S. mail, the *Caucasian* (the name changed to avoid the ban) had a large circulation, and Jack's letters were successful, Wyman says.[65] Now "nigh on eighty years old," Jack again writes as a presidential confidante offering apparent solace and commonsense advice to a president beleaguered by the conflicting demands of his party and a fractious cabinet. Like Charles A. Davis in his Downing letters, the anonymous Copperhead writer skillfully combined real events with the fiction of Jack's relationship, but he too had to react to these events as they unfolded in ways that strained and ultimately destroyed that relationship.

Jack is something of a fifth columnist, ridiculing the Union's floundering military efforts and provoking political dissension under the guise of good will to Lincoln. What emerged in 1862 as the overriding concern of the pro-Confederacy author, and of antislavery radicals as well, was the president's position on slavery, which would determine the nature of the war itself. In his inaugural address in 1861, Lincoln had disavowed any intent to interfere with slavery; as he appeared to vacillate, pressure came from many points of view for a stand against it, and as that pressure grew, so did the opposition. On 22 September 1862, Lincoln made a dramatic move with the preliminary Emancipation Proclamation, announcing that as of 1 January 1863 all persons held as slaves in territories under rebellion would be freed. The one hundred days that followed were tumultuous, with many fearing that he would reconsider, many others fearing he would not. Jack Downing, of course, argues against emancipation, and in his confidential conversations with Lincoln portrays the president as agreeable to cracker-barrel good sense but bedeviled by his cabinet. Jack has his say in the cabinet meetings too, stirring up trouble and drawing lively caricatures of the members—lively, but highly prejudicial, given the narrow interests of the Copperhead author. Alone with the president, Jack shows him the errors of his ways with homey exempla aplenty, and in October, Lincoln confesses "it's jest as you told me. That Proclymashin of mine ain't popular. . . . I know I'd been a great deal better off if I'd followed your advice all through these trubbils, but you see I had to go with my party."

Such admissions played to what appeared as real indecisiveness on Lincoln's part in these days, given military defeat in the battlefields and political setbacks at the polls during the Congressional elections—all of which intensified the pressure from all sides. The crisis came in December as a committee of Republican senators clamored for a reorganization of the cabinet, a move aimed chiefly at removing Secretary of State William Seward. Hearing of their proceedings, Lincoln admitted, "I have been more distressed than by any event of my life."[66] But on 19 December 1862 the president finessed the crisis with a brilliant diplomatic stroke, a surprise meeting of the committee and cabinet. On 31 December the cabinet and the president put the final touches on the Emancipation Proclamation, which was issued on 1 January 1863. Another political tumult ensued, but Lincoln had irrevocably changed the nature of the Civil War from a campaign not only to restore what he considered the Union but also to end slavery in it.

Jack Downing took credit for suggesting to the president the crucial meeting between the committee and the cabinet that "saved the nashun," and reported the confrontation in his own inimitable style, but Lincoln's bold, resolute stand against slavery meant that Jack no longer had a meaningful role to play in the administration. His next letter, dated 4 February 1863, he writes from Downingville, having broken with the president over "his Free Nigger Proclamashin": "I thought I should persuade him out of it, an tharby save the great disgrace an stane it would be on our country. But the truth is, the Kernel [Lincoln] an I had a row about it, an I left." The truth was, in fact, that despite the protest following the proclamation, the political climate had changed in Lincoln's favor, as Jack himself admits: even the "Demmycratic party didn't cum out bluntly agin this proclamashin, but kept on supportin the war." And even Downingville itself celebrated the return of its local hero in the Union cause—not Jack, but "Kernel Stebbins," who believes "freedom is to extend from the frozen planes of Alabama to the sunny banks of Newfoundland." After 1 January 1863, Jack writes fewer letters—twenty-three of the thirty in the series appear in eleven months of 1862; only seven in the next thirteen months. "I didn't feel like ritin in these times," he admits in March 1863. The author sends him back to Washington to help Lincoln with his message to Congress in December, but the pretense cannot be revived given the political realities. In the next-to-last letter Lincoln tells Jack "I wish now I had taken your advice," but even this fictitious Lincoln has to admit the emphatic truth: "I'me in the Abolishin bote, and you can't stop it now eny more than you kin put Lake Superior in a quart bottle." In the last letter, with Jack "completely disgusted" and with no place for Jack in the "real" world, the author resorts to a dream allegory about a graveyard where Lincoln, the cabinet, leaders of the war Democrats, and abolitionists lay to rest the Constitution and thus the Union.[67]

As for his place in the New England cracker-barrel tradition, this Jack Downing fails not only because, or when, he espouses the unabashed racism of Copperhead propaganda (modern readers should know that of seventeen daily newspapers in New York at the time, nine were pro-slavery and five were pro-Confederacy[68]), but because he is so exclusively the mouthpiece for that propaganda. As a result, the author has little care for anything else, say, for the literary niceties of characterization and some semblance of an identifiable dialect. Jack's many and elaborate rustic stories are often amusing enough even to ameliorate the intransigent ideology they illustrate—and Lincoln appropriately responds with stories of his own—but Jack's language is usually more phonetic than regional. Like his revelation of the president as a convivial but compulsive drinker-on-the-sly, his vulgar rendering of such names as "Hor*ass* Gree*lie*" (Republican editor of the *New York Tribune*) and "[Charles] Sum*nure*" (leading Senate anti-Southern radical) reflects the true tone of his characterization and the vicious, at heart humorless, intent of the author. Jack Downing's appearance in the 1860s, over thirty years after his creation by Seba Smith, is something of a tribute to the enduring popularity of that cracker-barrel characterization, but this last Jack Downing ultimately fails, perhaps, because he seems rather weary at eighty, and admittedly rather dated, what with repeated references to his earlier career with Andrew Jackson in an attempt to establish his literary lineage and cracker-barrel credibility.

Sam Slick

In creating Jack Downing, Seba Smith "had opened a new vein of literary ore," wrote Colonel James Watson Webb, editor of the *Morning Courier and New York Enquirer* (16 July 1845). In doing so, Smith had to contend with not only the "rascally counterfeiters" of Jack himself but also a Yankee cracker-barrel philosopher coined of the same ore but with a different stamp, Sam Slick. Always protective of his claim, Smith wrote in a survey of New England cracker-barrel humor in *May-Day in New-York* (1845) that "had Major Downing never written, the public never would have heard of Sam Slick," and later, more objective observers agree. V. L. O. Chittick, the fair-minded biographer of Thomas Chandler Haliburton, the man who created Sam Slick, agrees and even argues convincingly that not only was Haliburton considered by his fellow Nova Scotians "the Jack Downing of British North America" but also that he endeavored to be that.[69] Haliburton learned from Smith's example that a rustic character could say something worth listening to because he spoke in a vernacular that entertained and instructed, however ironically. Sam Slick was no mere imitation of Jack Downing, however. A clockmaker and peddler from Slickville, Connecticut, the creation of a Nova Scotian judge of decidedly Tory persuasions, Sam was a Connecticut Yankee as the consummate Yankee: bumptious, brash, and outspoken while not well spoken, he had the go-ahead philosophy of the archetypal democratic American who knew no bounds. Beginning in 1836, and over the next twenty years, Haliburton wrote seven books featuring Sam Slick (and others under his name), books that went through more than two hundred editions in the nineteenth century and into the twentieth, including translations into French and German. Joshua Silsbee brought Sam to the stage in the 1840s (see fig. 13), almanacs appeared under Sam's name, and Ann Stephens capitalized on the popularity of the family name with her characterization of Jonathan Slick.[70] In our own time, more has been written about Thomas Chandler Haliburton than about any nineteenth-century "American" humorist other than Mark Twain, due in large part to the exemplary work of Canadian scholars eager, but judiciously so, to reveal the worth of one of their own.

Sam first appeared in the Halifax *Novascotian* in September 1835, at the crest of Jack Downing's popularity, and proved popular enough within four months to encourage Haliburton to end publication there and add more letters and publish the first collection, *The Clockmaker; or, the Sayings and Doings of Samuel Slick, of Slickville*, late in 1836. By the end of the next year, editions had been published in England and the United States that enjoyed a warm reception from reviewers, and two more volumes in the series appeared in 1838 and 1840.

Despite the well-established example of Jack Downing, Haliburton approached the techniques of New England cracker-barrel humor tentatively in the early sketches. We see Sam indirectly, through the eyes of a Nova Scotian identified only as "the squire," who accompanies Sam on his clock-peddling peregrinations through the Nova Scotian countryside. In time, though, a format emerged that became the pattern for nearly all of the books: Sam as an irrepressible raconteur with cracker-barrel opinions on everything, with the squire as a frame narrator who initiates Sam's monologues, acts as a sounding board for his opinions, and provides a mild restraint on the Yankee's more outlandish pronouncements. Sam has rustic analogies for every occasion and does not hesitate to pile them one on the other. In the following consideration of matrimony, for example, he first compares marriage to a boy skating on thin ice, then immediately shifts to another, quite different, comparison:

You've seen a boy sliding on a most beautiful bit of ice, ha'nt you, larfin, and hoopin, and hallowin like one possessed, when presently sowse he goes in over head and ears? How he outs, fins, flops about, and blows like a porpus proper frightened, don't he? and when he gets out, there he stands, all shiverin and shakin, and the water a squish-squashin in his shoes, and his trowsers all stickin slimsey like to his legs. Well, he sneaks off home, lookin like a fool, and thinkin every body he meets is a larfin at him—many folks here are like that are boy, afore they have been six months married. They'd be proper glad to get out of the scrape too, and sneak off if they could, that's a fact. The marriage yoke is plaguy apt to gall the neck, as the ash bough does the ox in rainy weather, unless it be most particularly well fitted. You've seen a yoke of cattle that war'nt properly mated, they spend more strength in pullin again each other than in pulling the load.[71]

Typically, Sam's complex, enthusiastic metaphors very nearly overwhelm the point they were originally intended to make.

Sam expounded on a wide variety of topics—American eating habits, slavery, religion, English travelers, marriage, and women—but the dominant issue of the first volume, Haliburton's reason for initially taking on the cracker-barrel persona, was the Nova Scotians' failure to develop the resources of their province. Sam Slick, a Yankee peddler and thus the archetypal embodiment of American enterprising ingenuity, cataloged for Haliburton accurately and enthusiastically the many and sundry errors of the bluenoses, as the Nova Scotians were called. They devote too much time to raising horses, spend too much money on fancy houses rather than sensible barns, and get too involved in bickering about politics, according to Sam: *"Give up politics—it's a barren field, and well watched too; where one critter jumps a fence into a good field and gets fat, more nor twenty are chased round and round, by a whole pack of yelpin curs, till they are fairly beat out, and eend by bein half starved, and are at the liftin at last. Look to your farms—your water powers—your fisheries, and factories."*

In Judge Haliburton's own voice, such criticism would take on overtones of class and self-interest, but in the cracker-barrel tradition that Haliburton had adopted, Sam's rustic analysis amuses at the same time that it gives the further credence of plain good sense. "There's a moral, Sam, in everything in natur'," his father once told him, and the Yankee applies the principle liberally. The Nova Scotians, he says, "vegetate like a lettuce plant in a sarce garden, they grow tall and spindlin, run to seed right off, grow as bitter as gaul and die." Often Sam's dicta—"wise saws" that Haliburton at times italicizes—resemble the proverbial wisdom of Poor Richard: *"Poverty is keen enough, without sharpening its edge by poking fun at it,"* and *"power has a natural tendency to corpulencey,"* he remarks.[72] The conjoining of homespun sense and speech is in the best cracker-barrel tradition, of course, and for Haliburton's Canadian audience, Sam's belligerent nationalism ("the British can whip the world and we can whip the British," he likes to say), so endemic to the British characterization of Brother Jonathan, digs the sarcastic barbs just a bit deeper—and distances Haliburton himself from that sarcasm.

As the archetypal American, however, Yankee Sam Slick also embodied political principles that Haliburton, a Tory ideologue, could not abide, a contradiction that would trouble him throughout the Sam Slick volumes as he struggled to find a way to express those reservations within the conventions of the New England humor tradition in which he wrote. Sam's father, for example, admits that he has doubts about the necessity of the American Revolution, and although he had fought at Bunker Hill, he is haunted by the possibility that he had killed a British officer there in an impious war. However unlikely the confession may be, it expresses Haliburton's view of the American Revolution, but more important, it also expresses his opposition to proponents of Canadian independence and democratic reform in his own time. Sam himself voices Haliburton's reservations about democracy. Speaking of political practice in the United States, Sam admits, "Our folks have their heds a trifle too much, sometimes, particularly in Elections, both in freedom and speech. One hadn't ought to blart right out always all that comes uppermost." Hardly the orthodox opinion of the archetypal Yankee, particularly as a cracker-barrel philosopher that by his very nature tends to "blart right out all what comes uppermost," but Sam does pin the idea down with an appropriate, rustic analogy: "A horse that's too free frets himself and his rider too, and both on 'em lose flesh in the long run."

Toward the end of the first series, Haliburton finds that he must qualify even the virtues of progress that Sam had preached to the Nova Scotians from the beginning. Earlier, Sam had praised the factories at Lowell as a model to follow, but Reverend Hopewell, his minister in Slickville, later reminds him of their reprehensible influence. Factory towns will not only "corrupt our youth of both sexes and become hotbeds of iniquity" but also generate mobs, and "mobs will introduce disobedience and defiance of laws, and that must eend in anarchy and blood shed." Sam has to agree that the minister can "see near about as far into a millstone, as them that picks the hole into it." Reservations such as these are inappropriate to the Yankee persona Haliburton had adopted and inconsistent with the purposes for which he had adopted it. They foreshadow the more serious problems the Yankee persona posed for him in subsequent volumes in which he attempted to express opinions even more inappropriate to the Yankee voice.

Published in Nova Scotia in 1836, and more widely in 1837, the first *Clockmaker* book, despite its literally provincial import, was popular, particularly among English reviewers. Most of them misunderstood, or more likely simply ig-nored, Haliburton's Nova Scotian concerns, praising the novelty of the humor and above all the characterization of Sam Slick, who satisfied an English pen-chant for outlandish Americans. As for Sam's role as cracker-barrel philoso-pher, *Blackwood's Magazine* (Nov. 1837) said that Slick was "the general conduit of all opinions going at the same time," and thus exhibited "all the peculiarities of the native character in their most prominent point of view, to serve . . . for the portrait or the caricature of the Yankee." (The "or" is interesting in the ambiguity it creates as to whether Sam was an accurate or exaggerated Yankee.) Pleased with his initial success, Haliburton followed it up with a second series of *Clockmaker* stories in 1838 and a third in 1840. They too proved popular with reviewers, but reveal even more clearly Haliburton's persistent problems in the first series in making Sam an effective cracker-barrel philoso-pher of the kinds of opinions that he, Haliburton, wanted to express.

The second and third volumes made occasional jibes at bluenose foibles, but Haliburton felt that he had succeeded in his original intent and so turned to broader Canadian problems. (Explaining the difference, Sam says of the second series, "It ain't jist altogether so local, and it goes a little grain deeper into things.")[73] Haliburton had no use for reformers at home and abroad who pushed for independence and liberal reform, but with Sam as his principal spokesman, he had to balance the democratic political predilections inherent in the Yankee type with his own antidemocratic, conservative, pro-English views. Prodded by the still-unnamed but ubiquitous squire, Sam tries to draw a line between what is appropriate for America and what is suitable for its Northern neighbor. "Elective councils are inconsistent with colonial dependence," he considers, and as usual illustrates the opinion with a homey metaphor. "Its takin' away the crane that holds up the pot from the fire, to keep it from boilin' over, and clappin' it right on the coals: what a gallopin' boil it would soon come into, wouldn't it?" Usually, though, Sam finds in American experience itself symptoms of the many ills of liberalism in contrast to the salubrious traditions of conservative English practice. On religion, he does not quite come out in favor of the established church beloved by the squire, but Sam's story of Slickville's turning out the kindly Reverend Hopewell illustrates the virtues of tax-supported churches and the vices of the "voluntary system" in the United States. Sam even expresses serious doubts about crucial features of the American political system—rotation in office and universal suffrage—which result in American politicians being nothing but what Sam calls "popularity seeking patriots." At the end of the second series, Sam frets about the opinions in the book, and on reading the manuscript tells the squire, "You don't like republics, that's sartin. . . . Do you mean to write a satire on our great nation, and our free and enlightened citizens?" Nothing could be further from his mind, the squire assures; some of his best friends are Americans.

In the third *Clockmaker* book, as Sam continues to spout Tory ideology at the expense of American democratic practice, the squire begins to comment on the fundamental contradictions in a Yankee's espousing the virtues of English example and suggests to Sam that he is not a republican at all but a Tory. Apparently dissatisfied with continuing that inconsistency, Haliburton turned to Sam's Slickville minister, Reverend Hopewell, as spokesman. An elderly Episcopalian divine who had been unceremoniously thrown out by his parishioners (who then inexplicably became Unitarians), Hopewell voices British religious/political principles more attuned to those of the squire and Haliburton. The squire objects when Sam interrupts the minister's long monologues in favor of an established church for America and a limited monarchy, for the clockmaker "had a tendency to make the minister's conversations too desultory for one whose object was instruction."[74] Sam, as a result, becomes more arrogantly nationalistic and vain, and his anecdotes illustrate the loose morality that guides Yankee, which is to say American, economic speculation and political practice. By the end of the third series, Hopewell becomes the dominant voice of American right-headedness, and as he does so, the language he uses changes from a vernacular much like Sam's to diction that is measured and formal. In speaking with Sam, though, he returns to "the familiar and idiomatic language to which Mr. Slick was accustomed," as the squire says, because it was "better suited to the level of his understanding." With this judgment of vernacular speech, Haliburton brought into question the most basic, salient feature of the cracker-barrel philosopher.

In the two Sam Slick series that followed—*The Attaché; or, Sam Slick in England* in 1843 and 1844—Haliburton's reservations about Sam become fully realized. Surely Haliburton had been wanting to do it all along—to un- leash Sam as the living, ironic embodiment of the Yankee brag that America "is the top loftiest place in all creation." Strutting about as the American attaché in English society, among "benighted, ignorant, insolent foreigners," Sam calls them, he acts the ring-tailed boor in the name of "a free man and a Gentleman at large."

On English politics, Sam can still be sound enough on occasion. True, he has some harsh words for the Tories, but much worse are the "Masses, Repub- licans, Agitators, Repealers, Liberals," and, ultimately, the Whigs in "the great reform chain." His primary role in these books, however, is as an ironic per- sona, a parvenu par excellence, obstreperous in manner and irreverent in opinion. Dining among the fine folks, for example, is "both heavy work and light feedin'," and one dinner party is the same as every other: "The same powdered, liveried, lazy, idle, good-for-nothin', do-little, stand-in-the-way- of-each-other, useless sarvants. Same picturs, same plate, same fixin's, same don't-know-what-to-do-with-yourself-kinder-o'lookin'-master." (One has to wonder if Sam provided a convenient mask for Haliburton to register some- thing of his own colonial judgment of such matters.) By turns outrageously bombastic, vain, and self-righteous, Sam represented for Haliburton all of the social, political, and cultural evils of democratic society—a full-scale satiric attack not only on democratic America but also on liberal reformers in Canada and their cohorts in England. In time, Sam sets himself up as a "man of fashion" and in doing so "rendered himself ridiculous," the squire says. "It is impossible to express the pain with which I contemplated this awkward, over-dressed, vulgar, caricature."

With Sam as an ironic persona, so patently crass, his homey judgments reduced mostly to wrong-headed bombast, the identity of the anonymous squire, the character most like Haliburton himself, begins to emerge: his displeasure with and distaste for Sam become more explicit, and he even takes on a name, "Poker." Reverend Hopewell too takes on a larger role as Sam's temporizer and the voice of propriety and reason at their New World best. Haliburton knew what he was up to. In sending the first of the *Attaché* sketches to his publisher, Richard Bentley, Haliburton wrote that Hopewell "is rather a prominent character in all the books and will be still more so in the forthcoming one" because "there were things to be said too wise and too deep for Sam."[75] Hopewell understands and appreciates, for example, everything about England and its traditions, not only the state church but also social classes and entail. (Asked to preach in an English church, he is modestly pleased that his sermon has converted a nascent radical.) As for Sam, the good reverend had doubted his qualifications as attaché, and thus as representative American, from the beginning. Throughout the *Attaché* he and Poker join wringing hands in sober-sided apologia and lofty critiques on each occasion of Sam's intemperate opinion and behavior. "To a vulgar man like him," Poker intones, "totally ignorant of modes of life, a thousand little usages of society would unavoidably wholly escape his notice, while the selection, collocation, or pronunciation of words were things for which he had not perception and no use,"[76] to which Hopewell, typically, nods sagely. This pattern, Darlene Kelly says, "ultimately becomes monotonous, especially in the later [*Attaché*] books where it is used so routinely."[77] The *Attaché* series ends appropriately, though, and with some semblance of a plot, given the Yankee's ironic role here, when Sam himself admits the errors of his foolish pretensions. The good counsel of the squire and Hopewell has opened his eyes, he confesses. Ruefully echoing Reverend Hopewell's reservations about his qualifications as attaché to the Court of St. James, Sam admits he is out of place, that he has played the fool. Contrite, he plans to return home to take up clock making and peddling as more appropriate to his breeding and experience.

The two *Attaché* books received some good reviews, but Haliburton's brand of Tory ideology and colonial carping, more explicit in these books than in the *Clockmaker* series, were not particularly popular among readers; but worse, the novelty of Sam Slick as the comic Yankee had begun to wear thin as well. The *Spectator* (15 July 1843) clearly understood and praised Haliburton's contribution to cracker-barrel humor: "With the advantage derived from the slang and other peculiarities of Slick" he had given him "the power of 'making points' which often tell with a happy effect"; however, this reviewer concluded, in the latest books, the author "has reached the poorest of all repetitions, that of all repetitions, that of repeating himself." Although in America the *Knickerbocker* (Oct. 1843) observed that "the clock-maker has lost none of his shrewdness, his acute observations, nor his sparkling humor," C. C. Felton in the *North American Review* (Jan. 1844) launched a long and scathing attack on Haliburton's politics, his literary pretensions, and the whole Slick canon. Haliburton too knew that his cracker-barrel Yankee had run its course. "Here is an end to Sml. Slick," he wrote his publisher with formal finality in concluding a letter accompanying the last of the *Attaché* sketches.[78]

Nevertheless, Haliburton continued to capitalize on Sam's name by putting "by the author of 'Sam Slick the Clockmaker,' 'The Attaché,' etc." on the title pages of subsequent books: *The Old Judge* (1849), *Rule and Misrule of the English in America* (1851), and *Traits of American Humor* (1852). And, as have so many writers who create popular comic personae, however ambivalent they might feel about or be simply weary of their creations, Haliburton returned to Sam Slick in *Sam Slick's Wise Saws and Modern Instances* (1853) and its continuation, *Nature and Human Nature* (1855); however, the currency of Sam Slick—indeed, of the Yankee as representative American—had been spent by the 1850s. The review of *Wise Saws* in the *Acadian Recorder* (18 June 1853) surveyed succinctly the evolution of Sam's character in the various books, kindly tempering its criticism with the jeu d'esprit of an elaborate metaphor. Judge Haliburton must know, said this reviewer, "that the most delicious of *joints* becomes rather unpalatable, except to the most voracious; when served up too often." He continued the conceit in a judicious survey of the Sam Slick books: "We had the Clockmaker, in the 'first series' of that work, fresh, and most of readers [*sic*] thought, rich and racy. Then we had him 'twice-laid, cold,' in the 'second series.' Anon, he comes on 'deviled,' as the 'Attaché.' Now we have the remains 'hashed' and again placed before us. We expect to hear next that the Judge has made us soup from the bones." And in 1855 Judge

Haliburton tried, with the predicted results, in his last book featuring Sam Slick, *Nature and Human Nature.*

Although the Sam Slick books were published—and the early ones, at least, were popular—in the United States, Haliburton began the series for an audience primarily Nova Scotian, and then continued it over the years for an audience essentially English. And although Haliburton initially capitalized on the popularity of Jack Downing and got the example of the cracker-barrel philosopher from him, he cast his Yankee solidly in the broader British mold of the archetypal American common man, as seen in the later books with his careless blending of the backwoods Crockett and the Yankee Downing, a bone of contention critics then and since have picked at.

Haliburton's dominant concern—increasingly over the years, in all of his books, not just the Sam Slick ones—was England's colonial policy toward the Canadas: no democrat, he certainly did not want self-government, but neither did he want London to run things on its own. What Haliburton really wanted, Northrop Frye says, was "patronage on a grand scale. As for the kind of person who should be appointed—well, there are several hints, sometimes not very subtle hints, about one in particular who has deserved well of his country."[79] (Not very subtle, for example, is Sam's persistent prodding in the later books of the too-modest squire to promote his own cause in this regard.) Sam himself puts succinctly the fate that lay in store if policy did not change. Coaching Squire Poker for an important meeting with the minister of colonial affairs in London, Sam tells him what to say: *"If you don't make Englishmen of us, the force of circumstances will make Yankees of us, as sure as you are born."* The emphasis is Haliburton's, because that consequence was his greatest fear and the hole card in his strategy to change English policy. But that *Sam* should play it is typically inappropriate, for with his surly, boorish behavior, this Connecticut Yankee literally acts out what the consequences of that policy would be. Typical and at the same time inappropriate, because time and again Haliburton tried and failed to reconcile a fundamental dilemma in his portrayal of the New England cracker-barrel philosopher—the "impossible contradiction," Chittick calls it, "between Sam Slick as the typical New World democrat and at the same time the representative of steadfast conservatism, which had returned again and again to plague his creator."[80]

Given that "impossible contradiction," though, why did Haliburton return again and again to this Yankee as a cracker-barrel voice? Sam's name and the novelty of his characterization in the early *Clockmaker* volumes sold books, of course, but a better answer can be found in looking at what else Haliburton got from the Yankee persona, two very different kinds of humor that had nothing to do with colonial policy or Haliburton's apprehensions about democracy. Throughout all the books, Sam makes judgments and tells stories so racist, sometimes misogynist, that they go beyond anything that might be excused as "acceptable" even in an era less enlightened than our own, and his coarse jokes and sexual innuendoes are usually more smarmy than comic. No ironic persona to satirize Americans in these matters, Sam provides a convenient way for Haliburton to voice not so much his own views on such subjects as his sense of humor in general. His penchant for mild indecencies and double entendre appeared most prominently in *Letter Bag of the Great Western* (1840). A book attributed to Sam, though not written in his style, it was "an allfired smutty thing," Sam's "brother" Jonathan Slick lamented.[81] More conventional reviewers agreed, and, in fact, the charge of vulgarity dogged Haliburton throughout his long literary career, but he apparently enjoyed that brand of humor and found Sam an appropriate way to express it. Neither the righteous Reverend Hopewell nor the poker-faced squire, for example, would see the humor that Sam does in an embarrassed factory girl's description of her brother in the navy as a "rooster-swain." (Playing all too dumb about her squeamishness, Sam bullies her into admitting that her brother is a "cockswain.")

On the other hand, neither the minister nor the squire would or could tell with Sam's uninhibited vigor and authenticity another kind of humor, the "native American humor," that Haliburton also enjoyed, as is evident in the two anthologies he edited, *Traits of American Humor* (1852) and *The Americans at Home* (1854). Two examples illustrate Haliburton's skill in this tradition. "The Clockmaker"[82] shows Sam in the classic role of the Yankee peddler. Queried by the squire as to how he manages to sell so many clocks, "which certainly cannot be called necessary articles, among a people [the bluenoses] with whom there seems to be so great a scarcity of money," Sam replies, "It is done by a knowledge of *soft sawder* and *human natur'*," which he subsequently demonstrates. Stopping off at Deacon Flint's farm, the Yankee skillfully plays on the vanity of the deacon and his wife, who welcome the travelers into their home. That is "soft sawder," Sam confides to the squire. Then, when he leaves his last clock, ostensibly promised to neighbor Steel's wife, to the Flints's safekeeping for a time, that is "human natur'." Sam explains it all for the squire as they ride off: "Mrs. Flint will never let Mrs. Steel have the refusal—nor will the Deacon larn, until I call for the clock, that having once indulged in a superfluity, how difficult it is to give it up." Twelve thousand of the fifteen thousand clocks he has sold in the province over the years were left in just that way. "We trust to 'soft sawder' to get them into the house, and to 'human natur' that they never come out of it," the Yankee concludes (see fig. 18).

In a different type of story, "Italian Painting,"[83] Sam tells about the time he was commissioned to go to Italy to acquire some art for the Slickville, Connecticut, Athenaeum:

> I bought two Madonnas, I think they call them—beautiful little pictures they were too,—but the child's legs were so naked an ondecent, that to please the governor and his factory galls, I had an artist to paint trousers, and a pair of lace boots on him, and they look quite genteel now. It improved 'em amazin'ly; but the best o' the joke was those Macaroni rascals, seein' me a stranger, thought to do me nicely (most infarnal cheats them dealers too,—walk right into you afore you know where you be.) The older a pictur' was, and the more it was blacked, so you couldn't see the figurs, the more they axed for it; and they'd talk and jabber away about their Tittyan tints and Guido airs by the hour. How soft we are, ain't we? said I. Catch a weasel asleep, will you? Second-hand farniture don't suit our market. We want picturs, and not things that look a plaguy sight more like the shutters of an old smoke-house than paintins, and I hope I may be shot if I didn't get bran new ones for half the price they axed for them rusty old veterans.

As Sam said, the Slickville Athenaeum must have been "actilly a sight to behold." The story is worth quoting because it still amuses, not merely because it anticipates so clearly the ingenuous New World eye that Artemus Ward and Mark Twain cast on Old World art, albeit with different satiric purpose. Stories such as these reflect a Tory's satiric view of Yankee 'cuteness, Puritan prudery, and American taste, but Sam is not the caricature he too often becomes when more political issues were at stake. As a humorist in the cracker-barrel tradition, Haliburton was at his best in the first *Clockmaker* volume where the rustic Yankee's embodiment of American progress was well suited to the intentions of the author. In the subsequent volumes, Haliburton could not effectively reconcile his own uncompromising, irascible Toryism with the unrefined, democratic proclivities inherent in Sam Slick. When politics were not on the agenda, however, Haliburton often proved a skillful humorist. Among the heavy-handed philosophizing of Reverend Hopewell, the cautious admonitions of the squire, and the tedious, often tasteless recollections of Sam Slick can be found character sketches, horse trading yarns, Yankee tricks, and the kinds of comic anecdotes that capture the spirit of New England humor at its best.

James Russell Lowell

Haliburton's blurring of frontier and Yankee character and his blind pursuit of a discredited political agenda had done much to erode the popularity of Sam Slick, but Haliburton's failure to revive the popularity of his Yankee cracker-barrel philosopher in the 1850s was also due in part, says his biographer, to the appearance a few years before of the Biglow letters of James Russell Lowell, a Yankee cracker-barrel humorist whose message was more sincerely democratic and whose rustic New England speech had an authentic ring to it.[84] On the face of it, Lowell would seem an unlikely author of vernacular American humor. Born into a distinguished New England family and educated at Harvard, he pursued literary fame in more traditional, respectable, ways (and with far more success than Seba Smith). He published the medieval romance *The Vision of Sir Launfal*, the neoclassical satire *A Fable for Critics*, and an anthology of earlier poems all in 1848, the same year as his first collection of native humor, *The Biglow Papers*. Of the four, his satiric rustic letters in verse were the most popular, and along with the second series of *Biglow Papers*, published in 1866, they continue to provide the basis for Lowell's reputation as a writer.[85]

The Biglow Papers, First Series

Lowell admired and wanted for himself the "common touch" of Robert Burns's colloquial poems, Leon Howard says.[86] Although he had essayed a rustic, semiliterate characterization in a letter to William Story in 1844,[87] his first published Biglow letter did not appear until 17 June 1846, in the Boston *Courier*, edited by Joseph Buckingham. (As editor of the *New England Galaxy* in the 1820s, Buckingham had fostered New England humor, including the various Strickland letters.) In the early experiments with the character of Hosea, Lowell had delineated him as something of a mercenary coward, but he appeared in the first published letter in verse as a Yankee from a rural town named Jaalam, who had been to Boston and whose letter reported not his comic experiences with city slickers or a theater but his righteous indignation at a sergeant recruiting soldiers to fight in the Mexican War:

> Thrash away, you'll *hev* to rattle
>   On them kittle drums o' yourn,—
> 'Taint a knowin' kind o' cattle
>   Thet is ketched with mouldy corn;
> Put in stiff, you fifer feller,
>   Let folks see how spry you be,—
> Guess you 'll toot till you are yeller
>   'Fore you git ahold o' me![88]

War itself is un-Christian: "I call it murder,— / There you hev it plain an' flat; / I don't want to go no furder / Than my Testyment fer that," says Hosea. This war is particularly despicable because it promises to extend slavery, and he berates his fellow New Englanders for their complicity: "Aint it cute to see a Yankee / Take sech everlastin' pains, / All to git the Devil's thankee, / Helpin on 'em weld their chains?" He even proposes disunion, a highly radical stance for the time. For Lowell, Hosea's rustic Yankee represents not so much the farmer and laboring class, the general electorate, as he does the heritage of Puritan morality that refuses to be corrupted by the persuasions of unprincipled Yankee politicians or Southern slave owners.

The poem, published anonymously, was a popular, if controversial, success, and although Lowell later admitted that he had no definite intention of writing another such letter,[89] he did so, albeit more than a year later (18 Aug. 1847), and in the following thirteen months he wrote the eight other pieces published as *The Biglow Papers* in 1848. In continuing the series, Lowell wrote only one other letter in which Hosea speaks directly, creating instead ironic personae, characterizations of public figures, for example, who admitted to all of the callous intentions and hypocritical opinions that Lowell inferred from their public actions and statements. Browning's dramatic monologues may have had some influence here,[90] but Seba Smith and Charles Augustus Davis had used this device in their Downing letters. Whereas they sometimes confused the loyalties of Jack in doing so, however, Lowell avoided that confusion by making Hosea Biglow the author of the poems, not the principal speaker. That not only distanced Hosea from what they say but also distanced Lowell himself from the satiric intent of what appear to be Hosea's creations.

"A Letter from a Candidate for the Presidency in Answer to Suttin Questions Proposed by Mr. Hosea Biglow" represents the views of a presidential candidate, one of the "271 ginerals" responding to Hosea's request to give his position on the important issues of the day, according to a brief preface by Hosea. Typical of the responses he received, this candidate refuses to commit himself to any opinion, admitting that he will support whatever seems to offer the greatest chance to get him elected: "I'm an eclectic; ez to choosin' / 'Twixt this an' thet, I 'm plaguy lawth; / I leave a side thet looks like losin' / But (wile there's doubt) I stick to both." The only firm position he takes is opposing a national bank, an issue that Jackson had taken care of some twenty years earlier. The speaker is, in fact, a caricature of General Zachary Taylor, who had been nominated by the Whigs as a "peoples' candidate" who would embrace all political faiths, because Taylor himself professed none. Indeed, it was said that he had never even voted. In the letter-poem, a parody of a widely printed letter from Taylor to a J. S. Allison of Pennsylvania,[91] the candidate himself articulates these accusations—and in words of Lowell's choosing. Although the letter represents Taylor's public views, the private postscript promising Hosea the running of the lighthouse at Jaalam Point in exchange for his help in getting elected shows the candidate as venal at heart, a device reminiscent of one used by Seba Smith in a letter cited above from Joshua Downing to his nephew Jack.

Lowell favored this kind of ironic self-caricature in the first series of *Biglow Papers,* and "The Pious Editor's Creed," often anthologized in collections of American humor and literature, is one of the best of the type. Lowell probably had no specific editor in mind here;[92] rather, the speaker represents all editors who willfully "believe wutever trash / 'll keep the people in blindness," and Lowell skillfully constructed such poems to heighten the ironic, self-revealing satire he enjoyed writing. The presidential candidate cited above, for example, begins with a pious promise to answer Hosea's questions forthrightly: "I'm a straight-spoken kind of creetur / Thet blurts right out wut's in his head," and he seems to do so for two stanzas, but then with each succeeding verse he tumbles into self-serving vacillation. In "The Pious Editor's Creed," the first nine stanzas begin with a principle that indeed appears pious, but by the end of each stanza the principle becomes twisted into self-interest:

> I du believe in special ways
> > O' prayin' an' convartin';
> The bread comes back in many days,
> > An' buttered, tu, fer sartin;—
> I mean in preyin' til one busts
> > On wut the party chooses,
> An' in convartin' public trusts
> > To very privit uses.

Here Lowell heightens the hypocrisy with the editor's knowing pun on the word "preyin'." ("Take care of praying and preyin in fifth stanza," he told his editor.[93]) In the last four stanzas, *this* pious editor drops his pretense and enthusiastically embraces the tactics that Lowell considered all too typical of powerful, unprincipled editors.

Lowell used the ironic persona with particular skill with Birdofredum Sawin, the only character that he developed in detail and the author of three of the nine letters. In the first letter, Lowell portrays him (or rather has the Yankee portray himself) somewhat sympathetically as a weak-willed young country boy who had fallen for the blandishments of the recruiting sergeant described so derisively by Hosea. Now a soldier in the battlefield as a result of the recruiter's rhetoric, Birdofredum writes of his disillusionment with the promised charms of Mexico; he has to interrupt his narrative, for example, to discourage a large scorpion threatening his toes. He also exposes the lie behind the arguments of "Anglosaxon" racial superiority that had been used to justify the conflict, another manifestation of Manifest Destiny that Lowell deplored. Although told that Mexicans were not human beings but an "ourang outang nation" that could be killed without conscience, the rustic Yankee soldier has come to learn that they are not much different from him. Birdofredum (the name itself an ironic allusion to the rhetoric of Manifest Destiny) is no moral philosopher, though; when he says that "ninepunce a day fer killin' folks comes kind o' low fer murder," he objects as much to the pay as he does to the principle.

In his second letter, Birdofredom writes as a wounded veteran, and his matter-of-fact accounting of his many injuries—he has lost an eye, a leg, one hand, and the fingers from the other hand—evokes sympathy for this foot soldier and others like him as the innocent victims of politicians safe and comfortable back home. However, Lowell abruptly shifts the reader's sympathies in the last third of the letter by making Sawin an ironic persona, one who decides to exploit his injuries in a bid for political office; they are his only qualifications. Admitting to no principles, he will campaign on "hooraws" such as "the ONE-EYED SLARTERER, the BLOODY BIRDOFREDUM," because "Them's wut takes hold o' folks thet think, ez well ez o' the masses, / An' makes you sartin o' the aid o' good men of all classes." Also, as it seems necessary to be a Southerner to get elected, he proposes to buy an inexpensive baby slave "to suit the No'thern folks, who feel obleeged to say / They hate an' cuss the very thing they vote fer every day." The irony is Lowell's, not Birdofredum's. With this letter, published in July 1848 as the presidential election heated up, Birdofredum Sawin became another caricature of Whig nominee Zachary Taylor, a war veteran who professed no opinions, a Southerner who had once owned slaves.

Lowell's satiric intentions become explicit in Birdofredum's third letter, the last of the first series of *Biglow Papers*, when the Yankee decides to give up his own candidacy and throw his support to Taylor, the Whig nominee. His reasons for doing so serve as a veritable catalog of the hypocritical, conscienceless politics of the day, according to Lowell, but he satirized specifically Daniel Webster, who, although opposed to slavery, had defended Taylor's nomination.[94] Lowell's own sympathies lay with the Free-Soil party, which the disreputable Sawin has no stomach for. For one thing, he reports, the party includes teetotalers, but above all he cannot abide the party's humanitarian, abolitionist views. The letter ends with his relating his experiences of capturing a runaway slave family. When he tries to return them, they trick him by taking his wooden leg and then force him to work their fields. In a final comic and highly satiric reversal of stereotypical roles, the black man kicks him out for being lazy, adding, "The childrin's growin' up, an' you aint jest the model / I'd like to hev 'em immertate, an' so you'd better toddle!" Such humiliations heighten the indignant Sawin's contempt for abolitionists.

Although the assertions that the Biglow verses "were folded into almanacs and tacked up on blacksmith shops" as well as reprinted in Eastern newspapers[95] have not been sufficiently documented, there is no reason to doubt Lowell's statement in a December letter to Sydney Gay, editor of the *Standard*, that the first edition of fifteen hundred copies of the book sold within the first week of publication in November 1848.[96] That it was, apparently, a popular success but not a critical one among reviewers, Lowell admitted in the same letter. Poe, understandably enough, dismissed Lowell in the *Southern Literary Messenger* (Mar. 1849) as "one of the most rabid of the Abolition fanatics," but even editors of popular Northern journals generally ignored the book because, as Thomas Wortham says, they "rarely allowed the discussion of slavery and its abolition. It was not good business."[97]

The paucity of critical success did not trouble Lowell much, however: "I am quite satisfied with seeing the feathers fly," he wrote Gay in December. But he did begin to feel somewhat uneasy about the public fame his satiric verse had engendered. "He had acquired a public character as a popular comic writer," Leon Howard writes, "and he immediately became self-conscious about it."[98] Lowell would later say, perhaps too modestly, that he was "almost unread" writing under his own name and thus surprised, even pleased, at overhearing that he "was utterly incompetent" to have written the Biglow poems.[99] As early as 13 November 1847, however, when his authorship became known with the publication of the third letter, he wrote to his close friend

Charles Briggs that his literary identity was composed of "two utterly distinct characters: half of me is clear mystic and enthusiast, the other humorist." He also admitted, "I feel a little offended when my friends confound the two."[100] That confusion seems to have guided Lowell's choice of mottoes on the title page of the book when it was published in 1848. The first, from Francis Quarles— "The ploughman's whistle, or the trivial flute / Finds more respect than great Apollo's lute"—may be ambiguous, but it does seem to sanction, to defend, the vernacular conventions of the *Biglow Papers*. There is no ambiguity, however, in the second motto of Lowell's own creation, in Latin, a true apologia aimed at those readers who could translate it: "*Margaritas, munde porcine, calcasti: en, siliquas accipe*" ("O, swinish world, you have trampled pearls: so, take the husks"). And when he published the second series of letters in 1867, this former editor of the *Atlantic* and the *North American Review* made his concerns public in the introduction: "If I put on the cap and bells and made myself one of the court-fools of King Demos, it was less to make his majesty laugh than to win a passage to his royal ears for certain things which I had deeply at heart. I say this because there is no imputation that could be more galling to any man's self-respect than that of being a mere jester."[101] However much he might admit to the problem and try to explain it on his own terms, that identity would continue to plague him.[102]

In addition to a perceived problem of his literary identity, he faced a related dilemma inherent in the conventions of the cracker-barrel tradition that his *Biglow Papers* had become a part of. In the 13 November 1847 letter to Briggs, Lowell had written that he was sorry he had begun by making Hosea such a "detestable speller" and that he planned to get "him out of it gradually. I mean to altogether," by having Parson Wilbur propose a subscription to send Hosea to college. Again, this is just after his authorship became known with the third letter, and when Hosea "disappears." "The only further use I shall put Hosea to," he continued, "will be to stir up 'the Legislater' at the next session on the subject of allowing women to retain their own earnings, etc." However, Hosea did not appear again as spokesman *for* principles; Lowell had become not only self-conscious about his literary identity but also uncertain about the role that the rustic character could take in political satire. That is, having created in Hosea a character with high principles, Lowell found those principles incompatible with the Yankee's low way of expressing them.

Lowell's reservations about the appropriateness of the cracker-barrel voice for principled thinking can be seen in his creation of another character from the fictitious Jaalam, Parson Homer Wilbur. Hosea had mentioned him in the first letter, but Wilbur first appeared on his own in November 1847 as author of a letter defending Hosea and denying that Lowell was the author, and then again with a long preface to "The Pious Editor's Creed" and as author of "Leaving the Matter Open" in the *Standard* (27 July 1848). In the book, Wilbur dominates, with Lowell giving more than half of its pages to the learned parson, its apparent editor—a reminder, perhaps, that the real author of the book was himself a scholar and the author of a *book*, not newspaper "squibs," as Lowell called Hosea's letters in the press. As a literary characterization, the good parson certainly has his partisans among readers of the *Biglow Papers*,[103] and although his learned notes do often address the issues raised by the dialect letter-poems, his elaborate, scholarly analyses, abundant with Latin quotations and etymologies, too often undercut the moral thrust of the rustic, ironic speakers and reduce their humorous admissions of guilt to tediously pedantic inconsequentiality. The book becomes less the sharp, cracker-barrel satire of the newspaper letters and more the New England novel that Lowell intermittently intended to write—a book with Shandyesque overtones, Howard says.[104] In the *Courier,* "What Mr. Robinson Thinks" stands alone as Hosea's; in the book it is embedded in a long introduction by Reverend Wilbur on the "position of the satirist" and then followed by the minister's remarks on patriotism—ponderous, pedantic bookends to Hosea's sprightly, vernacular verse. Witty, amiable, learned to a stuffy but lovably comic fault, Homer Wilbur serves as James Russell Lowell's alter ego. Lowell used his own editorial writing for some of Wilbur's notes in the book, he signed his own initials to Wilbur's "Leaving the Matter Open" when it appeared in the *Standard,* and he signed Wilbur's name to a letter to Gay in 1848.[105]

Not only for serious literary purposes but also for high-minded satire, Hosea Biglow's vernacular had its limitations. In using the language of the rustic Yankee in the early *Biglow Papers,* Lowell wrote, "I feared the risk of seeming to vulgarize a deep and sacred conviction," and so, he says, he created Parson Wilbur "to rise above the level of mere *patois.*"[106] He put it another way in a letter: "I conceived my parson-editor with his pedantry and verbosity, his amiable vanity and superiority to the verses he was editing, as a fitting artistic background and soil." He added, "It gave me the chance, too, of glancing obliquely at many things which were beyond the horizon of my other characters."[107] "In other words," Walter Blair says, Lowell "doubted whether American common sense and *mere* American talk were really enough to reveal all the truth."[108]

For the scholarly Lowell, future Smith Professor of Modern Languages at Harvard, patois was much more appropriate for the shallow, less-sacred convictions of the ironic personae he turned to once his authorship of the rustic letters in verse was known and Hosea "disappeared" in November 1847. When the "Pious Editor" in letter six says on the subject of "Freedom's cause" being fought in France, "It's wal enough agin a king / To dror resolves an' triggers,— / But libbaty's a kind o' thing / Thet don't agree with niggers," *how* he speaks— the low dialect, and particularly the vulgar, racist term at the end—reinforces that *what* this editor says is, in every sense of the term, *cant*. Although spoken by an ironic persona here, the term is also Hosea's (never Lowell's, never Wilbur's), who had used it in his first letter.

Thus to the extent that Lowell feared patois could "vulgarize" sacred convictions, he found he could use it effectively to stigmatize not-so-sacred ones. The technique worked effectively in "Debate in the Senate" as well, which features the distinguished South Carolinian John C. Calhoun as the principal, if unprincipled, speaker. "Here we stan' on the Constitution, by thunder! / It's a fact o wich ther 's bushills o' proofs; / Fer how could we trample on 't so, I wonder, / Eft worn't thet it's ollers under our hoofs?" the poem begins. No doubt the distinguished Carolinian spoke a regional dialect, but the printed medium graphically exposes an incorrectness that becomes one with a willful lack of principle, given his knowing pun about "standing" on the Constitution. That the poem is "sot to a nusry rhyme," an appropriate verse form for the unlearned Hosea, further demeans the celebrated senator from South Carolina.

Lowell's most imaginative ironic personae, most adventurous, was Birdofredum Sawin, who, as we have seen, became an ironic persona at the end of his second letter. If Wilbur acts as Lowell's alter ego, Birdofredum is Hosea's, the unsavory "other I" who evolved from Lowell's early experiments with Hosea's characterization. Birdofredum reveals the other side of the common man, whose crude language is appropriate to his crude ideas. Where pious editors might speak hypocritically in poems written by Hosea, Birdofredum, although his vernacular is Hosea's, speaks for himself and with wrong-headed vigor. His are the last two letters of the series, written to influence the November election, and Lowell intended to get the book published in time to influence the election—and would have done so if he had not added so much about Wilbur, if he had not confused his literary self-consciousness with his political intentions. Lowell had learned something of a lesson in real-world democracy earlier, in 1845. When the annexation of Texas threatened to expand slavery, Lowell wrote, "After all, the saddest part of the matter is that the moral sense of the mass of the people should be so dead, their intelligence in political affairs so limited, that they can be willing not only to submit to this iniquity, but sustain it."[109] The immoral Sawin believes that too, and when he proposes a subscription to raise the money he needs to buy a slave baby, he seems confident that it will be successful. For Lowell, the nomination and election of Zachary Taylor sadly confirmed that such cynical confidence was well placed.

The Biglow Papers, Second Series

After the publication of the first *Biglow* series, James Russell Lowell turned to other literary pursuits and personal concerns, but the growing civil conflict would at times provoke him to try his hand again at cracker-barrel satire. In 1854, for example, angered by the Kansas-Nebraska Act, he attempted a letter in the Biglow style, but after a few weeks reported that he had "lost the hang of *that* schoolhouse."[110] Again, in 1859, as the English editions of the first series were coming out, he wrote that "friendly people" have asked "'write us more "Biglow Papers,"'" and I have even been simple enough to try, only to find that I could not."[111] Two years later, however, in response to a request by James T. Fields, editor of the *Atlantic* after Lowell, he apparently tried harder. Admitting "it was clean against my critical judgment for I don't believe in resuscitations,"[112] the first letter in the new series appeared in the January 1862 *Atlantic* and five more appeared each month through June. Then the comic muse abandoned him—"Better no crop than small potatoes. I want to have the *passion* of the thing on me again and beget lusty Biglows," he wrote Fields[113]—

and over the next four years he wrote only three more Biglow papers, which would be collected with two other pieces and published as *The Biglow Papers, Second Series* in 1867.

Lowell began the new series as he had ended the first one, with a letter from Birdofredum Sawin, who fills in the fourteen years since he had last written. After being kicked out by the slave family, he tells of roaming the South, being mistakenly charged with theft, thrown in jail and then released when the real culprit was apprehended. Despite such treatment, the Yankee finds the secessionist South to his liking, and despite his marriage to "Jerushy" back home, he weds the "Widder Shennon" and settles in at her plantation. Willfully disreputable and unprincipled as ever in his second letter, his enthusiastic espousal of Southern life—its camp-meeting style religion, biblical justifications of slavery that lead to specious claims of racial superiority and bogus nobility—is an ironic indictment of the whole culture, a judgment that some Southern scholars still find offensive.[114]

Birdofredum's letters in the second series are not so effective, nor were they as popular, as those in the first. They suffer from discursive prolixity, but also Lowell did not develop the characterization with consistent satiric purpose. At the end of the second letter, for example, Sawin catalogues the conditions in the North that in part determined him to stay with the Confederacy. Congress failed to act with conviction, he says, because it is made up of self-interested, time-serving politicians who value popularity more than principle. At the heart of the problem lies the belief that democracy means "votes can turn biled kebbage into brain, / An' ary man thet's pop'lar 's fit to drive a lightnin'-train."[115] As long as such conditions persist, he righteously concludes, he plans to remain in the South. And yet, of course, exactly these conditions would most suit the unsavory type that Birdofredum has revealed himself to be. Lowell, in using the Yankee to voice his own critique of Northern politics, asked readers suddenly to reverse their understanding of Sawin's judgment. Lowell tried to get too much out of this one characterization in the second series, which is perhaps why he gave him up after two letters and turned to other techniques.

With "A Message of Jeff Davis in Secret Session," Lowell returned to the ironically satiric dramatic monologue—a speaker's admitting to all of the sundry sins his enemies accused him of—that had been so effective in the first series. The satiric jist of the confidential message is that all is not well with the Confederacy, Davis's published pronouncements to the contrary. In secret session, the Confederate president admits that his government is in chaos, foreign powers refuse to give support, and Southern soldiers refuse to fight. In reality, of course, Davis and the Southern press told a much different story, but Lowell has him admit here that it is all propaganda: "It's ne'ssary to take a good confident tone / With the public; but here, jest amongst us, I own / Things look blacker 'n thunder. Ther' 's no use denyin'/ We 're clean out o' money, an' 'most out o' lyin'." So blatant are the ironic admissions that it seems difficult to believe that the characterization would have done much satiric damage to the Southern cause, but the letter remains one of the most entertaining in the series: the versification flows effortlessly, and Jeff Davis himself seems amused by the glib audacity of what he admits to. A less successful piece in the same vein is "Speech of Honourable Preserved Doe in Secret Caucus," a caricature of Northern "Peace Democrats" sympathetic to the South. Both the humor and the verse seem labored here, and the poem adds nothing new to the off-the-record caricature of a hypocritical politician.

What makes the second series so different from the first is Lowell's development of the character of Hosea, who appears in five letters and as the author of four others. Only in one, though, "Latest Views of Mr. Biglow," does he speak to the events of the day with the forthright fervor of his very first letter, but with a very different moral. Earlier, he had written "Ez fer war, I call it murder,—There you hev it plain an' flat," but in support of Lincoln's Emancipation Proclamation, Hosea argues that "it's war we 're in, not politics; / It's systems wrastlin' now, not parties; / An' victory in the eend 'll fix / Where longest will an' truest heart is." Hosea leaves no doubt that the longest will and the truest hearts could be found with the Union, but only if it lived up to the moral principles on which it was founded. In reality, though, the politics of parties did prevail in the present, and Hosea's other poems not so much address the issues of the day as they attempt to return to and revive those earlier principles. In doing so, these poems examine more fully the fundamental philosophical concerns of the first series and the problems Lowell faced in using the cracker-barrel voice to address those concerns, but the mood is melancholy, the result futility. In "Mason and Slidell, a Yankee Idyll," and "Sunthin' in the Pastoral Line," Hosea, as the titles suggest, evokes the picturesque, unsullied virtues of rural New England life that provided the foundation for his ethical stance of his first poem, but in his later poems, the Yankee embodiment of those virtues sees himself as an anachronism in contemporary life. Even his own village has abandoned the old country schoolhouse and has built a three-story high school "where they teach the Lord knows wut," he writes in "Sunthin' in the Pastoral Line." Reflective, he returns at night to his bench in the old school and recalls the virtues taught there when he was a boy: "Faith, Hope, an' sunthin', ef it is n't Cherrity, / It's want o' guile, an' thet's ez gret a rerrity."

Such reflections raise melancholy reservations about the possibility of instilling such virtues into the present crisis, and in both poems Lowell uses the device of a dream to invoke personifications of the past that try to revive the dispirited Yankee. "In Mason and Slidell," Hosea tells of dreaming about a conversation between the Concord Bridge and the Bunker Hill Monument. They first discuss England's hypocrisy in failing to support the North against slavery, and then turn to the errors of the North in pursuing its own lofty cause. Because of party politics, too much is done for expediency rather than for principle; the nation must rededicate itself to the convictions of the founding fathers that the bridge and the monument represent. "Young folks are smart, but all ain't good thet's new; / I guess the gran'thers they knowed sunthin', tu," says the former. "Amen to thet! build sure in the beginnin': / An' then don't never tech the underpinnin'," replies the latter.

In "Sunthin' in the Pastoral Line," Hosea dreams of his great, great, great grandfather, who tries to bolster the flagging spirits of his descendant. "The moral question 's ollus plain enough,—" Hosea says, "It's jes' the human-natur' side thet's tough," and he suggests that it may be best to test the weathervane of opinion to see where it points. His ancestor will have none of that: "God hates your sneakin' creturs thet believe / He 'll settle things they run away an' leave!" The poem, however, offers no clear resolution on the side of the past. As Hosea points out, the hardest problem is not gaining the black man's rights, but emancipating the white race: "One 's chained in body an' can be sot free, / But t' other's chained in soul to an idee." By implication, the lessons of the past are as anachronistic as the cracker-barrel philosopher himself, and both poems suggest a troubled futility: Hosea speaks to a nation that does not listen.

With "Sunthin' in the Pastoral Line," published in June 1862, Lowell's comic muse suddenly gave out. In August of that year, reflecting on the six pieces he had written in as many months, he wrote to *Atlantic* editor Fields with highly uncharacteristic, but revealing, profanity: "I look back and wonder how in great H. I ever did it."[116] Like so many in the North, Lowell had underestimated the depth of secessionist sentiment in the South, and with the deaths of family and friends in the protracted war, he found it difficult to express his mood in humorous cracker-barrel verse. Lincoln's Emancipation Proclamation revived his spirits for "Latest Views" (Feb. 1863), but it was the only letter for three years. "The War and its constant expectation and anxiety oppress me," he wrote Fields.[117]

The struggle to write in those troubled times itself became the subject of "Mr. Hosea Biglow to the Editor of the Atlantic Monthly" (Apr. 1865), a dejection ode in which the character of Hosea and his struggle to express himself become blurred with that of his creator. Urged by the editor to "citify" his English and write "sunthin' light an' cute, / Rattlin' an' shrewd an' kin' o' jingleish," Hosea says that he can write "long-tailed" if he wants to, "but when I'm jokin', no I thankee; / Then, 'fore I know it, my idees / Run helter-skelter into Yankee." Joking is not appropriate to Hosea's somber mood, however; the war has enervated his literary abilities, and not even nature can alleviate his dejection or inspire his muse: "In-doors an' out by spells I try; / Ma'am Natur' keeps her spin-wheel goin', / But leaves my natur' stiff and dry / Ez fiel's o' clover arter mowin'." That the cause of the dejection is Lowell's own becomes clear when Hosea speaks of the "three likely lads" who had died in the war, a reference to the deaths of Lowell's nephews. Thus Hosea's lament that he can "half despise myself for rhymin'" is surely in part Lowell's own as well. So too the climactic emotions of the impassioned prayer for peace that ends the poem: "Come, Peace! not like a mourner bowed / For honor lost an' dear ones wasted, / But proud, to meet a people proud, / With eyes thet tell o' triumph tasted!" These noble, deeply felt sentiments are Lowell's, not Hosea's, and are appropriately expressed in the "long-tailed" language of James Russell Lowell, not the cracker-barrel Yankee of Hosea Biglow.

With "Mr. Biglow's Speech in March Meeting" (May 1865), Lowell announced the end of the second *Biglow* series. The historical occasion of the poem was the political struggle over Reconstruction after the Civil War, but as was so often true in the *Biglow Papers*, particularly the later series, the poem is also about the cracker-barrel philosopher's dealing effectively with political realities. In the prose preface Hosea defends his unschooled style: "You kin spall an' punctooate thet as you please. I allus do, it kind of puts a noo soot of close onto a word, thisere funattick spellin' doos an' takes 'em out of the prissen dress they wair in the Dixonary." How he speaks is one with what he has to say, but he speaks, inexplicably, in the comically exaggerated eye dialect of the literary comedians. As such, it seems a parody of speaking according to "Natur," which, he says here, Parson Wilbur had always advised him to do.

In the poem, though, Hosea returns to his more natural New England dialect to address the more serious problem, the ironic dilemma of speaking "naturally" in a democracy, a problem posed earlier in "Mason and Slidell" and "Sunthin' in the Pastoral Line." In "March Meeting," he admits that he could never be elected, that he has no forum, no political constituency, because he speaks too honestly, again, too naturally: "I'm one o' them thet finds it ruther hard / To mannyfactur' wisdom by the yard, / An' maysure off, accordin' to demand, / The piece-goods el'kence that I keep on hand." Then, recalling Parson Wilbur's advice that speakers should tailor what they say to the intellect of their listeners, Hosea sets up the structural and thematic conceit of the poem by taking his message to the "March Meeting" of his cabbage patch. ("The kebbige-heads 'll cair the day et last," Wilbur had advised him accurately if ironically.) To this audience throughout most of the poem, with straight-forward wit and good, if earnest, humor, the Yankee has his say about President Andrew Johnson's Reconstruction policy of restoring Southern states to their former sovereignty without requiring them to guarantee political rights to freed slaves. To Johnson's premise that the Southern states had not lost their sovereignty by seceding, for example, Hosea responds with cracker-barrel common sense, "Ef they war'n't out, then why, 'n the name o' sin, / Make all this row 'bout lettin' of 'em in?"

In reality the opposition to Johnson's plan originated less in Hosea's kind of commonsense logic and more in the fear of giving political power to a solidly

Democratic South, and thus the poem is not so much about political realities as it is about Hosea's futile place in that political climate. Having reached a dead end for moral earnestness, Lowell brought back the ironic persona of Birdofredum Sawin, who could express more vividly the ugly reality of racism:

"Wut *is* there lef' I'd like to know,
Ef 't ain't the defference o' color,
To keep up self-respec' an' show
The human natur' of a fullah?
Wut good in bein' white, onless
It's fixed by law, nut lef' to guess,
We're a heap smarter an' they duller?"

For Birdofredum, in fact, the times seem right for the election of Jefferson Davis as president. From Hosea's mouth, the suggestion would be absurd; Birdofredum's way of thinking, his very character, makes it credible. "Thet tells the story! Thet's wut we shall git," Hosea concludes, so little wonder the poem ends with his hearing "a whisperin' in the air, / A sighin' like, of unconsoled despair."

"Mr. Biglow's Speech in March Meeting" provides an appropriate if unsatisfying ending to the second series of Biglow papers. Lowell had given more dimension to Hosea as his cracker-barrel voice in these letters, but unlike in the first series, they are as much about the problem of his speaking to a nation that will not listen to what he has to say about the events of day as they are about the events themselves. Hosea speaks passionately for high principles, but they seem as anachronistic as the vernacular language he uses to voice them. With Birdofredum, vernacular usage points up the irony of his blithe assumption of superiority.

"March Meeting" is an appropriate if unsatisfying ending to both series of *Biglow Papers* as well, for the poem takes up, but reaches no solution to, the underlying dilemma of the two series, the contrast between the ideal of democracy and democracy in fact. Hosea, the rustic Yankee, embodies that ideal, speaking to principle in the cracker-barrel language of the people, but the "March Meeting" of the title is ironic: Hosea addresses not that New England bastion of ideal American democracy but his cabbage patch. Lowell took the conceit from an earlier statement by Birdofredum Sawin that democracy could "turn biled kebbage into brains," and so, appropriately enough, in this "March Meeting" the "kebbage heads" applaud *his* sentiments as well as Hosea's. The conceit has comic possibilities, but they lead to only one conclusion, and in this last Biglow letter, Lowell took them to their limit by reducing democracy—and the place of the cracker-barrel philosopher in it—to the humor of the absurd. Tragically absurd, because to the end Lowell had looked beyond a particular political agenda—more than the other New England cracker-barrel humorists and more self-consciously than any humorist before Twain—and had struggled in his art and in his soul to reconcile the paradoxes not only of his cracker-barrel humor but of his time.

Conclusion

In his introduction to the 1867 edition of the second series of *Biglow Papers,* Lowell observed that as a political satirist he felt he could "claim to be an *emeritus,*" and the introduction seems written in that mood, that spirit, for Lowell was right: with the 1867 publication of the *Biglow Papers, Second Series,* the New England tradition of native American humor, as a tradition, ended. Although the introduction is still a valuable essay on New England humor, Lowell's conflicting intentions—to demonstrate the indigenous authenticity of Yankee vernacular and to make it respectable by identifying its roots in British usage—reveal him, like Hosea Biglow, as the product of an earlier age. The Civil War Jack Downing (in the *Caucasian*) and Hosea Biglow had kept New England cracker-barrel humor alive in the 1860s, but in the 1850s the tradition in other forms had waned. Yankee theater was an American *commedia del arte* that ended by midcentury with the deaths of those actors who had given it life, although a play or two would continue to be acted by others. As for humorous stories and poems, nothing memorable was added in the 1850s. Much the same can be said, in fact, for the backwoods tradition of native American humor, with the remarkable exception of George W. Harris. His first Sut Lovingood sketch appeared in the *Spirit of the Times* in 1854, and the publication of *Sut Lovingood: Yarns Spun by a Nat'ral Born Durn'd Fool* in 1867 can be said to mark the end of the frontier tradition. The decade of the 1850s was a time of collecting, of anthologizing the earlier American humor of many kinds, among them Thomas Chandler Haliburton's three-volume *Traits of American Humor* (1852), Samuel Avery's *Laughing Gas* (1854) and *The Book of 1000 Comicalities* (1859), and *American Wit and Humor* (1859), gathered from *Harper's Magazine.* Retrospective too is "The Library of Humorous American Works," inexpensive reprintings of earlier humor initiated by Carey and Hart in 1846 and taken over by T. B. Peterson in 1854.[1]

The conventions of New England humor—of the Yankee character, his speech, and his comic experiences—were limited, and it is the nature of the mass media then and now to destroy by relentless repetition what it makes popular, to turn character into caricature. (In New England humor, much was caricature to begin with.) An English reviewer of Joshua Silsbee's performance in London would seem to be saying exactly that in 1851 with the complaint—perhaps the plaint—that "Yankee peculiarities have almost been done to death."[2] As a result, vernacular humor was taking new directions in the 1850s. Charles Farrar Browne and Henry Wheeler Shaw were both New England born, and they drew on the precedents of Jack Downing and other Yankees, but Browne's Artemus Ward and Shaw's Josh Billings have characters of their own—and not New England ones. So too with Matthew Franklin Whittier, whose Ethan Spike letters appeared sporadically from 1846 to 1863. Although similarities to Jack Downing abound, and to Birdofredum Sawin as well, Spike represents the Yankee of popular literature in transition, one who "has little in common with the cracker-barrel oracle of Yankee humor," Daniel Royot writes. "Instead of the innocent pose, he assumes the boastful, cynical attitudes of the southern ring-tailed roarer,"[3] a merging of types also taking place with the stage Yankee and Sam Slick at midcentury.

These trends, however, may reflect a more profound truth than the fact that readers had simply tired of the comic rustic Yankee, that he had been "done to death," a truth echoed in the reflective tone of Lowell's introduction and his last Biglow letters: after midcentury and with the Civil War, the New England Yankee was no longer the archetypal American. He had become too localized, given the sectional differences inherent in the coming of the Civil War in the 1850s. With the war itself, as illustrated in figures 4 and 5, Brother Jonathan became identified irrevocably with the Union forces. Uncle Sam would be too (see fig. 6), but after the war he would emerge as the iconographical archetype of the nation. He wore the striped pants, swallow-tail coat, and top hat of the Yankees of an earlier day, but the avuncular figure had no geographical identity and therefore none of the controversial commitments that one would provoke.[4]

The rustic New Englander would have a place in humorous literature in the following decades, but a less prominent one in the national consciousness, and he took on a different form because he served a different purpose. Richard Dorson calls this characterization "a local-color Yankee," mature, sedate, and wise.[5] Neither the comic butt of cultural or political changes nor the impudent critic of them, he became the sentimental, even nostalgic, embodiment of an increasingly mythic rendering of the nation's past. Harriet Beecher Stowe's

Sam Lawson in *Oldtown Folks* (1869) and later books anticipates a type that would include Denman Thompson's long portrayal of Joshua Whitcomb in *The Old Homestead* (1886), Edward Westcott's highly popular 1899 novel *David Harum* (also put on stage and later on film, starring Will Rogers), and Rowland Robinson's Uncle Lisha and Sam Lovel. In books published in the late 1880s and the 1890s, Robinson portrayed lovingly the olden customs and speech of a New England folk "fortified against the march of improvement."[6]

Some sense of the changes taking place in American humor at midcentury can be read in the pages of *Yankee Notions*. If it is true, as Walter Blair has said, that by 1850 America "had discovered most of the things it was going to laugh at,"[7] then all of those "things" are surely represented in *Yankee Notions*. A New York monthly humor magazine founded in 1852 and persevering to 1875 in nearly eleven thousand pages, *Yankee Notions* is a serial anthology of virtually every form of American humor, in word and picture, good and bad, that America had laughed at and would laugh at—for the rest of the nineteenth century, at least. All of the major "schools" (or "traditions") that modern scholarship has designated are well represented: New England, backwoods, and the literary comedians, as well as others not so well documented, such as American Irish, Dutch, Negro, "Hoosier," and "Western" (as *Yankee Notions* itself designated them), and much that defies categorizing. Among the major American humorists of the first four decades, only Lowell is missing, his political edge perhaps too sharp.

But to categorize too precisely those types and those writers may be to miss much of the character and role of American humor by midcentury. Taken together, the humor in *Yankee Notions* seems above all "modern," representing in new ways the political, social, and cultural strains of an urban nation.[8] *Yankee Notions* did reprint very early American humor—reaching back to the Federalist mock pastorals of the late eighteenth century—but much more often it portrayed the comic pretensions of an urban middle class, its fashions, tastes, and romantic follies. It also portrayed persistently, but with less good humor, the seamy side of city low life—poverty, vice, and violence—and with no sympathy for or understanding of what caused those conditions or what might change them. In the abstract, usually in contrast to the Old World, *Yankee Notions* celebrated the long-held faith in the social and political promises of the free and enlightened "Universal Yankee Nation" in its subtitle, but it had little use for fulfilling those promises in fact. Given the reality of Southern slavery, the American black represented an equivocal embodiment of that fulfillment—Southern slaves were sentimentalized, urban blacks caricatured—and thus the Irish immigrant, unequivocally urban and "foreign," bore the brunt of the misgivings typically expressed in *Yankee Notions.*

The rustic Yankee had had a place, a comic role to play, in a nation that could still see itself as *becoming* modern, but the humor in *Yankee Notions* reveals that the nation *is,* and in that context the New England Yankee no longer had a place, or much of one. "A Yankee Trick" in *Yankee Notions* (Aug. 1858) illustrates that distinction. Here, an Irishman eagerly accepts a Yankee's offer to teach him a trick. "Pat, I'll bet liquor you can't hit my hand," the Yankee says, holding it against a brick wall. When Pat hauls off and strikes, the Yankee jerks his hand away, leaving Pat "peeling the skinned flesh off his knuckles." The traditional Yankee story would end here, but this story does not. Eager for his brother Jim, a more recent immigrant and "green as peas," to "larn a Yankee trick," but with no wall available, Pat holds his hand up to his face. Jim, of course, "sends him reeling to the earth with four broken teeth and a large quantity of blood for 'larnin him the Yankee thrick.'"[9]

The ruse itself is surely ancient, and this version may well have appeared in print before 1858, but I would like to think that it did not appear earlier than, say, 1849, the date of "Taking the Starch Out of 'Em," quoted at the beginning of this book. In that story, as in other stories of Yankee tricks in the New England tradition, the rustic Yankee is the central character, and although we might laugh at his lingo, we grin with approval when this Yankee Jonathan, Uncle Sam aborning, puts one over on some "green" city boys who think they are more knowing. In "A Yankee Trick," although the Yankee is named Jonathan, and although the story line lends itself to a good-humored celebration of the superiority of the archetypal American to the foolish immigrant, the story centers on the characterization of the "green" Irishman, *his* way of talking and his thickheaded inability to understand how the trick should be done. The rustic Yankee character, *his* vernacular and the trick he plays, despite the title, are subordinate, merely means to another end. In *Yankee Notions* in 1858, they seem vestigial—remnants from another time, another tradition.

Notes

The following abbreviations for periodicals are used throughout the notes and bibliography:

AL	*American Literature*
AlaR	*Alabama Review*
AQ	*American Quarterly*
AS	*American Speech*
EAL	*Early American Literature*
ELN	*English Language Notes*
JAF	*Journal of American Folklore*
MissQ	*Mississippi Quarterly*
MLN	*Modern Language Notes*
NEQ	*New England Quarterly*
PAAS	*Publication of the American Antiquarian Society*
PMLA	*Publication of the Modern Language Association*
PMHB	*Pennsylvania Magazine of History and Biography*
QJS	*Quarterly Journal of Speech*
SLJ	*Southern Literary Journal*
SP	*Studies in Philology*
SR	*Sewanee Review*
StAH	*Studies in American Humor*
Whig Rev	*Whig Review*
WMQ	*William and Mary Quarterly*

Chapter 1. New England Humor and the Dilemma of American Identity

1. Thomas Yarrow, *An Oration Delivered* (1778) and John Lathrop, Jr., *An Oration* (1776), quoted in Sacvan Bercovitch, *The American Jeremiad* (Madison: U of Wisconsin P, 1978), 141–42. Bercovitch says that the terms "political millennium" and "American millennium" became "virtually standardized in the early nineteenth century."
2. Albert Gallatin to Matthew Lyon, 7 May 1816, in Albert Gallatin, *Writings,* ed. Henry Adams (Philadelphia: Lippincott, 1879), 1: 700.
3. See George Templeton Strong, *Diary,* ed. Allan Nevins and Milton H. Thomas, 2 vols. (New York: Macmillan, 1952).

4. "What could have induced Neal to go to Europe and commence a systematic warfare upon the character, manners, and peculiarities of his countrymen, is to us, utterly inconceivable—a warfare which is not only unnatural but unprincipled?" asked the *New England Galaxy* 8 (2 Sept. 1852): 2.

5. George Bancroft, *Literary and Historical Miscellanies* (New York: Harper and Brothers, 1855), 415.

6. Albert Matthews, "Brother Jonathan," *Publication of the Colonial Society of Massachusetts* 7 (1901): 94–126, and "Brother Jonathan Once More," *Publication of the Colonial Society of Massachusetts* 32 (1935): 374–86. Also see Winifred Morgan, *An American Icon: Brother Jonathan and American Identity* (Newark: U of Delaware P, 1988). On the term *Yankee,* see the variety of nineteenth-century opinions in Oscar G. T. Sonneck, *Report on "The Star Spangled Banner," "Hail Columbia," "America," "Yankee Doodle"* (Washington, DC: Library of Congress, 1909), 80–95. See also the various entries for "Yankee" in *A Dictionary of Americanisms on Historical Principles.*

7. Good studies of Uncle Sam are Alton Ketchum, *Uncle Sam, the Man and the Legend* (New York: Hill and Wang, 1959); Albert Matthews, "Uncle Sam," *PAAS* 19 (1908): 21–65; the best is Winifred Morgan, above.

8. For a sound analysis of this dilemma, see Albert J. Von Frank, *The Sacred Game: Provincialism and Frontier Consciousness in American Literature, 1660–1860* (New York: Cambridge UP, 1985).

9. The seminal study of the significance of pastoralism in the American experience is Leo Marx, *The Machine and the Garden* (New York: Oxford UP, 1964). See also his "Pastoralism in America," in *Ideology and Classic American Literature,* ed. Sacvan Bercovitch and Myra Jehlen (New York: Cambridge UP, 1986), 36–69.

10. *Mark Twain, the Development of a Writer* (Cambridge: Harvard UP, 1962), 4.

11. On English travelers, see Max Berger, *The British Traveller in America, 1836–1860* (New York: Columbia UP, 1943), which is a continuation of Jane Mesick, *The English Traveller in America, 1785–1835* (New York: Columbia UP, 1922). Berger's and Mesick's bibliographies list more than three hundred books by English travelers from 1785 to 1860. For French visitors, see Frank Monaghan, *French Travellers in the United States, 1765–1932* (1933; rpt. New York: Antiquarian, 1961).

12. *Athenaeum,* 22 Oct. 1828, quoted in Nils Erik Enkvist, *American Humor in England before Mark Twain* (Abo, Finland: Abo Academi, 1953), 64.

13. Traveling in the United States in the 1830s, Michael Chevalier saw the national character represented by two leading types, the Yankee and the Virginian, but believed "if one wished to form a single type, representing the American character of the present moment as a single whole, it would be necessary to take at least three fourths of the Yankee and to mix it with hardly one fourth of the Virginian." Chevalier also saw a third type, the man of the West, and although his "features are not yet sharply defined," Chevalier predicted that the figure "seems ultimately destined to become superior to the others." See his *Society, Manners, and Politics in the United States,* ed. John William Ward (1839; rpt. Garden City, NY: Doubleday, 1961), 102, 107.

14. Enkvist, *American Humor,* 25. On American humor in France, see James C. Austin and Daniel Royot, *American Humor in France* (Ames: Iowa State UP, 1978).

15. Mesick, *The English Traveller in America,* 312.

16. Timothy Flint, *Recollections of the Last Ten Years* (1826; rpt. New York: De Capo, 1968), 32–33, passim.

17. Captain Frederick Marryat, *A Diary in America,* ed. Jules Zanger (1839; rpt. Bloomington: Indiana UP, 1960), 38.

18. An example of the precautions that should be taken in considering travel books as folk sources is the work of traveler John Bernard (1756–1828), an English actor who performed and traveled in the United States and Canada from 1797 to 1810. Two years after his death, his son, Bayle Bernard, edited and published his father's *Retrospections of the Stage,* which dealt with his father's life up to leaving England in 1797. In 1887 a more comprehensive work was published, *Retrospections of America* (1887; rpt. New York: Benjamin Blom, 1969), which was edited by Mrs. Bayle Bernard from "three different sets of extracts, all taken literally from the autobiography, and exact, so far as they went, but all incomplete" of the son's versions, according to Laurence Hutton and Brander Matthews in an introduction. However, the long disquisition and the many anecdotes illustrating Yankee 'cuteness—especially in chapter 2, dated 1797—seem more appropriate to a later time and to the literary inventiveness of the younger Bernard, a playwright who wrote for actors Hill and Silsbee and whom Hutton and Matthews think should be considered "one of the inventors of the Stage Yankee." I wonder then, if John Q. Anderson is correct in his essay "Some Migratory Anecdotes in American Folk Humor," *MissQ* 25 (1972): 447–57, when he ascribes to *Retrospections of America* "an early—perhaps the earliest—recorded version" of the "hat-in-the-mud" tale and dates it "from about 1780," according to the dating in Bernard's "autobiography."

19. Henry Cook Todd, *Notes Upon Canada and the United States,* 2d ed. (Toronto: Rogers and Thompson, 1840), 27–28.

20. James Fenimore Cooper, *Notions of the Americans,* introduced by Robert Spiller (1828; rpt. New York: Frederick Unger, 1963), 1: 55.

21. John Lambert, *Travels through Lower Canada and the United States of North America, 1806–1808* (1816), quoted in Enkvist, *American Humor,* 14. An elaborate example of how English writers would use a literary device for such matters, as Lambert did with his "narrative," is "On Americanisms, with a Fragment of a Trans-Atlantic Pastoral," *New Monthly Magazine* (Dec. 1820): 629–32. It features a dialogue between "two guessing Yankees" whose colloquially rich speech is elaborately foot-noted with mock seriousness.

22. In attributing this to Buckingham, I follow the assumption of Allen Walker Read, "The World of Joe Strickland," *JAF* 76 (Oct.–Dec. 1963): 308 n86.

23. Forthright repudiation of the rustic Yankee as the archetypal American is difficult to find, but one of the most interesting is that expressed by the *Voice of Industry* (11 Dec. 1846) declaring that the Yankee, "the personified nationality, is malignant, cheating,

hypocritical and diabolical." It may be that the socialistic *Voice* did not like the capitalistic ingenuity that the Yankee represented. The unrelentingly conservative Cooper was the only major American writer to so directly use the rustic Yankee character "as a national symbol, but a symbol of all the defects of democracy," in the words of William Walker, *James Fenimore Cooper* (New York: Barnes and Noble, 1962), 107. Walker's discussion in chapter 6, "Yankees and Yorkers," traces the evolution of the character in Cooper's books "over the years from a folk type to a full-fledged symbol of social evil."

24. Clarence Gohdes, *American Literature in 19th-Century England* (New York: Columbia UP, 1944), 78.

25. V. L. O. Chittick, *Thomas Chandler Haliburton* (New York: Columbia UP, 1924), 205, and Walter S. Avis, "A Note on the Speech of Sam Slick," in *The Sam Slick Anthology*, ed. Reginald Eyre Watters (Toronto: Clarke, Irwin, 1969), xix–xxix. To a nineteenth-century French critic, the Slick books were even more accurate than travel books: "He enters into the secret details of private life, and exhibits all which English travelers have left in shadow," wrote Philarète Charles in *Revue des Deux Mondes* (15 Apr. 1841), rpt. in Richard A. Davies, ed., *On Thomas Chandler Haliburton* (Ottawa: Tecumseh, 1979), 52.

26. Many of the reviews quoted here and in chapter 6 are reprinted or excerpted in Davies, *On Thomas Chandler Haliburton*, 11–92. Also see Enkvist, *American Humor*, 28–35.

27. About the popularity of Sam Slick in America, Chittick (*Thomas Chandler Haliburton*, 350) says, "There is no testimony that is both definite and reliable." In book publication, English editions far outnumbered American ones, and Sam was certainly not so popular in American journals and on stage as Jack Downing.

28. James Russell Lowell, *The Poetical Works of James Russell Lowell* (Boston: Houghton, Mifflin, 1890), 2: 208. Constance Rourke, *American Humor, a Study of the National Character* (New York: Harcourt, Brace, 1931), points out the obvious hybrid Yankee-frontiersman that Sam became. For a survey of opinion on the matter before the 1930s, see Chittick, *Thomas Chandler Haliburton*, 348–50. On the authenticity of Sam's speech, see Elna Bengston, *The Language and Vocabulary of Sam Slick* (Copenhagen: E. Munksgaard, 1956), and Avis, "Note on the Speech of Sam Slick."

29. One of the most detailed surveys was conducted in *Eliza Cook's Journal* and reprinted in the *Eclectic Magazine* (Sept. 1854): "The Americans of the United States in almost all of their literary varieties, are pretty close followers of English prototypes. Bryant is a smaller Wordsworth; Longfellow, a minor Tennyson; Washington Irving, a modern Addison; Cooper was the Walter Scott of the ocean and prairie. Prescott and Bancroft are the Robertson and Hume of the New World. . . . Emerson is, perhaps, the most original thinker and writer in the United States; and he, too, has been called the American Carlyle." It was this writer who concluded that the humor of the United States was "really native and original."

30. Quoted in Benjamin Spencer, *The Quest for Nationality* (Syracuse: Syracuse UP, 1957), 141.

31. Louis D. Rubin, Jr., ed., *The Comic Imagination in American Literature* (New Brunswick, NJ: Rutgers UP, 1973), 5.

Chapter 2. Early American Humor

1. Robert Secor, "The Significance of Pennsylvania's Eighteenth-Century Jest Books," *PMHB* 110 (1986): 261. Secor sees three reasons to consider early American jest books: for their "truly American material," for the insights into "language, tastes, and attitudes of the times," and for charting "the development of American humor." In doing so, he builds on the earlier work of P. M. Zall, "The Old Age of American Jest Books," *EAL* 15 (Spring 1980): 3–13, who finds more differences in style than in content and theme between English and American jest books. Both cite the still earlier work of Harry B. Weiss, "A Brief History of American Jest Books," *Bulletin of the New York Public Library* (1943): 273–89. Harrison T. Meserole, "'A Kind of Burr': Colonial New England's Heritage of Wit," in *American Literature: The New England Heritage,* ed. James Nagel and Richard Astro (New York: Garland, 1981), 11–28, takes a more *belletristic* approach to the question of whether "the literary heritage of New England includes a rich dimension of wit."

2. Robert K. Dodge, *Early Almanac Humor* (Bowling Green, OH: Bowling Green State UP, 1987), 4, 33. See also Marion Barber Stowell, "Humor in Colonial Almanacs," *StAH* 1, no. 3 (1976): 34–37. Tandy, *Crackerbox Philosophers in American Humor and Satire* (1925; rpt. Port Washington, NY: Kennikat, 1964), 13 says that Robert B. Thomas's *Old Farmer's Almanac* "has at least sixty incarnations of New England humors and foibles before 1830." Blair, *Native American Humor* (1937; rpt. San Francisco: Chandler, 1960), 20 calls that estimate conservative, but I am not much convinced that the wit or humor of characters such as "Old Betty Blab," "Ben Bluster," "Old Screwpenny," "Goody Slipshod" and such have the kinds of Yankee qualities that would link them with the later New England humor tradition. Native humor and almanacs became one with the coming of comic almanacs in the 1830s, taken up here in chapter 4.

3. Nathaniel Ward, *The Simple Cobler of Aggawam in America,* ed. P. M. Zall. (Lincoln: U of Nebraska P, 1969), 3. Zall's introduction provides an excellent analysis of the book's literary roots; for a good literary analysis of the work itself, see Robert D. Arner, "*The Simple Cobler of Aggawam:* Nathaniel Ward and the Rhetoric of Satire," *EAL* 5 (Winter 1970–71): 3–16.

4. Moses Coit Tyler, *A History of American Literature, 1607–1765* (1878; rpt. New York: Collier, 1962), 84.

5. W. Howland, Kenney, ed. *Laughter in the Wilderness: Early American Humor to 1783* (Kent, OH: Kent State UP, 1976), 74. Also see the chapter on Alsop in J. A. Leo Lemay, *Men of Letters in Colonial Maryland* (Knoxville: U of Tennessee P, 1972), 48–69.

6. Lemay, *Men of Letters,* 92–93.

7. Larzer Ziff, ed., *The Literature of America* (New York: McGraw-Hill, 1971), 1: 157, and Lemay, *Men of Letters,* 77–93. Lemay, *Men of Letters,* 90, says that "the structure and general contents of *The Sotweed Factor* were familiar to English and American

readers before the poem appeared in 1708" and cites "The New England Ballad" and "A West-Country Man's Voyage to New England." On Cooke's poem, also see Robert D. Arner, "Ebenezer Cooke's *The Sotweed Factor:* The Structure of Satire," *SLJ* 4, no. 1 (Spring 1972): 33–47; and Edward H. Cohen, *Ebenezer Cooke: The Sotweed Canon* (Athens: U of Georgia P, 1975). I think the intent is uncertain. It was traditional to make fun of English wrongheaded, low opinions of colonists, but also typical for English writers to satirize them as provincials—and for highminded colonists to poke fun at colonial low life. Just one of the critical issues is the curse that it ends with: if that is the persona speaking, why would Cooke find it necessary to tame it down in the third edition in 1731? As he had become a permanent resident of the colony, its "poet laureate," you would think he would be even more committed to satirizing English opinion. The drafts of the preface, reprinted and discussed by Cohen, indicate that Marylanders had been offended by it, and Cooke disavows authorship of the curse. In *"New England Annoyances": America's First Folk Song* (Newark: U of Delaware P, 1985), Lemay provides a thorough survey of seventeenth-century promotional and antipromotional literature and his interpretation of its place in American humor.

8. Benjamin Franklin, *Benjamin Franklin, Writings*, ed. J. A. Leo Lemay (New York: Library of America, 1987), 8. Subsequent references are to this edition.

9. George F. Horner, "Franklin's *Dogood Papers* Re-examined," *SP* 37 (1940): 501–23, places the Dogood Papers in its political context. J. A. Leo Lemay, "Benjamin Franklin," in *Major Writers of Early American Literature*, ed. Everett Emerson (Madison: U of Wisconsin P, 1972), 205–43, analyzes more fully the literary backgrounds and merits of the series.

10. Franklin's Poor Richard is often cited as an early Yankee prototype, but I cannot see that he anticipates the later tradition very clearly. There are not the conventional contrasts, no semblance of vernacular, and the pithy wisdom is virtually all borrowed, as Franklin himself admitted. In "Franklin's Poor Richard's Almanacs: 'The Humblest of his Labors,'" in *The Oldest Revolutionary: Essays on Benjamin Franklin*, ed. J. A. Leo Lemay (Philadelphia: U of Pennsylvania P, 1976), 77–89, I have argued that Poor Richard is an ironic persona.

11. John Adams, *Diary and Autobiography of John Adams*, ed. L. H. Butterfield et al. (Cambridge: Harvard UP, 1961), 1: 133.

12. Ignored by Adams's nineteenth-century editor Charles Francis Adams, they have been reprinted in the modern edition of his papers, Robert Taylor et al., eds., *Papers of John Adams* (Cambridge: Harvard UP, 1977), vol. 1. I prefer and will quote here the edition by Helen Saltman, "John Adams' Political Satires: The Humphrey Ploughjogger Letters" (Ph.D. diss., U of California, Los Angeles, 1981). Also see her "John Adams's Earliest Essays: The Humphrey Ploughjogger Letters," *WMQ* 37 (1980): 125–35.

13. In the *Portsmouth Mercury and Weekly Advertiser*, 28 Oct. 1765, reprinted in Saltman, "John Adams' Political Satires," 254–57.

14. Saltman, "John Adams' Political Satires," 63. Another series of letters featuring phonetic spelling, these by the semiliterate, democratic patriot "Indian Jacob," appeared in the Boston *Gazette* at about the same time. See Mark M. Lipper, "Comic Caricatures in Early American Newspapers as Indicators of the National Character" (Ph.D. diss., Southern Illinois U, 1973).

15. Kenney, *Laughter in the Wilderness,* 207. Kenney also includes in this observation Robert Hunter's *Androboros,* not taken up here.
16. Saltman, "John Adams' Political Satires," 99. Adams remembered them many years later with some ambivalence, writing to his son in 1792: "That my Confessions may be compleat I must tell you that I wrote a very foolish unmeaning thing in Fleets Paper in 1762 or 1763 under the signature of Humphrey Ploughjogger. In this there was neither good nor Evil, yet it excited more merriment than all my other writings together." Feb. 13, 1792, Taylor, *Papers of John Adams,* 58.
17. Blair, *Native American Humor,* 17.
18. Richard Beale Davis, ed., "The Colonial Virginia Satirist," in *Transactions of the American Philosophical Society* n.s. 57, pt. 1 (1967): 1–74.
19. The first scholarly study of the background of "Yankee Doodle" is Sonneck, *Report,* 79–156. For more recent studies, see S. Foster Damon, *Yankee Doodle* (Providence: Bibliographical Society of America, 1959), and especially J. A. Leo Lemay, "The American Origins of 'Yankee Doodle,'" *WMQ* 33 (July 1976): 435–64, who argues that both the tunes and words have American folk origins. Unless otherwise cited, texts for the song are taken from facsimiles in Sonneck.
20. William Gordon, *The History of the Independence of the United States of America,* (1788; rpt. Freeport, NY: Books for Libraries, 1969), 1: 481. It is not clear whether this is a true letter or a literary device that Gordon used for his history. I suspect the latter.
21. Sonneck, *Report,* 109.
22. In Frank Moore, ed., *Songs and Ballads of the American Revolution* (New York: Appleton, 1856), 363–66.
23. For a detailed consideration of this song, see John William Ward, *Andrew Jackson, Symbol for an Age* (1955; rpt. New York: Oxford UP, 1962), 13–29.
24. Lemay, "American Origins," dates an early version of this song as the summer of 1775.
25. On dating this song, see Lemay, "American Origins," 452 n88, who dates it 1775–85. The text used here is "The Yankees Return from Camp," from a facsimile in Sonneck, *Report,* 193. For one of the several Civil War renditions of the song, see Sylvia G. L. Dannett, *A Treasury of Civil War Humor* (New York: Thomas Yoseloff, 1963), 110–11.
26. F. O. Matthiessen, *American Renaissance* (New York: Oxford UP, 1941), 200.
27. George Thomas Tanselle, *Royall Tyler* (Cambridge: Harvard UP, 1967), 60. See also Arthur H. Nethercot, "The Dramatic Background of Royall Tyler's *The Contrast,*" *AL* 12 (1941): 435–46.
28. Royall Tyler, *The Contrast* (1790; rpt. New York: Burt Franklin, 1970), 6. All citations are from this edition.
29. Quoted in Matthews, "Brother Jonathan," 113. Taking a representative modern view, Richard Moody, *America Takes the Stage* (Bloomington: Indiana UP, 1955), 114, says "Jonathan displayed the admirable qualities of the 'true American' in contrast to the outmoded foreign artificialities of Dimple, Jessamy, Charlotte, and Letitia." Daniel F. Havens, *The Colombian Muse of Comedy* (Carbondale: Southern Illinois UP, 1973), 31, provides a nicely balanced study, but I particularly like the cogent analysis by Von Frank, *The Sacred Game,* 29–41.
30. In addition to the literary tradition of "Yankee Doodle" is Joseph Atkinson's comic opera *A Match for a Widow: or, the Frolics of Fancy,* written in 1785, performed in

Dublin in 1786, and printed in London in 1788, which has a Yankee servant named "Jonathan." According to Marston Balch, "Jonathan the First," *MLN* 46 (May 1931): 281–88, Tyler's and Atkinson's Jonathans "show many points of likeness. For example, each is the servant or orderly of the army officer who is the hero of the play. In this capacity each is introduced into a fashionable milieu so remote from his provincial experiences as to throw into high relief every trait of his speech, dress, and behavior, and to make him a comic figure, not only to the main characters, but to their household servants as well." Given the production and publication dates of the two plays, there is no reason to think that Tyler was familiar with the earlier work, although Balch speculates that word of "Atkinson's innovation in Dublin" may have reached Tyler.

31. Harold Ellis, "Joseph Dennie and His Circle: A Study in American Literature from 1792 to 1812," *Bulletin of the University of Texas, Studies in English* No. 40 (Austin: U of Texas P, 1915), 185.

32. The afterpiece for the evening, according to what Jonathan says, was *The Poor Soldier*. Tyler had seen the same program only a few weeks earlier, and Thomas Wignell, who first played Jonathan, was one of the leading players that night.

33. Frederick Tupper, "Royall Tyler, Man of Letters and Law," *Proceedings of the Vermont Historical Society* 4 (1928): 68. On Tyler's use of language, Robert B. Stein, "Royall Tyler and the Question of Our Speech," *NEQ* 38 (1965): 454–74, discusses the thematic importance of the language.

34. A possible exception may be Lazarus Beach's farce *Jonathan Postfree: or, The Honest Yankee* (1807) in which the Yankee is the title character. His ignorance of city life is made light of, but there are no clearly established comic scenes.

35. Tandy, *Crackerbox Philosophers*, 10.

36. On the American Della Cruscan movement, see M. Ray Adams, "Della Cruscanism in America," *PMLA* 79 (1964): 254–65; and Frederick Lewis Pattee, *The First Century of American Literature, 1770–1870* (1935; rpt. New York: Cooper Square, 1966), 107–18.

37. Wilford E. Binkley, *American Political Parties* (New York: Knopf, 1962), 50.

38. Blair, *Native American Humor*, 21 n2, says this "apparently originated" in the Portland, Maine, *Eastern Journal* (11 May 1795), and in addition to newspaper reprintings it also appeared in *The Spirit of the Public Journals for 1805* and in *The Maryland and Virginia Almanac* (Baltimore) *for 1806*.

39. Thomas Green Fessenden, *Original Poems* (Philadelphia: Lorenzo P, 1806), 15. An earlier edition of the book was published in London in 1804 by Albion Press.

40. Judith Yaross Lee discusses the Federalist writers' "intense, even racist use of dialect to characterize the democratic populace—a desirable strategy for raising fears of Jeffersonian mobocracy," in "Republican Rhymes: Constitutional Controversy and the Democratization of Verse Satire, 1786–1799," *StAH* n.s. 6 (1988): 30–39. I have long wondered why the anti-Federalists delineated no vernacular characterizations in response, and I think Lee may be correct in saying that "Republicans overcompensated with extremely correct verse forms, as if to prove that they could indeed write in learned forms if they tried."

41. It is not clear whether Fessenden wrote the reply. I believe he did not, for Tabitha's point of view in the poem does not appear along with a longer version of "Peter

Periwinkle . . ." titled "Love's Labour Lost" in Fessenden's *Original Poems*. Pattee, *First Century of American Literature*, 226 n5, says it is "undoubtedly the work of Tyler," but Marius B. Péladeau, ed. *The Verse of Royall Tyler* (Charlottesville: UP of Virginia, 1968) does not include it.

42. A different and longer broadside version of the piece is in the American Antiquarian Society, which dates it 1832–37.

43. Tyler's poem did inspire a mock pastoral of the more conventional courting kind, "Phelim O'Bluff's Epistle to Miss Bett Boldface," which was reprinted in several newspapers. A note to it in the Kennebeck, Maine, *Intelligencer* (23 Sept. 1796) directs the reader to an earlier literary column that featured Tyler's "ode," which in line thirty-seven refers to a person called "Bets."

44. Blair, *Native American Humor*, 24. A poem of the same kind is "A Country Ball Described," in the Amherst, New Hampshire, *Village Messenger* (25 Sept. 1797). The political intent behind this description of rustic revelry can be seen in the name assumed by the author, "A Friend to Order."

45. Tandy, *Crackerbox Philosophers*, 20, says there is an "early, unexpurgated" copy of the poem in the collection of the American Antiquarian Society. Some sections of this brittle broadside—perhaps offending ones—are missing, however. At issue may be the meaning Tandy gave the word "unexpurgated" in 1925. The text in question appears to be the same as another broadside version in the American Antiquarian Society in which Jonathan says "Why Sal, I's going to say as how— / you'll stay with me tonight, / I kind of love you Sal, I vow— / And mother said I might." In the version published in *Original Poems*, Jonathan suggests that they "spark" it that night.

46. An exception is "The Yankee Lover's Soliloquy" in *The Rover* (Oct. 1855), which attributes it to J. Swett, and in *Yankee Notions* (Oct. 1859). The poem has the chief features of many of the earlier mock pastorals, the galloping rhythms of the dactylic meter and rustic metaphors.

47. David Humphreys, *The Yankey In England* (1815), 14–15.

48. In his preface to *The Down-Easters* (1833), John Neal says that *The Yankey in England* is one of two works "containing so much as one single phrase of *pure Yankee*." See also Marie Killhoffer, "A Comparison of the Dialect of 'The Biglow Papers' with the Dialect of Four American Yankee Plays," *AS* 3 (1928): 222–36.

Chapter 3. New England Humor on Stage

1. William Dunlap, *History of the American Theatre*, 2d ed. (1832; rpt. New York: Burt Franklin, 1963), 162. Young Dunlap himself had been inspired by Tyler's success in 1787. His *The Modest Soldier, or Love in New York* (1788) included a Yankee servant, but the play was never produced and no copy survives.

2. Tandy, *Crackerbox Philosophers*, 5.

3. Dunlap, *History of the American Theatre*, 311.

4. Gohdes, *American Literature in 19th-Century England*, 73. The text used for analysis here is Charles Mathews, *The London Mathews: Containing an Account of this*

Celebrated Comedian's Trip to America (Baltimore: J. Robinson, 1824). For a study of Mathews's *Trip*, see Francis Hodge, *Yankee Theatre: The Image of America on Stage 1825–1850* (Austin: U of Texas P, 1964), 60–72; and Walter Blair, "Charles Mathews and his 'Trip to America,'" in *Prospects*, ed. Jack Saltman (New York: Burt Franklin, 1976), vol. 2: 1–23.

5. John Neal, "Story Telling," *New England Magazine* 8 (Jan. 1835): 1–12, recounts the early history of the story.

6. Charles Mathews, *The Life and Correspondence of Charles Mathews*, ed. Edmund Yates (London: Routledge, Warne, and Routledge, 1860), 261.

7. The play exists only in a manuscript version in the Enthoven Collection, Victoria and Albert Museum, London. The discussion here is based upon the description in Hodge, *Yankee Theater*, 72–76.

8. Hodge, *Yankee Theater*, 75.

9. Todd, *Notes Upon Canada*, 32. As Todd himself notes, however, Mathews did return to America, in 1834, and did so successfully, despite a press campaign calling for censure of his calumnies. Mathews, acknowledging the use he had made of Humphreys's work, deviously laid the blame for any misrepresentation to the American: "Wicked man, to caricature his own countrymen in such wretched style and clumsy fashion, and lead the English into error! Fie, Fie, Humphries [sic]!," in *Memoirs of Charles Mathews*, ed. Mrs. Mathews (London: Richard Bentley, 1839), 3: 540.

10. Of the nearly one hundred Yankee plays in Hodge's bibliography, only about 25 percent are extant, and most of that number are in manuscript. Hodge's bibliography does not include *Ebenezer Venture*, which was published. Many other titles appear in newspaper advertisements and theater playbills.

11. Samuel Woodworth, preface to *The Forest Rose; or, American Farmers* (New York: Samuel French, [1855]). Quotations are from this edition rather than the 1825 one because they probably more accurately reflect what later Yankee actors did with the role.

12. James Hackett, *Jonathan in England* (Boston: W. V. Spenser, [1859]). By necessity, as with all of the published plays discussed here, the analysis of *Jonathan in England* must be based on a text published several years after the original production, although as in the case with *The Yankee Peddler; or, Old Times in Virginia*, the differences between the later publications and the earlier performances may not be great.

13. Sol Smith, *Theatrical Management in the West and South for Thirty Years* (New York: Harper, 1898), 212–13. Other popular Yankee characters originated by James Hackett are Industrious Doolittle in *The Times; or, Life in New York* (1829), and *Job Fox; or, The Yankee Valet* (1834). Hackett also played the frontiersman, Col. Nimrod Wildfire, in James Kirke Paulding's *The Lion of the West* (1831).

14. Quoted in Nils Erik Enkvist, *Caricatures of Americans on the English Stage Prior to 1870* (1951; rpt. Port Washington, NY: Kennikat, 1968), 51.

15. Hodge, *Yankee Theater*, 141.

16. George H. Hill, *Scenes from the Life of an Actor* (New York: Garret, 1853), 55.

17. Joseph Jones, *The Green Mountain Boy* (New York: Samuel French, [1860]). The last performance listed in this edition is 1860, with John S. Clarke playing the role of

Jedediah. Scenes from the play used here are from Hill, *Scenes from the Life*, 163–83, because they are probably closer to Hill's original performance. Certainly they differ from the later published edition.

18. Morris Barnett, *Yankee Peddler; or, Old Times in Virginia* (New York: Samuel French, [1854]). Hodge, *Yankee Theater*, 282, says this is a revised version by Barnett and "was apparently rewritten for Dan Marble." According to Hodge's description of and quotations from the Hill version in manuscript in the Lord Chamberlain Collection, British Museum, it does not seem to differ significantly from the Samuel French edition. That edition lists Marble as playing the role in St. Louis in 1841, Hill playing it in Louisville in 1845, and H. F. Stone doing so in Chicago in 1853.

19. W. K. Northall, ed., *Life and Recollections of Yankee Hill* (New York: W. F. Burgess, 1850), 37. Hill was sensitive to the undesirable Yankee traits attributed to the American character. He liked the English people he met because they were without "that eternal ghost of trade haunting them and obtruding the unsocial question of 'How much can I get out of this fellow?' at every new introduction, as in America" (Hill, *Scenes from the Life*, 131). Sol Smith too was concerned with English opinions fostered by the stage Yankee. "That Solon Shingle business is shameful, a burlesque upon this country & its jurisprudence. I am glad that the Britishers would not stand it long," he wrote in a letter dated August 21, 1865, quoted in *Catalogue Thirteen, Autograph Letters* (Philadelphia: David J. Holmes, n.d.), 29.

20. Hill, *Scenes from the Life*, 128–29.

21. Quoted in Northall, *Life and Recollections*, 49. A number of English and Scottish reviews are reprinted in *Life and Recollections*, 47–62, 64–70. Hill also appeared in *Casper Hauser* and *A Down East Bargain*. Americans were very much interested in the reception of their actors abroad, which was reported in the press. In the 1830s, the *Spirit of the Times*, although it later featured frontier humor, was particularly interested in the careers of Yankee actors. Examples include "Mr. Hackett" (9 June 1832); "Yankee Hill in London" (31 Dec. 1836); and "Lord Hackett" (11 Mar. 1837).

22. In Northall, *Life and Recollections*, 51.

23. Joseph Jones, *The People's Lawyer* (New York: Samuel French, n.d.). This edition gives a performance by Hill at the National Theater in Boston in 1839, but C. Burke and George Locke are also listed as having played the Yankee role. Silsbee too played it, but it was Burke, according to Brander Matthews, who first made Solon Shingle an older Yankee, the interpretation that John Owens gave to his long and highly popular version of the role beginning in the 1860s. See "Americans on the Stage," *Scribners' Monthly* (18 July 1879), 331.

24. "Hill the Yankee Comedian," *Courier and New York Enquirer*, 7 Aug. 1833. *The Spirit of the Times*, 24 Nov. 1832, said that Hill's performance at the Park Theater in New York was a "lower grade" than Hackett's but admitted that in "many points actually surpassed the far-famed attempts of Hackett in the same line."

25. The only biography of Marble is Jonathan F. Kelly, *Dan Marble: A Biographical Sketch* (New York: Dewitt and Davenport, 1851).

26. Cornelius A. Logan, *The Vermont Wool Dealer* (Boston: Walter H. Baker, 1851). Quotations are from this edition.

27. Hodge, *Yankee Theater*, 222.
28. Cornelius A. Logan, *Yankee Land* (Boston: William V. Spencer, [1854]). This is a rewrite of *The Wag of Maine*, which Hackett played in 1834. This edition lists performances by five other actors in the role of Lot Sap Sago, the last in 1854. Marble played it under the title *Yankee Land* in 1842; another version, played in 1844, was titled *Hue and Cry*, which he used in performances after that date.
29. These reviews are quoted in Enkvist, *Caricatures*, 97–98.
30. Lawrence LaBrée, *Ebenezer Venture; or, Advertising for a Wife* (New York: Samuel French, [1841]). Quotations are from this edition.
31. Henry Nash Smith, *Virgin Land, the American West as Myth and Symbol* (Cambridge: Harvard UP, 1950), 64.
32. The version used here is from George H. Hill, *Little Hill's Yankee Story Book* (Philadelphia: Turner and Fisher, 1836), 10–13, which says "Recited by Mr. Hackett." However, Hodge, *Yankee Theater*, 94–96, reprints a rather different, manuscript version of the story from Hackett's London performance in *Sylvester Daggerwood*. The story indeed became a popular theater piece: the *Boston Evening Transcript*, 12 Apr. 1833, announced that a Mr. D. A. Stone would "make his first appearance here and recite the celebrated story of Uncle Ben." On the origins, see note 5 above.
33. Jonathan Kelly's biography of Marble includes a number of the stories the actor told on stage.
34. Joseph Ireland, *Records of the New York Stage* (1886–87; rpt. New York: Burt Franklin, 1968), 2: 106. The only biographical sketch I have found is Thomas W. Valentine, *The Valentines in America, 1644–1874* (New York: Clark and Maynard, 1874), 35. William Valentine, "generally called, 'Dr. Valentine, *the Humorist,'*" was born in New York in 1802. He studied medicine, but "gave humorous lectures through the country for many years, and as a delineator of character and scenes, he had few superiors." Valentine was also a ventriloquist and "an excellent performer on the flute."
35. In William Valentine, *Dr. Valentine and Yankee Hill's Metamorphoses, being the Second Series of Dr. Valentine's Comic Lectures* (New York: Garrett, 1852), 11–15. The contents of this are much the same as in *Comic Metamorphoses* (New York: Dick and Fitzgerald, 1855). Valentine's publications would appear to be as eccentric as he was. The cover of one edition has the following information: *Dr. Valentine's Comic Lectures* (New York: W. F. Burgess, 1850), but the inside title page reads *A Budget of Wit and Humor . . .* (Philadelphia: C. Marshall, 1849). And this volume has the same contents as William Valentine, *Dr. Valentine's Comic Lectures* (New York: Burgess, 1850).
36. The quotations used here are from Northall, *Life and Recollections*, 152–71.
37. This is in a prefatory note to "Yankee Cabala" in Northall, *Life and Recollections*, 127. Another example of humor on the subject is "A Modern Astronomer," written by "Enoch Fithister," in *The Carpet Bag*, 6 Dec. 1851.
38. "Lecture on New England" appears in Hill, *Scenes from the Life*, 183–95.
39. Quoted in Enkvist, *Caricatures*, 110.
40. Joseph Ireland, *Records of the New York Stage from 1750–1860* (New York: T. H. Morrell, 1866–67), 2: 506. Mrs. Williams's sister, Malvina Florence, née Pray, also acted the part of the "Yankee gal," and both, with their husbands playing the Irish comic parts they specialized in, toured England in the 1850s. See Enkvist, *Caricatures*, 119–23.

Chapter 4. New England Humor in Print

1. In his study of national types in American short fiction before 1800, Jack Moore concluded that he could not write a chapter on Yankee stories "simply because there were too few of them," in his "Native Elements in American Magazine Short Fiction, 1741–1800" (Ph.D. diss., U of North Carolina, 1963), 5.

2. The Portland, Maine, *Eastern Argus* in 1815 printed four humorous pieces that give some credence to that conclusion. In "A True Story," 24 May 1815, a Yankee in a stagecoach endures the criticism of things American by his English companions. When lightening strikes a tree and upsets the coach, he retorts, "There, blast you! cries Jonathan, quite in a passion, / Have you got better THUNDER in England than that?" As a brief prose anecdote, the same story was printed in the *Yankee*, 10 Jan. 1846, attributing it to the Vicksburg *Intelligencer*. "Extracts from Jonathan's Memorandum of a Tour to See York State," 8 Nov. 1815, gives a homey account of city fashions. As both of these were attributed to other papers, no doubt further research into newspapers of the time would turn up more humor in the same vein.

3. Some of the poems were also circulated as broadsides. The American Antiquarian Society's copy of "Jonathan's Visit to a Wedding" also has a comic "Negro" sermon, "Rev. Mr. Quambo's Sarmont."

4. Virtually everything cited in this chapter appeared more than once, and although I will usually indicate that, I do not assume that the source I cite is the first one. For a good discussion of reprintings, see Richard Dorson, *Jonathan Draws the Long Bow* (Cambridge: Harvard UP, 1946), 13–15.

5. See Read, "The World of Joe Strickland," 277–308.

6. Charles Nichols, "Notes on the Almanacs of Massachusetts," *PAAS* n.s. 22 (1912): 38. In bad taste would be the following from *Marsh's Komick All My Nac (for) 1852*: Mrs. Partington, reading about Jenny Lind's having a "fellow feeling in her bosom" for the needy and unfortunate, exclaimed, "A feller feeling in her bosom!" she exclaims. "La me, if that aint just the way the fellers used to do when I was a girl." And in the *Boston Evening Transcript*, 5 Jan. 1831, "A Parent" complained of the recently published almanac *Food For Fun* that promised twelve new Yankee stories: "Had the stories been called *Rochesterian* stories, they would have been rightly named. There is not one of them but is calculated to corrupt the morals of youth, and most of them are licentiously indecent." Some of the stories are neither new nor offensive, but stories such as the one of the Yankee who tricks his wife into believing that she is the one who defecated in bed are definitely not the type of thing usually put into print.

7. Henig Cohen and William B. Dillingham, eds., *Humor of the Old Southwest*, 2d ed. (Athens: U of Georgia P, 1975), xvii, divide frontier humor into twenty categories.

8. William Walcutt's "Joel Wetsel, A Story of the Backwoods," in the *Republic* (Oct. 1852): 96–98, develops the conflict into a short story.

9. Hodge, *Yankee Theater*, 111. Stories of the type include "A Militia Captain" and "Grand Review" in the *Boston Evening Transcript*, 10 May and 29 March 1831, respectively. For visual representation, see David Claypoole Johnston's "Marching in the Line of Review" in his annual collection titled *Scraps* (Boston, 1837), 3, and "A Militia Fight," signed by "Downer" in the *American Comic Almanac* (1835), 50. "The

Yankee Militia Muster," in *The Comic Songster* (Philadelphia, 1836), 11–14, is a musical stage rendition.

10. Edgar Allan Poe, review of Augustus Baldwin Longsteet's *Georgia Scenes, Southern Literary Messenger* 2 (Mar. 1836): 292. Poe was correct in believing that Longstreet had not written the piece.

11. For some background on the phenomenon, see Chandos Michael Brown, "A Natural History of the Sea Serpent: Knowledge, Power, and the Culture of Science in Antebellum America," *AQ* 42 (1990): 402–36.

12. Patricia and Milton Rickels, *Seba Smith* (Boston: G. K. Hall, 1977), 123. The Rickelses see similarities between Jack Robinson and Jim Doggett in Thomas Bang Thorpe's earlier story, "The Big Bear of Arkansas." In each, they conclude, "the readers' sympathies and identification lie with the folk raconteur, not the condescending auditors of the story" (112).

13. Of the same type would be "The Yankee Engineer," in *Graham's* (Jan. 1840): 32–35, and "Deacon Carpenter's Hard Case," *Godey's Lady's Book* (May 1843): 212–16.

14. The story also appeared in *Bentley's Miscellany* (Mar. 1848), and in a collection of Burton's writings titled *Waggaries and Vagaries* (1842), which went through several editions in the 1840s and 1850s, sometimes under the title *The Yankee Among the Mermaids*. One other story in the collection features an entertaining rustic Yankee. "Thaumaturgia" is a long story of Eph Brattle, who barges in on the devil's birthday party whistling "Yankee Doodle" and ends up on a trip to New York with Apicius, the Negro king of Numidia; the Earl of Rochester; Cato; and Queen Zenobia. Burton also edited *Burton's Comic Songster* (1838) and *Cyclopedia of Modern Wit and Humor* (1859), both of which went through several editions.

15. Linguists have not studied this dialect for accuracy, but the methods used for the study of the authenticity of literary dialect make it virtually inconceivable that it is authentic. On literary dialect, see George Krapp, "The Psychology of Dialect Writing," *Bookman* 62 (Dec. 1926): 522–27; Sumner Ives, "A Theory of Literary Dialect" and Paul Bowdre, Jr., "Eye Dialect as a Literary Device," both in *A Various Language, Perspectives on American Dialects,* ed. Juanita V. Williamson and Virginia M. Burke (New York: Holt, Rinehart and Winston, 1971), 145–77 and 178–86. James Russell Lowell's use of New England dialect in *The Biglow Papers,* however, has been examined carefully. James Walker Downer concludes that "his characterization of the dialect primarily by incidence of phoneme, is successful, suggesting to the informed reader the actual sounds, the intonation, the rhythm, and the cadence of Yankee speech." See "Features of New England Rustic Pronunciation in James Russell Lowell's 'Biglow Papers'" (Ph.D. diss., U of Michigan, 1958), 3. For the place of dialect in American literary history, see Richard Bridgman, *The Colloquial Style in America* (New York: Oxford UP, 1966).

16. All quotations from Jonathan Slick are taken from Ann Stephens, *High Life in New York* (New York: Bunce and Brothers, 1854).

17. Bridgman, *The Colloquial Style in America,* 23.

18. Mesick, *The English Traveller in America,* 82.

19. Northall, *Life and Recollections,* 75–78. A different version appeared as "Yankee Inquisitiveness" in Howard Paul, *The Courtship and Adventures of Jonathan Homebread* (New York: Dick and Fitzgerald, 1860), 251–56.

20. The repartee here is much like that in "Arkansas Traveler," which was in circulation in print and on stage in mid-nineteenth century America and is still performed today by bluegrass musicians.

21. Quoted here is Frances Whitcher, *The Widow Bedott Papers* (New York: J. C. Derby, 1856). The Widow Bedott stories first appeared in Joseph Neal's *Saturday Gazette and Literary Museum* in 1846 and were collected in book form as *The Widow Bedott Papers* in 1856, which sold more than 100,000 copies. In 1879, David Ross Locke, creator of Petroleum V. Nasby, made the widow a stage character for Neil Burgess with *The Widow Bedott; or, A Hunt for a Husband,* which played in theaters toward the end of the nineteenth century. See Jane Curry, "Yes, Virginia, There Were Female Humorists: Frances Whitcher and Her Widow Bedott," *University of Michigan Papers in Women's Studies* 1 (1974): 74–90. George Hill's "A Family Picture," *Life and Recollections,* 104–8, has a similar ending.

22. Perry Miller, *Errand Into the Wilderness* (1956; rpt. Harper and Row, 1964), 8.

23. Edward Ward, *A Trip to New-England with a Character of the Country and People, both Indians and English* (1699; rpt. New York: Columbia UP, for the Facsimile Text Society, 1933), 5, 7.

24. "Joseph Beachnut and the Tooth Powder," in Hill, *Little Hill's Yankee Story Book,* 30–32; "Sutler Savencoon's Speckle-ation in Sand-Bag Hams," *Jonathan Jaw Stretcher's Yankee Story All-My-Nack* (Boston: B. W. Cottrell, [1851]).

25. The next week (22 Jan. 1819) the *Galaxy* printed "Yankee Puns—No. II." In this poem, a Yankee sold some cattle, promising the buyer that he had never known them to "kick before." The buyer, finding they did indeed kick, accused the Yankee of cheating. Strictly speaking, though, the peddler had not lied: "'Stop, sir, look sharp,' says Clod, 'you'll find, / When e'er they kick, they kick *behind*.'"

26. A much altered version also made the rounds as "Sleepy Davy.—A Sporting Sketch" in *Spirit of the Times,* 29 July 1845.

27. See also "Ten Upon Eleven," *Constellation,* 12 May 1832. Here a Frenchman tells a Yankee that horse he is selling is "ten upon eleven" years old. The new Englander, after buying the horse, learns that "ten upon eleven" is a literal version of "twenty-one" in French. See too "The Frenchman's Trick," *Spirit of the Times,* 18 Apr. 1835.

28. On rustic Yankee courtship in popular humor and belles lettres, see Lawrence Buell, *New England Literary Culture: From Revolution Through Renaissance* (New York: Cambridge UP, 1986), 343–46.

29. *John Beedle's Sleighride, Courtship and Marriage* (New York: C. Wells, 1841), 2. This quotes *Bicknell's Reporter,* which attributes the work to John Neal, a misattribution that continues to the present day, although the title page says "attributed to Capt. M'Clintock, of the U.S. Army."

30. Voss, "The Evolution of Lowell's 'The Courtin',"" *AL* 15 (1953): 49–50.

31. Lowell, *Poetical Works* 2: 205.

32. For examples of backwoods and New England courtship in Southern newspapers, see Eugene Current-Garcia, "Newspaper Humor in the Old South, 1835–1855," *AlaR* 2 (Apr. 1949): 102–21; James L. W. West, "Early Backwoods Humor in the Greenville *Mountaineer, 1826–1840," *MissQ* 25 (Winter 1971): 69–82, along with his "Backwoods Humor in the Greenville *Mountaineer,* 1830–1850," TS, Furman U Library; and Nancy

B. Sederberg, "Antebellum Southern Humor in the *Camden Journal*: 1826–1840," *MissQ* 27 (Winter 1973–74): 41–74; Fritz Oehlschlaeger, *Old Southwest Humor from the St. Louis "Daily Reveille," 1844–1850* (Columbia: U of Missouri P, 1990).

33. See Bernard Bowron, Leo Marx and Arnold Rose, "Literature and Covert Culture," in *Studies in American Culture,* ed. Joseph J. Kwiat and Marcy C. Turpie (Minneapolis: U of Minnesota P, 1960), 84–95; and Marvin Fisher, "The Iconology of Industrialism, 1830–60," *AQ* 13 (Fall 1961): 347–64.

34. It also appeared as a broadside. The *Galaxy* reprinted the poem from the *Republican Sentinel,* but in a prefatory note, took credit for the inspiration with "the enumeration of *notions* sold by 'John Brown of Natick town,' which appeared in the *Galaxy* a few years since [19 June 1818]." In the same vein is "New Year's Presents, or Sandy's Description of Jos. Bonfanti's Fancy Store, 279 Broadway," in the *New England Galaxy* (21 Jan. 1825) and later in newspapers.

35. Paul, *The Courtship and Adventures,* 35–44, 49–59.

36. "How a Raw Yankee Enlisted," *Yankee Notions* 1 (Sept. 1852): 86; "A Yankee at the Adams House," *Yankee Blade* 6 (30 Oct. 1847): 2.

37. Mark Twain described much the same experience while watching the can-can in Paris in *Innocents Abroad* (1869).

38. Linda Ann Finton, "Women Vernacular Humorists in Nineteenth-Century America: Ann Stephens, Francis Whitcher, and Marietta Holley" (Ph.D. diss., U of California, Berkeley, 1978), 52.

39. Gary Lindberg, *The Confidence Man in American Literature* (New York: Oxford UP, 1982), 93–96, discusses the peddler stereotype along with that of the self-made man as revealing "the doubleness of nineteenth-century American attitudes toward success." Warwick Wadlington, *The Confidence Game in American Literature* (Princeton: Princeton UP, 1975), 12, sees another kind of doubleness: "Although there is a comic relish in the frontier trickster's duplicity, there is also a recognition of the more grotesque impulses of the confidence man, often combined . . . with a satire of Jacksonian faith in the common man and rugged individualism." See also "The Yankee Peddler and the Con Man," a chapter in Emily Stipes Watts, *The Businessman in American Literature* (Athens: U of Georgia P, 1982), 34–44.

Chapter 6. The New England Cracker-barrel Philosophers

1. Worth some attention is the character of "Uncle Dan," the work of Thomas M. McKnight and subsequently Len Sullivan. McKnight, owner of the *Mooresville* (North Carolina) *Tribune,* began the weekly column in the 1940s and syndicated it in other, mostly small-town weekly, newspapers around the country. Editors were free to change the names of the characters who appeared and to make place names local. Len Sullivan began contributing in the mid-1960s and kept it going after McKnight's death in 1968. At its peak, in the early 1960s, the column was carried by 120 papers; in 1990, the number was down to thirty, "and dropping like flies," according to Sullivan. "The format is a bit jaded, I'm sure," he adds, "and the audience for such corn pone is

dwindling. But our nemesis is the chain publishers who don't look above the bottom line." Len Sullivan, letter to the author, 25 Mar. 1991. Also in the cracker-barrel tradition is *The West Virginia Hillbilly,* a weekly from Richwood, West Virginia, the work of Jim Comstock. Started in 1956, it folded in 1958, revived the next year. After selling out his interest, Comstock revived the paper again in 1992. See Jim Comstock, *The Best of "Hillbilly,"* ed. Otto Whittaker (New York: Pocket Books, 1969).

2. See John William Ward, *Andrew Jackson, Symbol for an Age* (1955; rpt. New York: Oxford UP, 1962) and Marvin Meyers, *The Jacksonian Persuasion, Politics and Belief* (1957; rpt. Stanford: Stanford UP, 1960).

3. Ralph Waldo Emerson, *The Journals and Miscellaneous Notebooks of Ralph Waldo Emerson,* ed. Alfred R. Ferguson (Cambridge: Harvard UP, 1964), 4: 297.

4. Douglas T. Miller discusses the history of these points of view in "Pernicious Tendency of Parties," a chapter in his *The Birth of Modern America* (New York: Pegasus, 1970), 140–72.

5. Richard P. McCormick, *The Second American Party System: Party Formation in the Jacksonian Era* (Chapel Hill: U of North Carolina P, 1966), 30.

6. Miller, *The Birth of Modern America,* 158.

7. Gerald J. Baldasty, "The Press and Politics in the Age of Jackson," *Journalism Monographs* no. 89 (Aug. 1984): 23.

8. Herbert Ershkowitz, "Andrew Jackson, Seventh President and the Press," *Media History Digest* 5, no. 2 (1985): 10–16, 40. Amos Kendall, Isaac Hill, and Francis Blair, prominent members of Jackson's Kitchen Cabinet, had been editors, and Vice-President Martin Van Buren had earlier headed the party's committee to raise funds to establish and circulate party newspapers.

9. Frank Luther Mott, *American Journalism, a History: 1690–1960,* 3d ed. (New York: Macmillan, 1962), 254.

10. The cracker-barrel Davy Crockett had little to do with the real Crockett, who would be recreated in myth following his death at the Alamo. For examples of the latest work on Crockett and excellent bibliographies, see *Davy Crockett: The Man, the Legend, the Legacy, 1786–1986,* ed. Michael A. Lofaro (Knoxville: U of Tennessee P, 1985); and *Crockett at Two Hundred: New Perspectives on the Man and the Myth,* ed. Michael A. Lofaro and Joe Cummings (Knoxville: U of Tennessee P, 1989).

11. Tandy, *Crackerbox Philosophers,* ix.

12. See Read, "The World of Joe Strickland," for a thorough and thoughtful consideration of the Strickland tradition.

13. New York *Enquirer,* 9 June 1827, in Read, "The World of Joe Strickland," 288–89.

14. Read, "The World of Joe Strickland," 284 n24.

15. Read, "The World of Joe Strickland," 301, 307 n69; West, "Early Backwoods Humor," 78.

16. *Daily Courier,* 15 Apr. 1830. Virtually everything that has been written about Jack Downing has been based on the letters that appear in the 1833 collection. An examination of the early letters as they appeared in the *Courier* shows more accurately the evolution of Seba Smith as a cracker-barrel humorist. That is, when he began the letters in January 1830, he had no idea what direction they might take and certainly

how popular they would be. The early *Courier* letters, for example, reveal that he experimented with cracker-barrel correspondents other than Jack, such as Ned and Jackson Downing.

17. For many years, the only study of Seba Smith (and his wife, Elizabeth Oakes Smith) was Mary Alice Wyman, *Two American Pioneers, Seba Smith and Elizabeth Oakes Smith* (New York: Columbia UP, 1927). A more recent work, and one that offers more interpretation of Smith's Downing letters and his belles lettres generally, is Milton and Patricia Rickels, *Seba Smith* (Boston: Twayne, 1977). Wyman contains more biographical, factual information, but it is not always accurate.

18. Rickels, *Seba Smith*, 38–39.

19. *United States Telegraph*, Washington, DC, 6 Sept. 1833; *Boston Post*, 9 Nov. 1833; *Elton's Comic All-My-Nack for '37* (New York: R. H. Elton, [1836]). On a more serious note, the *Boston Evening Transcript*, 10 Aug. 1833, reported that a Mr. W. W. Wilson was charged with counterfeiting a three dollar bill of the Nahant, Massachusetts, bank, one signed "Andrew Jackson, President and Jack Downing, Cashier." Wilson called it an experiment but was "bound in the sum of $500 to answer at the Municipal Court."

20. Ketchum, *Uncle Sam*, 63.

21. Ironically, he would be challenged again in 1830. See Cameron C. Nickels, "Seba Smith Embattled," *Maine Historical Society Quarterly* 13 (1973): 7–27.

22. Seba Smith, *The Life and Writings of Major Jack Downing*, 3d ed. (Boston: Lilly, Wait, Colman, and Holden, 1834), 43. Subsequent quotations will be from this edition unless otherwise indicated.

23. Marquis James, *The Life of Andrew Jackson* (Indianapolis: Bobbs-Merrill, 1938), 641.

24. Wyman, *Two American Pioneers*, 64. See also Rickels, *Seba Smith*, 58–60, and Ward, *Andrew Jackson*, 83–87.

25. Ward, *Andrew Jackson*, 84.

26. Ward, *Andrew Jackson*, 87. Ward is incorrect, though, in attributing the "Amazin' Smart Skoller" version to Seba Smith. The Smith book he cites, *Jack Downing's Letters by Major Jack Downing* (a reprint of *May Day in New York*, 1845) and that he incorrectly dates as 1834, does not make that claim. See Ward, *Andrew Jackson*, 240 n27.

27. "Marriage Extraordinary," Boston *Evening Transcript*, 12 July 1833; Boston *Evening Gazette*, 24 Aug. 1833.

28. Quoted in Smith, *Life and Writings*, 269.

29. Seba Smith, Charles Augustas Davis, et al., *Letters Written During the President's Tour* (1833; Freeport, NY: Books for Libraries, 1969). *The Cincinnati Daily Gazette* had printed "with great frequency, many specimens of Downing letters," Wyman, *Two American Pioneers*, 75 says. A second edition of this volume appeared in 1838. Another collection of Smith, Davis, and counterfeit letters was published in Philadelphia: *The Select Letters of Major Jack Downing* (1834; Upper Saddle River, NJ: Gregg, 1970). Both of these facsimile editions are erroneously attributed to Smith.

30. Charles Augustus Davis, *Letters of J. Downing* (New York: Harper, 1834), 89. All quotations and references will be from this edition.

31. James, *The Life of Andrew Jackson*, 658. According to James 877–88 n39, "about twenty letters" passed between Biddle and Davis from September 1833 to October 1834.

32. See the entry for Davis in Jacob Blanck, comp., *Bibliography of American Literature* (New Haven: Yale UP), 2: 411–14.

33. Wyman, *Two American Pioneers,* 4. The conflict Smith now faced in trying to redeem the satiric intent of the letters is clear in contrasting one of the resolutions of the Downingville caucus, chaired by Uncle Joshua, to nominate Jack for governor, to a resolution published in the *Eastern Argus,* 14 Sept. 1818, of a political caucus, chaired by Samuel Andrews, to recommend Albion K. Parris for senator. In Downingville: "Resolved, therefore, That we recommend him to the electors of this State as a candidate for said office, and that we will use all fair and honorable means, and if necessary, will not stick at some a little *dis* honorable, to secure his election." In Bridgeton: "Resolution: Whereupon it was unanimously resolved that the delegates present will use all lawful and honorable means in their power to promote the election of said Albion K. Parris." The first clearly parodies the second, satirically revealing the hypocrisy of such public resolutions.

34. Seba Smith, letter to Elizabeth Oakes Smith, 5 Nov. 1833, Alderman Library, U of Virginia. Elizabeth did not like the Major's portrait either—"the look is not honest"— nor did Seba's mother and brother; letter to Seba Smith, 11 Nov. 1833, Alderman Library, U of Virginia. Smith used the same picture for the *Downing Gazette* in 1834 and the *Rover* in 1844, but he was still not comfortable with it. In the latter, Jack complains to the editor, who says that the portrait "is a very striking likeness of what the Major was in the early part of his public career. But we know there is such a thing in portrait painting as getting *too strong* a likeness, and perhaps that is the case in the present instance."

35. On Johnston's career, see Malcolm Johnson, *David Claypoole Johnston: American Graphic Humorist, 1798–1865,* exhibition catalog, 1970; and David Tatham, "D. C. Johnston's Pictorialization of Vernacular Humor in Jacksonian America," in *American Speech: 1600 to the Present,* ed. Peter Benes. Dublin Seminar for New England Folklife: *Annual Proc.* 25–26 June 1983 (Boston: Boston U, 1985): 107–19. In our time, scholars selecting the Downing canon have tended to ignore the political satire of the letters, preferring instead the humor and local color sentiments of the introduction. Walter Blair, in *Native American Humor,* reprints the part about Jack's grandfather and four letters that feature the Downingville milieu. James Miller, Jr., ed., *Heritage of American Literature* (New York: Harcourt, Brace, Jovanovich, 1991), vol. 1 represents Downing only with an excerpt from the preface. Daniel Hoffman, in *Form and Fable in American Fiction* (New York: Oxford UP, 1961), 49 seems to have in mind only the preface when he extols Downingville's "paradisal" innocence: the people have, like Jack, knowledge, but it is "instinctual knowledge, not the hard, mean knowledge gained by experience. Their innate good natures and their birthright of Yankee wisdom make such characters as Major Downing inviolable against chicanery."

36. Robert V. Remini, *Andrew Jackson and the Bank War* (New York: Norton, 1967), 129. "In introducing and ultimately enforcing acceptance of his doctrine" that the president is the direct representative of the American people, Remini concludes, "Jackson liberated the president from the position of prime minister, responsible only to the Congress. In effect he altered the essential character of the presidency" (147).

37. Wyman, *Two American Pioneers*, 85. The Library of Congress has twenty-six numbers of *Major Downing's Advocate;* the New York Public Library has issues of *Major Downing's Advocate and Mechanics' Journal* from 9 July 1834, the first issue, to 1 Nov. of that year.

38. On Smith's influence upon Crockett, see Joseph Arpad, "Introduction," in *A Narrative of the Life of David Crockett,* by David Crockett (1834; rpt. New Haven: College and UP, 1972), 29–31. Arpad says the connection between Downing and Crockett had been attempted two years earlier when the Jackson, Tennessee, *Southern Statesman* reprinted Jack's letters, and on 17 Sept. 1833 printed a letter from the *Daily Courier* inviting Crockett to join Jack in Washington. "In the same issue," says Arpad, "appeared Crockett's reply which accepted the invitation and promised to couch his observations in Downing's characteristic vernacular and point of view."

39. Ward, *Andrew Jackson*, 79.

40. Wyman, *Two American Pioneers*, 49, suggests that Augustin Smith Clayton may have "assisted" in the correspondence, but she also proposes Clayton as the author of Crockett's *Tour to the North and Down East* (1836) as well as the *Autobiography.* Arpad, "Introduction," 32, says Pennsylvania Whig congressman William Clark wrote the former. Scholars generally agree that Thomas Chilton, congressman from Kentucky, generously helped in writing the latter.

41. James Atkins Shackford, *David Crockett, the Man and the Legend* (1956; rpt. Chapel Hill: U of North Carolina P, 1986), 58. Later in his book, Shackford suggests that *both* Davis and Smith sat down to dinner with Crockett, "either literally or figuratively" (197) and that Davis influenced Smith's stronger anti-Jackson stand in the *Gazette.* However compatible they were politically, Seba Smith protested relentlessly Davis's literary theft of Jack Downing. Shackford has no evidence to support his conclusions and ignores facts that would argue against it.

42. Rickels, *Seba Smith*, 27.

43. Current-Garcia, "Newspaper Humor," 107 n22, says that the Columbus, Georgia, *Enquirer* began reprinting Downing letters in July 1833 "and continued doing so as often as the exchanges made them available, until as late as September 12, 1854." They appeared in other Georgia papers as well, including the *States Rights' Sentinel,* edited by backwoods humorist Augustus Baldwin Longstreet. See Wyman, *Two American Pioneers,* 83 for the midwestern letters.

44. *The Life of Andrew Jackson by Jack Downing* (Philadelphia: T. K. Greenbank, 1834). As the style and substance make clear, this is by neither Davis nor Smith. *Jack Downing's Song Book* (Providence: Weeden and Cory, 1835). According to Wyman, *Two American Pioneers,* 78, this was "a collection of popular songs, which appears to have been suggested by one of the Davis letters." The book is dedicated to Jackson, but the songs have no political import.

45. William Murrell, *A History of American Graphic Humor* (New York: Whitney Museum of Art, 1933), 1: 127. Good collections of these can be found in the Print Department of the Boston Public Library, the American Antiquarian Society, and the Library of Congress.

46. Murrell, *History of American Graphic Humor,* 132.

47. Hodge, *Yankee Theater,* 145.

48. Hodge, *Yankee Theater,* 235. Hodge, *Yankee Theater,* 145 also reports the opening on 24 Apr. 1834 of W. F. Gates's *Life in New York, or the Major's Come.* At the same time in Boston, the *Evening Transcript,* 28 Apr. 1834, advertised *Major Jack Downing At Home and Abroad,* and on 23 June wrote that a "Mr. Blake" played him at the Warren Theater. He was also the leading character in *Moonshine, or Lunar Discoveries,* Sept. 1835. Finally, in the 1960s, William Mooney presented at the Players Theater off Broadway, "*Major Jack Downing Goes to Portland,* by Seba Smith," according to Rickels, *Seba Smith,* 139.

49. Wyman, *Two American Pioneers,* 86–87. Wyman is not correct, however, in saying that the letters continued only until April 1839. Poe also seemed to believe that Brooks had written these letters. See *Graham's Magazine* 19 (Dec. 1841): 283.

50. Reprinted in Stephen Hess and Milton Kaplan, *The Ungentlemanly Art, a History of American Political Cartoons* (New York: Macmillan, 1975), 38.

51. The pen was a "precarious business for main dependence," Smith wrote to Rufus Griswold in 1842: "It will do for a staff, but not for a crutch. However, since Mrs. Smith and myself have each a staff, if we walk together, I hope we may be able to keep from falling" (Wyman, *Two American Pioneers,* 115). Elizabeth's literary reputation would soon overshadow Seba's, fulfilling intellectual ambitions she had had since a child. She enjoyed, as Seba did not, the stimulating literary and social life that the city had to offer in the 1840s. Poe admitted her into the august ranks of the literati. See Mary Alice Wyman, ed., *Selections from the Autobiography of Elizabeth Oakes Smith* (New York: Columbia UP, 1924), as well as her *Two American Pioneers.* Also see Kent Ljungquist and Cameron C. Nickels, "Elizabeth Oakes Smith on Poe: A Chapter in the Recovery of His Nineteenth-Century Reputation," in *Poe and His Times,* ed. Benjamin Franklin Fisher IV (Baltimore: Edgar Allan Poe Society, 1990), 235–47.

52. Smith protested the literary theft of the counterfeiters, however, in *John Smith's Letters with Picters to Match,* (New York: Samuel Colman, 1839). This brief series of letters had appeared in the *New York Mirror* in 1839 under the name John Smith, Jack Downing's cousin. John wrote in the Downing style about the "Aroostook War," a Canadian–U.S. boundary dispute in Maine that had national attention but did not result in partisan politics. As a result, the letters reflect more New England local color than political satire.

53. Five "chapters" in a series titled "Major Jack Downing's Second Life" appeared in the 2, 9, 23, 30 May and 13 June issues of the *New World.* Three of them would be included in *May Day in New York* (1845).

54. Introduced to Henry Clay as Jack Downing, Smith said he felt "awkward" (letter to Elizabeth Oakes Smith, 1 Nov. 1833, Alderman Library, U of Virginia). Also, asked if he would attend a Bowdoin College commencement in 1852 and contribute something as Jack Downing, Smith replied, "I am afraid 'Major Downing' would be somewhat out of place in a commencement exercise" (letter to unknown addressee at Bowdoin, 6 Aug. 1852, Alderman Library, U of Virginia). And again, in a letter to Nehemiah Cleveland asking for information about his Bowdoin classmates, Smith wrote of himself that he had published "but one volume that I think of much account, and that is the

'New Elements of Geometry'" [1850]. The Downing letters "were remarkable for their extensive popularity, which I conceive arose more from peculiar circumstances than from their intrinsic merits" (letter to Cleveland, 6 Feb. 1854, Alderman Library, U of Virginia). Finally, in a letter to Philadelphia publishers Carey and Hart in 1841, he confessed that the popularity of Downing letters "has always been a matter of great wonderment to me" (Seba Smith to Carey and Hart, 20 Dec. 1841, Pennsylvania Historical Society).

55. See Daniel Royot, "The Rover," in *American Humor Magazines and Comic Periodicals,* ed. David E. E. Sloane (New York: Greenwood P, 1987), 239–41. The *Rover* appeared in semiannual volumes beginning in mid-March and mid-August. Volume 3, for example, begins 23 March 1844.

56. Because so few issues of *Bunker Hill* are extant, information and quotations used here are taken from the *Rover,* which liberally reprinted various pieces from it.

57. The success of the *New York American Republican* "was so immediate that by the fall of that year [1844] it boasted a circulation second only to the New York *Sun,* and a weekly edition was being published to satisfy out-of-city readers. The columns of this paper were filled constantly with articles against foreigners and Catholics," says Ray Allen Billington, *The Protestant Crusade, 1800–1860* (1938; rpt. New York: Rinehart, 1952), 109–10.

58. Louis Dow Scisco, *Political Nativism in New York State* (1901; rpt. New York: Ames, 1968), 16.

59. According to the Rickels, *Seba Smith,* 124, "With only two omissions and with very few changes, the series [in the *National Intelligencer*] was reprinted" in the book. Also, one sketch from *John Smith's Letters* was revised and included. In addition to Wyman and the Rickels on this series, also see John H. Schroeder, "Seba Smith's Political Satire," *NEQ* 50 (1977): 214–33.

60. Shackford, *David Crockett,* 197.

61. Seba Smith, *My Thirty Years Out of the Senate* (New York: Oakesmith, 1859), 256. All quotations are from this edition.

62. The Rickels, *Seba Smith,* 126–27 argue that Smith does protest as well "the essential evil of war."

63. In the manuscript collection of the Alderman Library of the University of Virginia is a letter February 1851 in Smith's hand and signed "Squire Downing," who speaks of Jack Downing as "my dead and gone uncle." Written in the Downing cracker-barrel style, the letter pokes fun at "wimmens' rites," interesting given Elizabeth Oakes Smith's commitment to that cause.

64. Before book publication in 1859, the whole series had appeared in *Emerson's Magazine* from October 1857 through June 1858. Although *Speech of John Smith, Esquire, Not Delivered at Smithville, September 15, 1861* (New York: Bryant, 1864) has been attributed to Smith, he almost certainly did not write it. Not only was Smith in very poor health at the time, but the piece is not written in his style, and its rejection of peace until slavery has been eradicated does not reflect Smith's sentiments about slavery.

65. Wyman, *Two American Pioneers,* 91. The text used for citations here is *Letters of Major Jack Downing, of the Downingville Militia,* 3d ed. (New York: Van Evrie, Horton, 1866). Announcing the publication of the second edition on 11 March 1865, the *Day Book* reprinted several short, appreciative notices from other papers.

66. J. G. Randall, *Lincoln the President: Springfield to Gettysburg* (New York: Dodd, Mead, 1945), 2: 243.

67. The 5 March 1864 issue of the *Day Book* announced the publication of a lithograph cartoon, "Major Downing's Dream," which it called "a telling political caricature."

68. Mott, *American Journalism*, 339–40.

69. Chittick, *Thomas Chandler Haliburton*, 371.

70. A series titled "Letters of Fashionable Life" by a cousin, Ezekiel Slick, appeared in *Yankee Notions* in 1853, and in 1858 S. A. Hammet used Sam's name in *Piney Woods Tavern; or Sam Slick in Texas*. Later, an anonymous author signed "Sam Slick, Jr." to *Adventures of an Office Seeker* (Richmond: Everett Waddy, 1904), which appears to be a political autobiography, and there is William Stanley Hoole's *Sam Slick in Texas* (San Antonio: Naylor, 1945).

71. Thomas Chandler Haliburton, *The Clockmaker*, 5th ed. (London: Richard Bentley, 1839), 1: 197–98. Subsequent references to the first *Clockmaker* are from this edition.

72. On the connection between Poor Richard and Sam Slick, see Daniel Royot, "Sam Slick and American Popular Humor," in *The Thomas Chandler Haliburton Symposium*, ed. Frank M. Tierney (Ottawa: U of Ottawa P, 1985), 123–33.

73. Thomas Chandler Haliburton, *The Clockmaker, Second Series* 5th ed. (London: Richard Bentley, 1839), 2: 318. All references to the second series are to this edition.

74. Thomas Chandler Haliburton, *The Clockmaker, Third Series* (London: Richard Bentley, 1840), 3: 264. Subsequent references to the third series are from this edition.

75. Thomas Chandler Haliburton, *The Letters of Thomas Chandler Haliburton*, ed. Richard A. Davies. (Toronto: U of Toronto P, 1988), 128.

76. Thomas Chandler Haliburton, *The Attaché*, rev. ed. (New York: Dick and Fitzgerald, n.d.), 259. This edition combines the two series.

77. Darlene Kelly, "Haliburton's International Yankee," in *The Thomas Chandler Haliburton Symposium*, ed. Tierney, 147.

78. Haliburton, *Letters*, 137.

79. Northrup Frye, "Haliburton: Mask and Ego," in *On Thomas Chandler Haliburton*, ed. Davies, 211.

80. Chittick, *Thomas Chandler Haliburton*, 558.

81. Stephens, *High Life in New York*, 144.

82. Haliburton, *The Clockmaker* 1: 9–15.

83. Haliburton, *The Clockmaker* 2: 141–53.

84. Chittick, *Thomas Chandler Haliburton*, 544. On his part, Lowell considered Sam Slick "a libel on the Yankee character."

85. *The Biglow Papers* have always been the source of Lowell's reputation in England, according to Nils Erik Enkvist, "The Biglow Papers in Nineteenth-Century England," *NEQ*, 26 (June 1953): 219–36.

86. Leon Howard, *Victorian Knight-Errant: A Study of the Early Literary Career of James Russell Lowell* (Berkeley: U of California P, 1952), 233. In "An Incident in a Railroad Car," describing how men "rude and rough" eagerly listened to someone reading Burns, Lowell spoke of his desire "to write some earnest verse or line, / Which, seeking not the praise of art, / Shall make a clearer faith and manhood shine / In the untutored heart."

87. This is reprinted in Gertrude Reese Hudson, *Browning to His American Friends* (London: Bowes and Bowes, 1965), 225.

88. The first five "papers" appeared in the *Boston Courier,* the last four in the *National Anti-Slavery Standard.* Although I have looked at these original printings, quotations here will be taken from the CEAA edition prepared by Thomas Wortham, *James Russell Lowell's "The Biglow Papers" [First Series]* (De Kalb: Northern Illinois UP, 1977).

89. Lowell, *Poetical Works* 2: 156.

90. Howard, *Victorian Knight-Errant,* 242–43.

91. Arthur M. Voss, "Backgrounds of Lowell's Satire in 'The Biglow Papers,'" *NEQ* 23 (1950): 55.

92. Voss, "Backgrounds," 54 does say that Lowell may have had in mind the editor of the Boston *Morning Post* as the model for this; Howard, *Victorian Knight-Errant,* 265 suggests that Lowell was thinking of William Cullen Bryant, editor of the New York *Evening Post.*

93. James Russell Lowell, *Letters of James Russell Lowell,* ed. Charles Eliot Norton (Boston: Houghton, Mifflin, 1904), 1: 178.

94. Voss, "Backgrounds," 56.

95. Tandy, *Crackerbox Philosophers,* 46; Walter Blair, *Horse Sense in American Humor* (Chicago: U of Chicago P, 1942), 94.

96. Lowell, *Letters* 1: 198.

97. Thomas Wortham, "Introduction," in Wortham, *Lowell's "The Biglow Papers,"* xxviii.

98. Howard, *Victorian Knight-Errant,* 239.

99. Lowell, *Poetical Works* 2: 157.

100. Lowell, *Letters* 1: 163, 164. Several years later, in 1859, as two English publishers competed to get the *Biglow Papers* into print, his feelings about that identity had sharpened: "I confess I am a little jealous of people who like my humorous poems best. I guess they are right 'up to date'—but I feel also as if it were a little unfair to the other half of me . . . ," quoted in Wortham, *Lowell's "The Biglow Papers,"* xxi.

101. *The Poetical Works of James Russell Lowell* 2: 157.

102. Arthur Voss, *"The Biglow Papers* in England," *American Literature* 21 (1949–50): 341 n6, writes that in 1880, with Lowell appointed to the prestigious post of United States Minister to England, a magazine there printed a cartoon entitled "Hosea Biglow goes to Court" with the caption "Popular notion of the newly-accredited American Minister, His Excellency Mr. James R. Lowell (Hosea Biglow), going to present his credentials to the Queen."

103. Wortham, *Lowell's "The Biglow Papers,"* xxvi says that Wilbur's "pedantry—a misuse of intellectual labor—is undeniable, but its extent and its damaging effect on the volume have been exaggerated by most critics."

104. Howard, *Victorian Knight-Errant,* 240.

105. Lowell, *Letters* 1: 187.

106. Lowell, *Poetical Works* 2: 156.

107. Lowell, *Letters* 1: 40.

108. Blair, *Horse Sense in American Humor,* 100–101.

109. James Russell Lowell, *The Anti-Slavery Papers* (1902; rpt. Negro Universities P, 1969), 1: 13.
110. James Russell Lowell, *New Letters of James Russell Lowell,* ed. Mark A. DeWolfe Howe (New York: Harper, 1932), 50.
111. Lowell, *Letters* 2: 38.
112. Lowell, *Letters* 2: 68.
113. Lowell, *Letters* 2: 70.
114. See Richard Croom Beatty, *James Russell Lowell* (1942; rpt. Hampton, CT: Archon, 1969). Voss, "Backgrounds," 59 suggests that Lowell was responding to an attack upon him by a Southern reviewer in *Debow's Review.*
115. Lowell, *Poetical Works* 2: 296. All quotations from the second series are from this edition.
116. Lowell, *Letters* 2: 72.
117. Lowell, *Letters* 2: 93.

Conclusion

1. See Nellie Smither, "Library of American Works: A Bibliographical Study" (Master's thesis, Columbia U, 1936). Smither says that thirty-three titles had been issued as of 1869 and reprinted many times after that year and that the paper-backed editions were still being sold in 1881.
2. Quoted in Enkvist, *Comic Caricatures,* 109.
3. Daniel Royot, "Whittier, Matthew Franklin," in *Encyclopedia of American Humorists,* ed. Steven H. Gale (New York: Garland, 1988), 483. See also Lloyd Wilfred Griffin, "Matthew Franklin Whittier, 'Ethan Spike,'" *NEQ* 14 (1941): 646–63. Other hybrid Yankees would include Nehemiah Slim, who reported his adventures in California in *Yankee Notions* in 1855, and also letters from Ezekiah Stubbins in the same magazine in 1864. More in the tradition is a series of poems in *Vanity Fair* in 1860 and 1861 featuring Jonathan's rustic opinions on events of the day, including the war.
4. The metamorphosis of the figure had begun early. Although Brother Jonathan resurfaced in political cartoons in the mid-1840s, Winifred Morgan, *An American Icon,* 84 writes that by the 1850s and thereafter "the same visual representation was frequently labeled Uncle Sam," and "except for occasional relics, Brother Jonathan practically disappeared from the American scene after the Civil War." The English would continue to prefer "Jonathan" as the American sobriquet.
5. Richard Dorson, "The Yankee on Stage," *NEQ* 30 (1940): 484.
6. Rowland Robinson, *Uncle Lisha's Shop,* 6th ed. (New York: Field and Stream, 1904), n. p. Other titles are *Sam Lovel's Camps* (889), *Danvis Folks* (1894), and *Uncle Lisha's Outing* (1902). At the turn of the century, the older Yankee returned to some of the traditional roles in popular literature. Thomas Fleming's *Around the "Pan" with Uncle Hank* (New York: Nut Shell, 1901), featuring Hank Slocum, "a Yankee farmer from 'way doawn East,' where they grow them long and lean, and as shrewd as it is possible for humanity to be," went through many editions. Other examples would be William T.

Call, *Josh Hayseed in New York* (New York: Excelsior, 1887) and Hilda Brenton, *Uncle Jed's Country Letters* (Boston: Henry A. Dickerman, 1902), letters from Pine Hollow, New Hampshire. The most popular of these is Cal Stewart's characterization of "Uncle Josh," influenced by Denman Thompson's stage characterization of Joshua Whitcomb. Stewart's "Pumpkin Centre" stories were first recorded on wax cylinders in the late 1890s and subsequently on records and in print through the 1920s. See the four-part essay by Jim Walsh in *Hobbies*, Jan.–Apr. 1951.

7. Blair, *Native American Humor*, 104. On *Yankee Notions*, see my entry in Sloane, *American Humor Magazines and Comic Periodicals*.

8. David Sloane, "Introduction," *The Literary Humor of the Urban Northeast: 1830–1890* (Baton Rouge: Louisiana State UP, 1983), 19, speaks of a school of northeastern literary humor that is independent of the frontier tradition but that has elements too frequently "separated unreflectively into such categories as Yankee, Knickerbocker, literary comedian, or nothing at all, since most of the post–Civil War writers of the Northeast do not fit comfortably into any category."

9. In recent years the story has circulated orally with a student at an "A. & M." university as the comic victim.

Bibliographic Essay

The scholarly study of American humor began in the 1920s with Jennette Tandy's *Crackerbox Philosophers in American Humor and Satire* (1925), V. L. O. Chittick's *Thomas Chandler Haliburton* (1924), and Mary Alice Wyman's *Two American Pioneers: Seba Smith and Elizabeth Oakes Smith* (1927), all originally dissertations at Columbia University. The next decade saw the publication of two major, more general works: Constance Rourke's *American Humor, A Study of National Character* (1931) and Walter Blair's *Native American Humor* (1937). Although still considered classics, these books reflect the concerns and ideological inclinations of their age in their search for what Van Wyck Brooks called in 1918 a "usable past" in American literature that would offer something of value to an age that seemed characterized by spiritual poverty on the one hand and material prosperity on the other. Vernon Louis Parrington's *Main Currents in American Thought* (1927–30) articulated the ideological thrust in this search for what he called "definitely American" in the nation's past. Parrington had no doubt that "democracy" and "American" were one: "The point of view from which I have endeavored to evaluate the materials is liberal rather than conservative, Jeffersonian rather than Federalistic," he wrote in the preface to the first volume. Both Rourke and Blair wrote in that Progressive spirit of essential Americanism, although Rourke's work is more transparently thesis-ridden in this respect than Blair's, whose book is also replete with original research carefully acknowledged and written in a lucid, unselfconscious style that Rourke apparently never aspired to.

Subsequent humor scholarship built on these works, taking two directions. First, it argued that native American humor reflected a real, folk, American experience, a point of view that tended to deny that the humor was self-consciously literary; it was, rather, the spontaneous, natural expression of the common man and free of politically ulterior intent. Subsequent scholarship also turned its attention almost exclusively to frontier or backwoods humor (the humor of "the old Southwest," Blair called it) rather than to the New England tradition of native humor. (Rourke and Blair discuss New England humor in their pioneer studies, but later works—Rourke on Crockett and Blair on Mark Twain—indicate that their hearts were in the old Southwest, not the Northeast.) The value of much of this scholarship cannot be denied, and the neglect of New England humor has seldom been overtly parochial or invidious.

There are two reasons for the attention to frontier humor, both of them having more to do with twentieth-century interests than nineteenth-century realities. First is the importance of the frontier tradition on the work of Mark Twain. That is the thrust of two early and influential books, Franklin Meine's *Tall Tales of the Southwest* (1930) and Bernard DeVoto's *Mark Twain's America* (1932), the latter a determined effort to defend frontier humor from Van Wyck Brooks's attack in *The Ordeal of Mark Twain* (1920) and thus Twain's own origins as examples of a vital and usable past.

The second, and more significant, reason for the attention given to Southwestern humor is that the frontier experience and its central character of the frontiersman have had persistent symbolic import for modern America, because frontier humor evokes (has been used to invoke) still meaningful, nostalgic qualities of rugged individualism and heroic exploits in a yet-wild and virgin land. It is, in a word, "masculine," a word, in fact, that appears often and with approbation in much of the commentary about the frontier tradition. (In urging the first generation of American literature historians to escape the genteel tradition, Parrington had encouraged them "to enter into a world of masculine intellects and material struggles.")

Despite the initial interest in New England humor by Wyman and Chittick, only two books that had something to do with that humor subsequently emerged from that era, Richard Dorson's *Jonathan Draws the Longbow* (1946) and B. A. Botkin's *A Treasury of New England Folklore* (1947), the latter significant chiefly for the early humor it reprints. More valuable are two later works, Francis Hodge's *Yankee Theatre: The Image of America on Stage 1825–1850* (1964) and Allan Walker Read's "The World of Joe Strickland" in the *Journal of American Folklore* (1964). For the most part, however, scholarship on New England humor continued to languish. Jesse Bier's 1968 dismissal of it as "a fit subject only for federal writers of the lean thirties, professional folklorists, and indefatigable students of 'American civilization'" has been quoted, and as late as 1975 Lewis Leary's "A 'Want-List' for the Study of American Humor" (a Modern Language Association address reprinted in *Studies in American Humor,* 1975) mentioned no New England humorist.

In the years since, however, much good work has appeared. Although my study focuses on New England humor beginning with the Revolution, scholarship on various writers and aspects of colonial American humor is thorough, thoughtful, and ready for synthesis. For my purposes here, I single out J. A. Leo Lemay's wide-ranging essay on "Yankee Doodle" (1976), which updates the work of Oscar G. T. Sonneck and S. Foster Damon on the subject.

As for the nineteenth-century tradition, Richard A. Davies's *On Thomas Chandler Haliburton* (1979) brings together a wide variety of previously published material, including contemporary reviews of Haliburton's work; *The Thomas Chandler Haliburton Symposium* (1985), edited by Frank Tierney, brings new perspectives to it, as does Davies's 1988 edition of Haliburton's letters. Patricia and Milton Rickelses's *Seba Smith* (1977) provides the analysis of the Jack Downing letters that Wyman's chiefly biographical (but for that reason indispensable) book lacks. Winifred Morgan's *An American Icon: Brother Jonathan and American Identity* (1988) draws from many sources but is particularly valuable because it focuses on nineteenth-century pictorial delineations of the Yankee. Although not solely about New England humor, David Sloane's *The Literary Humor of the Urban Northeast: 1830–1890* (1983) sees new and interesting connections among "types" and "periods" of American humor that literary historians must necessarily designate.

The one scholar who has consistently offered sound judgment backed with thorough research on New England humor is Daniel Royot. Some of his contributions over the years are in the following bibliography, and although not as easily accessible because it is in his native French, Royot's *L'humour Americain* (1980) did what I thought I would do, write the first book devoted solely to the New England tradition. Royot's approach differs significantly from my own, and for that reason I like to think of our work as complementary.

Surveys of, and collections of essays on, American humor generally either ignore or tend to give (perhaps necessarily in the surveys) New England humor cursory attention, but three reference books deserve note here. *American Humor Magazines and Comic Periodicals* (1987), edited by David Sloane, is a masterpiece of information of diverse kinds on the subject. The two volumes of *American Humorists, 1800–1850* (1982), edited by Stanley Trachtenberg, and Stephen H. Gale's *Encyclopedia of American Humorists* (1988) provide new biographical information, although the latter is rather uneven in its coverage.

To end with a "want list" of my own for the further study of New England humor, I would like to see all of this good work begin to find its way into the writing of scholars of nineteenth-century American culture who have tended to rely too easily upon what was done by the first generation of humor scholars, in particular Constance Rourke. There is also more to be done on New England humor itself, more to be found and more to be said about it. I believe there must be more New England humor—more American humor generally—lurking in newspapers and magazines between the Revolution and 1820 that would reveal more clearly than I do here the evolution of the humorous rustic Yankee characterization. I am convinced too that more needs to be known and is worth knowing about Ann Stephens's very popular characterization of Jonathan Slick. We also need accurate, informative editions of Seba Smith's and Charles Augustus Davis's Jack Downing letters, as well as Thomas Chandler Haliburton's Sam Slick volumes. Also, James Russell Lowell's second series of *Biglow Papers* deserves the kind of attention that Thomas Wortham gave to the first. My contention that the tradition of New England humor "ended" in the 1860s needs scrutiny. I believe it did in the sense I describe, but I would like to see more done on its later manifestations, as in the work of Rowland Robinson, Cal Stewart, and the stage Yankee. Finally, in that regard, now that we know more about New England humor, something meaningful can be written on its place in the humor of Mark Twain, say, the personal, cultural, and literary dilemmas reflected in his 1889 masterpiece *A Connecticut Yankee in King Arthur's Court*. It may well mark the "end" of the New England tradition of native American humor.

Selected Bibliography

Primary Works

Newspapers

Albany Journal, Albany, NY.
American Republican, New York.
Boston Evening Transcript.
Boston Post.
Connecticut Courant, Hartford.
Constellation, New York.
Courier, Boston.
Daily Advertiser, New York.
Daily Courier, Portland, ME.
Day Book, also titled *New York Weekly Caucasian*, New York.
Dover Enquirer, Dover, NH.
Downing Gazette, Portland, ME.
Eastern Argus, Portland, ME.
Evening Chronicle, Amesbury, MA.
Evening Gazette, Boston.
Exeter Newsletter, Exeter, NH.
Farmer's Weekly Museum, Walpole, NH.
Independent Chronicle and Boston Patriot.
Litchfield Enquirer, Litchfield, CT.
Major Downing's Advocate, New York.
Major Downing's Advocate and Mechanics' Journal, New York.
Morning Courier and New York Enquirer, New York.
New World, New York.
New York Daily Express.
New York Mirror.
Oxford Observer, Norway, ME.
Pittsburgh Gazette, Pittsburgh, PA.
Portland Advertiser, Portland, ME.
The Tickler, Philadelphia.
United States Telegraph, Washington, DC.
Working Man's Advocate, New York.
Yankee Farmer and Newsletter, Portland, ME.

Journals

Appleton's Journal, New York.
Brother Jonathan, New York.
Bunker Hill, New York.
Burton's Gentleman's Magazine, Philadelphia.
The Carpet Bag, Boston.
Comic Monthly, New York.
Emerson's United States Magazine and Putnam's Monthly, New York.
The Family Reader, Portland, ME.
Galaxy of Comicalities, Philadelphia.
Godey's Lady's Book, Philadelphia.
Graham's Magazine, Philadelphia.
Great Republic, New York.
The Harbinger, New York.
The Humorist, or Laughing Their Way, New York (?).
The Humorist, or Real Life in New York.
John-Donkey, Philadelphia.
The Joker, New York.
Knickerbocker, New York.
The Lantern, New York.
Maine Farmer, Augusta, ME.
Major Jack Downing's Magazine, Boston.
National Anti-Slavery Standard, Boston.
New England Galaxy, Boston.
New England Magazine, Boston.
New Monthly Magazine, Boston.
New Yorker, New York.
Port Folio, Philadelphia.
Republic, New York.
The Rover, New York.
Spirit of the Times, New York.
United States Magazine and Democratic Review, New York.
Vanity Fair, New York.
Voice of Industry, Boston.
The Yankee, Boston.
Yankee Blade, Boston.
Yankee Doodle, New York.
Yankee Notions, New York.

Comic Almanacs

(Titles may vary, as in "Almanack" or "All-My-Nack.")

American Comic Almanac, Boston.
Boston Comic Almanac.
Broad Grins; or, Fun for the New Year, Boston.
The Comic Token, Boston.
Crystal Palace Almanac, New York.
The Devil's Comical Oldmanick, New York and Philadelphia.
Elton's Comic All-My-Nack, New York.
Finn's Comic Almanac or United States Calendar, Boston.
Fisher's Comic Almanac, Boston and New York.
Food for Fun, or the Humorist's Almanac, Boston.
Frank Leslie's Comic Almanac, New York.
General Taylor's Old Rough and Ready Almanac, Philadelphia.
Hood's Komick Almanac, Troy, NY.
Jonathan Jaw Stretcher's Yankee Story All-My-Nack, Boston.
Josh Billings' Farmer's Almanac, New York.
The Komical Komic Almanac, New York.
Marryatt's Comic Naval Almanac, New York.
Marsh's Crystal Palace Comic Almanack, New York.
Marsh's Komick All My Nac, New York.
National Comic Almanac, Boston.
New American All-i-make.
New Comic Almanac, New York.
Old American Comic Almanac, Boston.
Old American Comic Almanac and the People's Almanac, Boston.
Old Fogy's Comic Almanac, New York.
People's Comic Almanac, New York.
Ripsnorter Comic Almanac, New York.
Rough and Ready Almanac, Cincinnati.
Sam Slick's Almanac, New York.
Turner's Comic Almanac, Boston, New York, and Philadelphia.
Uncle Phillip's Comic Almanac, New York.
Uncle Sam's Large Almanac, Philadelphia.
United States Comic Almanac.
Wyman's Comic Almanac, New York.

Books

Alsop, George. *A Character of the Province of Maryland*, ed. Newton D. Mereness. 1666. Rpt. Cleveland: Burrows, 1902.

American Jestbook, Containing a Curious Variety of Jests. Philadelphia: Carey and Spotswood, 1789.

American Joe Miller. Philadelphia: Carey and Hart, 1841.

American Joe Miller. Philadelphia: Daniels and Getz, 1853.

American Magazine of Wit. New York: H. C. Southwick, 1808.

American Wit and Humor. New York: Harper, 1859.

The Aurora Borealis, or Flashes of Wit Calculated to Drown the Dull Cares and Eradicate the Blue Devils. Boston: Editors of the *Galaxy of Wit*, 1831.

Avery, Samuel, ed. *The Book of 1000 Comicalities*. New York: Dick and Fitzgerald, 1859.

———. *Laughing Gas*. New York: Dick and Fitzgerald, 1854.

Barnum, Phineas T. *Funny Stories*. New York: Routledge, 1890.

Brenton, Hilda. *Uncle Jed's Country Letters*. Boston: Henry A. Dickerman, 1902.

Broad Grins; or, Fun for the New Year. New York: Arthur Ainsworth, 1832.

Burton, William, ed. *Burton's Comic Songster*. Philadelphia: James Kay, 1837.

———, ed. *Cyclopedia of Modern Wit and Humor*. New York: Appleton, 1859.

———. *The Yankee Among the Mermaid and Other Waggeries and Vagaries*. Philadelphia: T. B. Peterson, 1843.

Call, William T. *Josh Hayseed in New York*. New York: Excelsior, 1887.

Chaplet of Comus. Boston: Munroe and Francis, 1811.

Chips from Uncle Sam's Jack-Knife. New York: Dick and Fitzgerald, n.d.

Cohen, Henig, and William B. Dillingham, eds. *Humor of the Old Southwest*. 2d ed. Athens: U of Georgia P, 1975.

Comic Metamorphoses. New York: Dick and Fitzgerald, 1855.

The Comic Songster. Philadelphia, 1836.

The Comic Token for 1835, A Companion to the Comic Almanac. New York: Charles Ellms, [1835].

Comstock, Jim. *The Best of "Hillbilly."* Ed. Otto Whittaker. New York: Pocket Books, 1969.

Davis, Charles Augustus. *Letters of J. Downing*. New York: Harper, 1834.

Dexter, Timothy. *A Pickle for the Knowing Ones: Or Plain Truths in a Homespun Dress*. Salem, MA, 1802.

Fessenden, Thomas Green. *Original Poems*. Philadelphia: Lorenzo, 1806.

Finn, Henry J. *American Comic Annual*. Boston: Richardson, Lord, and Holbrook, 1831.

Flashes and Sparks of Wit and Humor by Our American Humorists. New York: M. J. Meyers, 1880.

Fleming, Thomas. *Around the "Pan" with Uncle Hank*. New York: Nut Shell, 1901.

Flowers of Wit; or, the Laughing Philosopher and Budget of Comicalities. Baltimore: C. V. Nickerson, 1832.

Franklin, Benjamin. *Benjamin Franklin, Writings*, ed. J. A. Leo Lemay. New York: Library of America, 1987.

Funnidos, Rignum [John Ballantyne]. *American Broad Grins*. 2d ed. London: Roberty Tyas, 1838.

Funny Stories; or, the American Jester. New York: Duyckinck, 1814.

The Galaxy of Wit. 2 vols. Boston: J. Reed, 1826.

Greene, Asa. *A Yankee Among the Nullifiers.* New York: Stodart, 1833.

———. *Travels in America, by George Fibbleton, Esq., Ex-Barber to His Majesty, the King of Great Britain.* New York: Pearson, 1833.

Haliburton, Thomas Chandler. *The Attaché.* Rev. ed. New York: Dick and Fitzgerald, n.d. Combines first and second series.

———. *The Clockmaker.* 5th ed. London: Richard Bentley, 1839.

———. *The Clockmaker, Second Series.* 5th ed. London: Richard Bentley, 1839.

———. *The Clockmaker, Third Series.* London: Richard Bentley, 1840.

———, ed. *Traits of American Humor.* 3 vols. London: Colburn, 1852.

Hammet, S. A. *Piney Woods Tavern; or Sam Slick in Texas.* Philadelphia, 1858.

Holley, Marietta. *Samantha Rastles the Woman Question,* ed. Jane Curry. Urbana: U of Illinois P, 1983.

Hoole, William Stanley. *Sam Slick in Texas.* San Antonio: Naylor, 1945.

Horn, James. *Horn's Last Budget of Fun.* New York, 1851.

The Humorist; a Collection of Entertaining Tales. Baltimore: Nickerson, Lucas and Dearum, 1829.

Ingersoll, Charles Jared. *Inchiquin, the Jesuit's Letters.* New York: I. Riley, 1810.

Irving, Washington. *A History of New York,* ed. Michael L. Black and Nancy B. Black. 1809. Rpt. Boston: Twayne, 1984.

Jack Downing's Song Book. Providence: Weeden and Cory, 1835.

Jerdan, William, ed. *Yankee Humor and Uncle Sam's Fun.* London: Ingram, Cooke, 1853.

Johnston, David Claypoole. *Scraps.* No. 1 (New Series). Boston, 1849.

Kelly, Jonathan F. *Dan Marble: A Biographical Sketch.* New York: Dewitt and Davenport, 1851.

Kettell, Samuel, ed. *Specimens of American Poetry.* 3 vols. 1829. Rpt. New York: Benjamin Blom, 1967.

———. *Yankee Notions.* Boston: Otis and Broaders, 1838.

Letters of Major Jack Downing, of the Downingville Militia. 3d ed. New York: Van Evrie, Horton, 1866.

The Life of Andrew Jackson by Jack Downing. Philadelphia: T. K. Greenbank, 1834.

Lowell, James Russell. *James Russell Lowell's The Biglow Papers [First Series]: A Critical Edition,* ed. Thomas Wortham. De Kalb: Northern Illinois UP, 1977.

———. *The Poetical Works of James Russell Lowell.* Vol. 2. Boston: Houghton Mifflin, 1890.

McClintock, William. *John Beedle's Sleighride, Courtship and Marriage.* New York: C. Wells, 1841.

Meine, Franklin J., ed. *Tall Tales of the Southwest.* New York: Knopf, 1930.

Momus at Home. Ithaca, New York: Wells and Selkreg, 1842.

Neal, Joseph C. *Charcoal Sketches; or, Scenes in a Metropolis.* 4th ed. Philadelphia: Carey and Hart, 1839.

Northall, William Knight, ed. *Life and Recollections of Yankee Hill.* Burgess, 1850.

Paul, Howard. *The Courtship and Adventures of Jonathan Homebred.* New York: Dick and Fitzgerald, 1860.

Paulding, James Kirke. *The Diverting History of John Bull and Brother Jonathan, by Hector Bull-Us.* 1812. Rev. ed. New York: Harper, 1835.

———. *John Bull in America; or, the New Munchausen.* New York: Charles Wiley, 1822.

Porter, William T., ed. *A Quarter Horse Race in Kentucky.* Philadelphia: T. B. Peterson, 1846.

Punch's Comic Songster. New York: Nafis and Cornish, [1840s].

Robinson, Rowland. *Danvis Folks.* Boston: Houghton Mifflin, 1894.

———. *Sam Lovel's Camp.* New York: Forest and Stream, 1889.

———. *Uncle Lisha's Shop.* 6th ed. New York: Forest and Stream, 1904.

Shillaber, Benjamin. *Knitting Work: A Web of Many Textures.* Brown, Taggard, and Chase, 1859.

Smith, Seba. *Jack Downing's Letters.* Philadelphia: T. B. Peterson, 1845.

———. *John Smith's Letters with Picters to Match.* New York: Samuel Colman, 1839. Same contents as *May-Day in New York,* below.

———. *Life and Writings of Major Jack Downing.* 3d ed. Boston: Lilly, Wait and Holden, 1834.

———. *May-Day in New York.* New York: Burgess and Stringer, 1845.

———. *My Thirty Years Out of the Senate.* New York: Oaksmith, 1859.

———. *'Way Down East; or Portraitures of Yankee Life.* Philadelphia: John Potter, 1854.

Smith, Seba, et al. *Letters Written During the President's Tour.* 1833. Rpt. Freeport, NY: Books for Libraries, 1969.

———. *The Select Letters of Major Downing.* 1834. Rpt. Upper Saddle River, NJ: Gregg, 1970.

Spencer, Albert H., ed. *Spencer's Book of Comic Relations.* New York: Dick and Fitzgerald, 1867.

Spirit of the Farmer's Museum. Walpole, NH: D. and T. Carlisle, 1801.

Spirit of the Public Journals. 1806. Rpt. New York: Arno, 1970.

Stephens, Ann. *High Life in New York.* New York: Bunce, 1854.

Stewart, Cal. *Uncle Josh's Punkin Centre Stories.* Chicago: Stanton, 1903.

Story, Issac. *A Parnassian Shop.* Boston: Russell and Cutler, 1801.

Thompson, William Tappan. *Major Jones' Courtship.* 2d ed. Philadelphia: Carey and Hart, 1844.

Tyler, Royall. *The Verse of Royall Tyler,* ed. Marius B. Péladeau. Charlottesville: UP of Virginia, 1968.

———. *The Yankey in London.* New York: Issac Day, 1809.

Ward, Nathaniel. *The Simple Cobler of Aggawam in America,* ed. P. M. Zall. Lincoln: U of Nebraska P, 1969.

Whitcher, Frances. *The Widow Bedott Papers.* Boston: J. C. Derby, 1856.

The Yankee Songster's Pocket Companion. Gardiner, ME, [1828].

Yankee Tales. London: Cameron and Fergusen. [Series with titles that include *The Coon Hunt, The Fire Hunt,* and *How Josh Jefferson Jenks Got a Start in the World*]. 1870s.

Theater Works

Barker, James Nelson. *Tears and Smiles*. Philadelphia: T. and G. Palmer, 1808.

Barnett, Morris. *Yankee Peddler; or, Old Times in Virginia*. New York: Samuel French, [1854].

Beach, Lazurus. *Jonathan Postfree; or, the Honest Yankee*. Philadelphia: Longworth, 1807.

The Better Sort; or, The Girl of Spirit. Boston: Isaiah Thomas, 1789.

Colman, George. *Who Wants a Guinea?* London: Longman, 1805.

Dunlap, William. *Trip to Niagara*. New York: E. B. Clayton, 1830.

Durivage, O. *The Stage-Struck Yankee*. Boston: William V. Spencer, [1854].

Hackett, James. *Jonathan in England*. Boston: Spenser, [1859].

Hill, George H. *Little Hill's Yankee Story Book*. Philadelphia: Turner and Fisher, 1836.

———. *Scenes from the Life of an Actor*. New York: Garrett, 1853.

Humphreys, David. *The Yankey in England*. N.p., 1815.

Hutton, Joseph. *Fashionable Follies*. Philadelphia: James Lakin, 1815.

Jones, Joseph. *The Green Mountain Boy*. New York: Samuel French, [1860].

———. *The People's Lawyer*. New York: Samuel French, n.d.

LaBrée, Lawrence. *Ebenezer Venture; or, Advertising for a Wife*. New York: Samuel French, [1841].

Lindlsey, A. *Love and Friendship; or, Yankee Notions*. New York: Longworth, 1809.

Logan, Cornelius A. *The Vermont Wool Dealer*. Boston: Walter H. Baker, 1851.

———. *Yankee Land*. Boston: William V. Spencer, [1854].

Low, Samuel. *The Politician Out-witted*. New York: W. Ross, 1789.

Mathews, Charles. *The London Mathews: Containing an Account of this Celebrated Comedian's Trip to America*. Baltimore: J. Robinson, 1824.

Paulding, James Kirke, and William Irving. *The Bucktails; or, Americans in England*. In *American Comedies*. Philadelphia, 1847.

Robinson, J. *The Yorker's Strategem; or, Banana's Wedding*. New York: T. and J. Swords, 1792.

Tyler, Royall. *The Contrast*. 1790. Rpt. New York: Burt Franklin, 1970.

Valentine, William. *Dr. Valentine's and Yankee Hill's Metamorphoses, being the Second Series of Dr. Valentine's Comic Lectures*. New York: Garrett, 1852.

———. *Dr. Valentine's Comic Lectures*. New York: Burgess, 1850.

Woodworth, Samuel. *The Forest Rose; or, American Farmers*. New York: Samuel French, [1855].

Secondary Works

Adams, John. *Diary and Autobiography of John Adams,* ed. L. H. Butterfield, et al. Vol. 1. Cambridge: Harvard UP, 1961.

Adams, M. Ray. "Della Cruscanism in America." *PMLA* 79 (1964): 254–65.

"American Humor." *The Eclectic Magazine of Foreign Literature, Science, and Art* 33 (Sept. 1854): 137–44. From *Eliza Cook's Journal.*

"American Humor." *The Eclectic Magazine of Foreign Literature, Science, and Art* 35 (June 1855): 267–72. From *Eliza Cook's Journal.*

"American Humor." *North British Review* 33 (Nov. 1860): 460–85.

"American Wit." *Living Age* 84 (Mar. 1865): 505–9. From *Saturday Review.*

Anderson, John Q. "Some Migratory Anecdotes in American Folk Humor." *MissQ* 25 (1972): 447–57.

"Are We A Good-Looking People?" *Putnam's* (Mar. 1853): 308–16.

Arner, Robert D. "Ebenezer Cooke's *The Sotweed Factor:* The Structure of Satire." *SLJ* 4, no. 1 (Spring 1972): 33–47.

———. "*The Simple Cobler of Aggawam:* Nathaniel Ward and the Rhetoric of Satire." *EAL* 5, no. 3 (Winter 1970–71): 3–16.

Arpad, Joseph. "Introduction." *A Narrative of the Life of David Crockett,* by David Crockett, 7–37. 1834. Rpt. New Haven: College and UP, 1972.

Austin, James C. and Daniel Royot. *American Humor in France.* Ames: Iowa State UP, 1978.

Avis, Walter S. "A Note on the Speech of Sam Slick." *The Sam Slick Anthology,* ed. Reginald Eyre Watters. Toronto: Clarke, Irwin, 1969.

Balch, Marston. "Jonathan the First." *MLN* 46 (1931): 281–88.

Baldasty, Gerald J. "The Press and Politics in the Age of Jackson." *Journalism Monographs* no. 89 (Aug. 1984): 1–28. Columbia, SC.

Bancroft, George. *Literary and Historical Miscellanies.* Harper and Brothers, 1855.

Beatty, Richard Croom. *James Russell Lowell.* 1942. Rpt. Hampton, CT: Archon, 1969.

Bengston, Elna. *The Language and Vocabulary of Sam Slick.* Copenhagen: E. Munksgaard, 1956.

Bercovitch, Sacvan. *The American Jeremiad.* Madison: U of Wisconsin P, 1978.

Berger, Max. *The British Traveller in America, 1836–1860.* New York: Columbia UP, 1943.

Bernard, John. *Retrospections of America,* ed. Mrs. Bayle Bernard. 1887. Rpt. New York: Benjamin Blom, 1969.

Bier, Jesse. *The Rise and Fall of American Humor.* New York: Holt, Rinehart, Winston, 1968.

Billington, Ray Allen. *The Protestant Crusade, 1800–1860: A Study of the Origins of American Nativism.* 1938. Rpt. New York: Rinehart, 1952.

Binkley, Wilford E. *American Political Parties.* New York: Knopf, 1962.

Blair, Walter. "Charles Mathews and His 'Trip to America.'" *Prospects,* ed. Jack Salzman. Vol. 2: 1–23. New York: Burt Franklin, 1976.

———. *Horse Sense in American Humor.* Chicago: U of Chicago P, 1942.

———. "'A Man's Voice Speaking': A Continuum in American Humor." *Veins of Humor,* ed. Harry Levin, 185–204. Cambridge: Harvard UP, 1972.

———. *Native American Humor.* 1937. Rpt. San Francisco: Chandler, 1960.

————. "The Popularity of Nineteenth-Century American Humor." *AL* 3 (1931): 175–93.

Blair, Walter, and Hamlin Hill. *American Humor, from Poor Richard to Doonesbury.* New York: Oxford UP, 1978.

Blane, William Newnham. *An Excursion through the United States and Canada During the Years 1822–1823.* 1824. Rpt. New York: Negro Universities P, 1964.

Botkin, B. A., ed. *A Treasury of New England Folklore.* New York: Crown, 1947.

Bowdre, Paul, Jr. "Eye Dialect as a Literary Device." *A Various Language, Perspectives on American Dialects,* ed. Juanita V. Williamson and Virginia M. Burke. 178–86.

Bowron, Bernard, Leo Marx, and Arnold Rose. "Literature and Covert Culture." *Studies in American Culture,* ed. Joseph J. Kwiat and Mary C. Turpie, 84–95. Minneapolis: U of Minnesota P, 1960.

Bradsher, Earl. "The Rise of Nationalism in American Literature." *Studies for William A. Reed,* ed. N. M. Caffee and Thomas Kirby, 269–87. Baton Rouge: Louisiana State UP, 1940.

Branch, Edgar M. *The Literary Apprenticeship of Mark Twain.* Urbana: U of Illinois P, 1950.

Bridgman, Richard. *The Colloquial Style in America.* New York: Oxford UP, 1966.

Brown, Carolyn S. *The Tall Tale in American Folklore and Literature.* Knoxville: U of Tennessee P, 1987.

Brown, Chandos Michael. "A Natural History of the Sea Serpent: Knowledge, Power and the Culture of Science in Antebellum America." *AQ* 42 (1990): 402–36.

[Buckingham, Joseph]. "Yankeeisms." *New England Magazine* 3 (Nov. 1832): 377–81.

Buell, Lawrence. *New England Literary Culture: From Revolution Through Renaissance.* New York: Cambridge UP, 1986.

Chevalier, Michael. *Society, Manners, and Politics in the United States,* ed. John William Ward. 1839. Rpt. Garden City, NY: Doubleday, 1961.

Chittick, V. L. O. *Thomas Chandler Haliburton.* 1924. Rpt. New York: AMS, 1966.

Clapp, William W., Jr. *A Record of the Boston Stage.* 1853. Rpt. Boston: Greenwood, 1969.

Clemens, Cyril. "Benjamin Shillaber and his *Carpet Bag*." *NEQ* 14 (1941): 519–37.

Coad, Oral S. "The Plays of Samuel Woodworth." *SR* 27 (1919): 163–75.

Cohen, Edward H. *Ebenezer Cooke: The Sotweed Canon.* Athens: U of Georgia P, 1975.

Cohen, Henig, and William B. Dillingham, eds. *Humor of the Old Southwest.* 2d ed. Athens: U of Georgia P, 1975.

Cooper, James Fenimore. *The American Democrat.* 1838. Rpt. New York: Vintage, 1956.

————. *Notions of the Americans.* Introduced by Robert Spiller. Vol. 1 1828. Rpt. New York: Frederick Unger, 1963.

Cox, S. S. "American Humor." *Harper's New Monthly Magazine* 50 (Apr. 1875): 690–701; (May 1875): 847–59.

Current-Garcia, Eugene. "Newspaper Humor in the Old South, 1835–1855." *AlaR* 2 (Apr. 1949): 102–21.

Curry, Jane. "Introduction." *Samantha Rastles the Woman Question,* by Marietta Holley, 1–19. Urbana: U of Illinois P, 1983.

————. "Yes, Virginia, There Were Female Humorists: Frances Whitcher and Her Widow Bedott." *University of Michigan Papers in Women's Studies* 1 (1974): 74–90.

Curvin, Jonathan W. "The Stage Yankee." *Studies in Speech and Drama in Honor of Alexander M. Drummond.* 139–51. Ithaca, NY: Cornell UP, 1944.

Damon, S. Foster. *Yankee Doodle*. Providence: Bibliographical Society of America, 1959.

Dannett, Sylvia G. L. *A Treasury of Civil War Humor*. New York: Thomas Yoseloff, 1963.

Davies, Richard A., ed. *On Thomas Chandler Haliburton*. Ottawa: Tecumseh, 1979.

Davis, Richard Beale, ed. "The Colonial Virginia Satirist." *Transactions of the American Philosophical Society* n.s. 57, pt. 1 (1967): 1–74.

DeVoto, Bernard. *Mark Twain's America*. 1932. Rpt. Boston: Houghton, Mifflin, 1967.

Dicker, Harry, and Elliott Shapiro. *Early American Sheet Music, Its Lure and Lore, 1768–1889*. New York: Bowker, 1941.

Dodge, Robert K. *Early Almanac Humor*. Bowling Green, OH: Bowling Green State UP, 1987.

Dolan, J. R. *The Yankee Peddlers of Early America*. New York: Bramhall, 1964.

Dorson, Richard. *American Folklore*. Chicago: U of Chicago P, 1959.

——. *Jonathan Draws the Long Bow*. Cambridge: Harvard UP, 1946.

——. "The Yankee on Stage—a Folk Hero of American Drama." *NEQ* 13 (1940): 467–93.

Downer, James Walker. "Features of New England Rustic Pronunciation in James Russell Lowell's 'Biglow Papers.'" Ph.D. diss., U of Michigan, 1958.

Duberman, Martin. *James Russell Lowell*. Boston: Houghton Mifflin, 1966.

Dudden, Arthur Power, ed. *American Humor*. New York: Oxford UP, 1987.

Dunlap, William. *History of the American Theatre*. 2d ed. 1832. Rpt. New York: Burt Franklin, 1963.

Ellis, Harold M. "Joseph Dennie and His Circle: A Study in American Literature from 1792 to 1812." *Bulletin of the University of Texas, Studies in English*. No. 40. Austin: U of Texas P, 1915.

Ellison, George R. "William Tappan Thompson and the *Southern Miscellany*, 1824–1844." *MissQ* 23 (1970): 155–68.

Emerson, Ralph Waldo. *The Journals and Miscellaneous Notebooks of Ralph Waldo Emerson*, ed. Alfred R. Ferguson. Vol. 4. Cambridge: Harvard UP, 1964.

Emery, Michael, and Edwin Emery. *The Press in America, an Interpretation of the Mass Media*. 6th ed. Englewood Cliffs, NJ: Prentice-Hall, 1988.

Enkvist, Nils Erik. *American Humor in England before Mark Twain*. Abo, Finland: Abo Akademia, 1953.

——. "The *Biglow Papers* in Nineteenth-Century England." *NEQ* 26 (1953): 219–36.

——. *Caricatures of Americans on the English Stage Prior to 1870*. 1951. Rpt. Port Washington, NY: Kennikat, 1968.

"English Strictures Upon this Country." *New England Magazine* (Nov. 1834): 411–12.

Ershkowitz, Herbert. "Andrew Jackson, Seventh President and the Press." *Media History Digest* 5, no. 2 (1985): 10–16, 40.

Evans, Estwick. *A Pedestrious Tour of Four Thousand Miles through the Western States and Territories*. Vol. 5 of *Early Western Travels*, ed. Reuben Gold Thwaites. 1819. Rpt. Cleveland: Arthur H. Clark, 1904.

Felton, C. C. Review of *The Attaché; or, Sam Slick in England*, by Thomas Chandler Haliburton. *North American Review* 58 (Jan. 1844): 211–24.

Finton, Linda Ann. "Women Vernacular Humorists in Nineteenth-Century America: Ann Stephens, Frances Whitcher, and Marietta Holley." Ph.D. diss., U of California, Berkeley, 1978.

Fisher, Marvin. "The Iconology of Industrialism, 1830–60." *AQ* 13 (1961): 347–64.

Flint, Timothy. *Recollections of the Last Ten Years*. 1826. Rpt. New York: De Capo, 1968.

———. "Sketches of the Literature of the United States." *Athenaeum* (4 July 1835): 511–12; (11 July 1835): 526–27; (1 Aug. 1835): 584–86.

Franklin, John Hope. *The Emancipation Proclamation*. Garden City, NY: Doubleday, 1963.

Frye, Northrop. "Haliburton: Mask and Ego." *On Thomas Chandler Haliburton*, ed. Richard A. Davies, 211–15. Ottawa: Tecumseh, 1979.

Gale, Stephen H., ed. *Encyclopedia of American Humorists*. New York: Garland, 1988.

Gallatin, Albert. *Writings*, ed. Henry Adams. Vol. 1. Philadelphia: Lippincott, 1879.

Gohdes, Clarence. *American Literature in 19th-Century England*. New York: Columbia UP, 1944.

Gordon, William. *The History of the Independence of the United States of America*. Vol. 1. 1788. Rpt. Freeport, NY: Books for Libraries, 1969.

Granger, Bruce. *Political Satire in the American Revolution, 1763–1783*. Ithaca, NY: Cornell UP, 1960.

Griffin, Lloyd Wilfred. "Matthew Franklin Whittier, 'Ethan Spike.'" *NEQ* 14 (1941): 646–63.

Haliburton, Thomas Chandler. *The Letters of Thomas Chandler Haliburton*, ed. Richard A. Davies. Toronto: U of Toronto P, 1988.

Hauck, Richard Boyd. *A Cheerful Nihilism: Confidence and 'The Absurd' in American Humorous Fiction*. Bloomington: Indiana UP, 1971.

———. "The Literary Contents of the New York 'Spirit of the Times': 1831–1865." Ph.D. diss., U of Illinois, 1965.

Havens, Daniel F. *The Colombian Muse of Comedy*. Carbondale: Southern Illinois UP, 1973.

Hawthorne, Nathaniel. "Thomas Green Fessenden." *Nathaniel Hawthorne, Tales and Sketches*, ed. Roy Harvey Pearce. 571–84. New York: Library of America, 1982.

Hess, Stephen, and Milton Kaplan. *The Ungentlemanly Art, a History of American Political Cartoons*. New York: Macmillan, 1975.

Review of *High Life in New York,* by Ann Stephens. *Illustrated London News* 5 (28 Sept. 1844): 202.

Hill, George Handel. *Scenes from the Life of an Actor*. New York: Garret, 1853.

"Hill the Yankee Comedian." *Courier and New York Enquirer* (7 Aug. 1833).

Hodge, Francis. "Charles Mathews Reports on America." *QJS* 36 (1950): 492–99.

———. *Yankee Theatre: The Image of America on Stage 1825–1850*. Austin: U of Texas P, 1964.

Hoffman, Daniel. *Form and Fable in American Fiction*. New York: Oxford UP, 1961.

Horner, George F. "Franklin's *Dogood Papers* Re-examined." *SP* 37 (1940): 501–23.

Howard, Leon. *Victorian Knight-Errant: A Study of the Early Literary Career of James Russell Lowell*. Berkeley: U of California P, 1952.

Hudson, Gertrude Reese. *Browning to His American Friends*. London: Bowes and Bowes, 1965.

[H. W.]. "Yankeeana." *London and Westminster Review* 32 (Dec. 1838): 137–45.

Ireland, Joseph. *Records of the New York Stage*. 2 vols. 1886–87. Rpt. New York: Burt Franklin, 1968.

Ives, Sumner. "A Theory of Literary Dialect." *A Various Language, Perspectives on American Dialects,* ed. Williamson and Burke, 145–77. New York: Holt, Rinehart and Winston, 1971.

James, Marquis. *The Life of Andrew Jackson*. Indianapolis: Bobbs-Merrill, 1938.

James, Reese D. *Old Drury of Philadelphia, A History of the Philadelphia Stage, 1800–1835.* 1932. Rpt. New York: Greenwood, 1968.

Janson, Charles W. *The Stranger in America.* London: Albion, 1807.

Jenkins, Reese D. "Lowell's Criteria of Political Values," *NEQ* 7 (1934): 115–41.

Johnson, E. W. "American Letters, Their Character and Advancement." *American Whig Rev* (June 1845): 576–80.

Johnson, Malcom. *David Claypoole Johnston: American Graphic Humorist, 1798–1865.* Exhibition catalog, 1970.

Jones, Howard Mumford. *The Theory of American Literature.* Rev. ed. Ithaca, NY: Cornell UP, 1965.

Kelly, Darlene. "Haliburton's International Yankee." *The Thomas Chandler Haliburton Symposium,* ed. Frank Tierney, 135–49. Ottawa: U of Ottawa P, 1985.

Kelly, Jonathan F. *Dan Marble: A Biographical Sketch.* New York: DeWitt and Davenport, 1851.

Kenney, W. Howland, ed. *Laughter in the Wilderness: Early American Humor to 1783.* Kent, OH: Kent State UP, 1976.

Ketchum, Alton. *Uncle Sam: the Man and the Legend.* New York: Hill and Wang, 1959.

Killhoffer, Marie. "A Comparison of the Dialect of 'The Biglow Papers' with the Dialect of Four American Yankee Plays." *AS* 3 (1928): 222–36.

Kittredge, George Lyman. *The Old Farmer and His Almanac.* Boston: William Ware, 1904.

Kobre, Sidney. *The Development of American Journalism.* Dubuque, IA: William C. Brown, 1969.

Krapp, George. "The Psychology of Dialect Writing." *Bookman* 62 (1926): 522–27.

[L.]. "Jottings on Art and Artists #2." *New World* (25 Feb. 1843): 246–47.

Lauber, John. *"The Contrast:* A Study in the Concept of Innocence." *ELN* 1 (Sept. 1963): 33–37.

Leary, Lewis. "A 'Want List' for the Study of American Humor." *StAH* 2, no. 2 (Oct. 1975): 116–30.

Lease, Benjamin. *That Wild Fellow, John Neal.* Chicago: U of Chicago P, 1972.

Lee, Judith Yaross. "Republican Rhymes: Constitutional Controversy and the Democratization of Verse Satire, 1786–1799." *StAH* n.s. 6 (1988): 30–39.

Legaré, Hugh S., and J. W. Simmons. "Introduction." *Southern Literary Gazette* 1 (Sept. 1828): 1–8.

Lemay, J. A. Leo. "The American Origins of 'Yankee Doodle.'" *WMQ* 33 (1976): 435–64.

―――. "Benjamin Franklin." *Major Writers of Early American Literature,* ed. Everett Emerson, 205–43. Madison: U of Wisconsin P, 1972.

―――. *Men of Letters in Colonial Maryland.* Knoxville: U of Tennessee P, 1972.

―――. *"New England Annoyances": America's First Folk Song.* Newark: U of Delaware P, 1985.

Review of *Letters of J. Downing,* by Charles Augustus Davis. *Literary Gazette* no. 912 (12 July 1834): 480–81.

Levy, Lester. *Flashes of Merriment: A Century of Humorous Songs in America 1805–1905.* Norman: U of Oklahoma P, 1971.

―――. *Picture the Songs.* Baltimore: Johns Hopkins UP, 1976.

Lindberg, Gary. *The Confidence Man in American Literature.* New York: Oxford UP, 1982.

Lipper, Mark M. "Comic Caricatures in Early American Newspapers as Indicators of the National Character." Ph.D. diss., Southern Illinois U, 1973.

Ljungquist, Kent, and Cameron C. Nickels. "Elizabeth Oakes Smith on Poe: A Chapter in the Recovery of His Nineteenth-Century Reputation." *Poe and His Times,* ed. Benjamin Franklin Fisher IV, 235–47. Baltimore: Edgar Allan Poe Society, 1990.

Lofaro, Michael A., ed. *Davy Crockett: The Man, the Legend, the Legacy.* Knoxville: U of Tennessee P, 1985.

Lofaro, Michael A., and Joe Cummings, eds. *Crockett at Two Hundred: New Perspectives on the Man and the Myth.* Knoxville: U of Tennessee P, 1989.

Logeman, Henri. "The Etymology of 'Yankee.'" *Studies in English Philology, a Miscellany in Honor of Frederick Klaeber,* ed. Kemp Malone and Martin B. Ruud. 403–13. Minneapolis: U of Minnesota P, 1929.

Lowell, James Russell. *The Anti-Slavery Papers.* 1902. Rpt. Negro Universities P, 1969.

———. *Letters of James Russell Lowell,* ed. Charles Eliot Norton. 3 vols. Boston: Houghton Mifflin, 1904.

———. "Nationality in Literature." *North American Review* 69 (July 1849): 196–216.

———. *New Letters of James Russell Lowell,* ed. Mark A. DeWolfe Howe. New York: Harper, 1932.

Luther, Frank. *Americans and Their Songs.* New York: Harper, 1945.

Lynn, Kenneth. *Mark Twain and Southwestern Humor.* Boston: Little, Brown, 1959.

Marryat, Frederick. *A Diary in America,* ed. Jules Zanger. 1839. Rpt. Bloomington: Indiana UP, 1960.

Marx, Leo. *The Machine in the Garden.* New York: Oxford UP, 1964.

———. "Pastoralism in America." *Ideology and Classic American Literature,* ed. Sacvan Bercovitch and Myra Jehlen, 36–69. New York: Cambridge UP, 1986.

Mathews, Charles. *The Life and Correspondence of Charles Mathews,* ed. Edmund Yates. London: Routledge, Warne, and Routledge, 1860.

———. *Memoirs of Charles Mathews,* ed. Mrs. [Anne] Mathews. 4 vols. London: Richard Bentley, 1838.

———. *A Continuation of the Memoirs of Charles Mathews,* ed. Mrs. [Anne] Mathews. 2 vols. Philadelphia: Lea and Blanchard, 1839.

Matthews, Albert. "Brother Jonathan." *Publication of the Colonial Society of Massachusetts* 7 (1901): 94–126.

———. "Brother Jonathan Once More." *Publication of the Colonial Society of Massachusetts* 32 (1935): 374–86.

———. "Uncle Sam." *PAAS* 19 (1908): 21–65.

Matthews, Brander. "Americans on the Stage." *Scribner's Monthly* 18 (July 1879): 321–33.

Matthiessen, F. O. *American Renaissance.* New York: Oxford UP, 1941.

McCormick, Richard P. *The Second American Party System: Party Formation in the Jacksonian Era.* Chapel Hill: U of North Carolina P, 1966.

Meine, Frank. "The Carpet Bag." *Collector's Journal* 4 (1933): 411–13.

———. "Vanity Fair." *Collector's Journal* 4 (1934): 461–63.

Meserole, Harrison T. "'A Kind of Burr': Colonial New England's Heritage of Wit." *American Literature: The New England Heritage,* ed. James Nagel and Richard Astro, 11–28. New York: Garland, 1981.

Mesick, Jane. *The English Traveller in America 1785–1835.* New York: Columbia UP, 1922.

Meyers, Marvin. *The Jacksonian Persuasion, Politics and Belief.* 1957. Rpt. Stanford: Stanford UP, 1960.

Micklus, Robert. *The Comic Genius of Dr. Hamilton.* Knoxville: U of Tennessee P, 1990.

Miller, Douglas T. *The Birth of Modern America 1820–1840.* New York: Macmillan, 1985.

Miller, Perry. *Errand Into the Wilderness.* 1956. New York: Rpt. Harper and Row, 1964.

Mintz, Lawrence E., ed. *Humor in America: A Research Guide to Genres and Topics.* New York: Greenwood, 1988.

Monaghan, Frank. *French Travellers in the United States, 1765–1932.* 1933. Rpt. New York: Antiquarian, 1961.

"Monthly Commentary." *American Monthly Magazine* 3 (Mar. 1837): 305–306.

Moody, Richard. *America Takes the Stage.* Bloomington: Indiana UP, 1955.

Moore, Frank, ed. *Songs and Ballads of the American Revolution.* New York: Appleton, 1856.

Moore, Jack. "Native Elements in American Magazine Short Fiction, 1741–1800." Ph.D. diss., U of North Carolina, 1963.

Morgan, Winifred. *An American Icon: Brother Jonathan and American Identity.* Newark: U of Delaware P, 1988.

Mott, Frank Luther. *American Journalism, a History: 1690–1960.* 3d ed. New York: Macmillan, 1962.

———. *A History of American Magazines.* Vols. 1–2. Cambridge: Harvard UP, 1938, 1939.

Murrell, William. *A History of American Graphic Humor.* Vol. 1. New York: Whitney Museum of American Art, 1933.

"National Postures." *New England Magazine* (Sept. 1834): 225–33.

"Neal—Brother Jonathan." *New England Galaxy* 8 (2 Sept. 1852): 2.

Neal, John. "British Travelers in America." *Monthly Magazine* 2 (Dec. 1826): 608–14.

———. "Character of the Real Yankees; What They are Supposed to be and What They Are." *New Monthly Magazine* 17 (Sept. 1826): 247–56.

———. *The Down-Easters.* 2 vols. New York: Harper, 1833.

———. "Speculations of a Traveller Concerning the People of the United States." *Blackwood's Magazine* 16 (July 1824): 91–97.

———. "Story Telling." *New England Magazine* 8 (Jan. 1835): 1–12.

———. *Wandering Recollections of a Somewhat Busy Life.* Boston: Roberts, 1869.

———. "The Yankee Tongue—And Its Corruptions." *Brother Jonathan* (26 Aug. 1843): 494–95.

Nethercot, Arthur H. "The Dramatic Background of Royall Tyler's *The Contrast.* AL 12 (1941): 435–46.

Nevins, Alan, and Frank Weitenkampf. *A Century of Political Cartoons.* New York: Scribner's, 1944.

Nichols, Charles. "Notes on the Almanacs of Massachusetts." *PAAS* n.s. 22 (1912): 15–134.

Nickels, Cameron C. "Federalist Mock Pastorals: The Ideology of Early New England Humor." *EAL* 17 (1982): 139–51.

———. "Franklin's Poor Richard's Almanacs: 'The Humblest of his Labors.'" *The Oldest Revolutionary: Essays on Benjamin Franklin,* ed. J. A. Leo Lemay, 77–89. Philadelphia: U of Pennsylvania P, 1976.

————. "*Yankee Notions*." *American Humor Magazines and Comic Periodicals*, ed. David E. E. Sloane, 322–25. New York: Greenwood, 1987.

Northall, W. K., ed. *Life and Recollections of Yankee Hill*. New York: W. F. Burgess, 1850.

"Notions of Sam Slick." *Bentley's Miscellany* 14 (1843): 81–94.

Oehlschlaeger, Fritz. "A Bibliography of Frontier Humor in the St. Louis *Daily Reveille*, 1844–46." *StAH* n.s. 3, no. 4 (1984–85): 267–89.

————. "A Bibliography of Frontier Humor in the St. Louis *Daily Reveille*, 1847–50." *StAH* 4, no. 4 (1985): 262–76.

————. *Old Southwest Humor from the St. Louis* Daily Reveille, *1844–1850*. Columbia: U of Missouri P, 1990.

"On Americanisms, with a Fragment of a Trans-Atlantic Pastoral." *New Monthly Magazine* 14 (Dec. 1820): 629–32.

Opie, Iona, and Peter Opie, eds. *The Oxford Dictionary of Nursery Rhymes*. New York: Oxford UP, 1951.

O'Sullivan John. "Introduction." *United States Magazine and Democratic Review* 1 (Oct. 1837): 1–14.

————. "The Poetry of the West." *United States Magazine and Democratic Review* 9 (July 1841): 23–44.

[P. Q.]. "National Literature." *American Monthly Magazine* 1 (1829): 379–85.

Parker, Theodore. "The Writings of Emerson." *Massachusetts Quarterly Rev* 3 (Mar. 1850): 200–254.

Parkman, Francis. "English Travellers of Rank in America." *North American Review* 154 (Jan. 1852): 197–216.

Pattee, Fred Lewis. *The First Century of American Literature, 1770–1870*. 1935. Rpt. New York: Cooper Square, 1966.

[Peter]. "Yankeeisms." *New England Galaxy* 8 (18 Nov. 1825): 3.

Poe, Edgar Allan. "A Chapter on Autography." *Graham's Magazine* 19 (Dec. 1841): 273–86.

————. Review of Augustus Baldwin Longstreet's *Georgia Scenes*. *Southern Literary Messenger* 2 (Mar. 1836): 287–92.

————. Review of Seba Smith's *Powhatan: A Metrical Romance in Five Cantos*. *Graham's Magazine*. 19 (July 1841): 46-47.

"Prospectus" for the *National Journal*. Washington, DC: 1823.

Quinn, Arthur Hobson. *A History of the American Drama from the Beginnings to the Civil War*. New York: Harper, 1923.

[Q. Q.]. "Yankee Notions." *New Monthly Magazine* 42 (Oct. 1836): 160–67.

Randall, J. G. *Lincoln the President: Springfield to Gettysburg*. Vol. 2. New York: Dodd, Mead, 1945.

Read, Allan Walker. "The World of Joe Strickland," *JAF* 76 (1963): 277–308.

Reese, James D. *Old Drury of Philadelphia: A History of the Philadelphia Stage, 1800–1825*. 1932. Rpt. New York: Greenwood, 1968.

Reilly, Bernard. *American Political Prints, 1766–1876: A Catalog of the Collections in the Library of Congress*. Boston: G. K. Hall, 1991.

Remini, Robert V. *Andrew Jackson and the Bank War*. New York: Norton. 1967.

Reynolds, David S. *Beneath the American Renaissance: The Subversive Imagination in the Age of Emerson and Melville.* New York: Alfred A. Knopf, 1988.

Rickels, Patricia and Milton. *Seba Smith.* Boston: G. K. Hall, 1977.

Rourke, Constance. *American Humor, a Study of National Character.* New York: Harcourt, Brace, 1931.

Royot, Daniel. *L'humour Americain: Des Puritans aux Yankees.* Lyon: Presses Universitaires de Lyon, 1980.

———. "*The Rover.*" *American Humor Magazines and Comic Periodicals,* ed. David E. E. Sloane, 239–41. New York: Greenwood, 1987.

———. "Sam Slick and American Popular Humor." *The Thomas Chandler Haliburton Symposium,* ed. Frank Tierney, 123–33. Ottawa: U of Ottawa P, 1985.

———. "Whittier, Matthew Franklin." *Encyclopedia of American Humorists,* ed. Stephen H. Gale, 482–84. New York: Garland, 1988.

Rubin, Joan Shelley. *Constance Rourke and American Culture.* Chapel Hill: U of North Carolina P, 1980.

Rubin, Louis D., Jr., ed. *The Comic Imagination in American Literature.* New Brunswick, NJ: Rutgers UP, 1973.

Saltman, Helen Saltzberg. "John Adams' Earliest Essays: The Humphrey Ploughjogger Letters." *WMQ* 37 (1980): 125–35.

———. "John Adams' Political Satires: The Humphrey Ploughjogger Letters." Ph.D. diss., U of California, Los Angeles, 1980.

Schlesinger, Arthur M. *The Age of Jackson.* Boston: Little, Brown, 1950.

Schmitz, Neil. *Of Huck and Alice: Humorous Writings in American Literature.* Minneapolis: U of Minnesota P, 1983.

Schroeder, John A. "Seba Smith's Political Satire." *NEQ* 50 (1977): 214–33.

Schudson, Michael. "The Revolution in American Journalism in the Age of Egalitarianism: The Penny Press." *A Social History of American Newspapers.* 12–60. New York: Basic Books, 1978.

Scisco, Louis Dow. *Political Nativism in New York State.* 1901. Rpt. New York: Ames, 1968.

Scudder, Horace. *James Russell Lowell, a Biography.* 2 vols. Boston: Houghton, Mifflin, 1901.

Secor, Robert. "The Significance of Pennsylvania's Eighteenth-Century Jest Books." *PMHB* 110 (1986): 259–87.

Sederberg, Nancy B. "Antebellum Southern Humor in the *Camden Journal:* 1826–1840." *MissQ* 27 (Winter 1973–74): 41–74.

Shackford, James Atkins. *David Crockett, the Man and the Legend.* 1956. Rpt. Chapel Hill: U of North Carolina P, 1986.

Singletary, Otis A. *The Mexican War.* Chicago: U of Chicago P, 1960.

Sklar, Robert. "Humor in America." *A Celebration of Laughter,* ed. Werner M. Mendel, 9–30. Los Angeles: Mara, 1970.

Sloane, David E. E., ed. *American Humor Magazines and Comic Periodicals.* New York: Greenwood, 1987.

———, ed., *The Literary Humor of the Urban Northeast: 1830–1890.* Baton Rouge: Louisiana State UP, 1983.

Smith, Henry Nash. *Mark Twain, the Development of a Writer.* Cambridge: Harvard UP, 1962.

————. *Virgin Land, the American West as Myth and Symbol.* Cambridge: Harvard UP, 1950.

Smith, Sol. *Theatrical Management in the West and South for Thirty Years.* New York: Harper, 1898.

Smither, Nellie. "Library of Humorous American Works: A Bibliographical Study." Master's thesis, Columbia U, 1936.

Sonneck, Oscar G. T. *Report on "The Star Spangled Banner," "Hail Columbia," "America," "Yankee Doodle."* Washington, DC: Library of Congress, 1909.

Spencer, Benjamin. *The Quest for Nationality.* Syracuse UP, 1957.

Stein, Roger B. "Royall Tyler and the Question of Our Speech." *NEQ* 38 (1965): 454–74.

Stephen, Leslie. "American Humor." *Cornhill Magazine* 13 (Jan. 1866): 28–43.

Stewart, Donald H. *The Opposition Press of the Federalist Period.* Albany: State U of New York P, 1969.

Stowell, Marion Barber. *Early American Almanacs.* New York: Burt Franklin, 1977.

————. "Humor in Colonial Almanacs." *StAH* 1, no. 3 (1976): 34–47.

Review of *The Stranger in America,* by F. Lieber, and *Letters of J. Downing,* by Charles Augustus Davis. *Quarterly Review* 53 (Apr. 1838): 396–406.

Strong, George Templeton. *Diary,* ed. Allan Nevins and Milton H. Thomas. 2 vols. New York: Macmillan, 1952.

Tandy, Jennette. *Crackerbox Philosophers in American Humor and Satire.* 1925. Rpt. Port Washington, NY: Kennikat, 1964.

Tanselle, George Thomas. *Royall Tyler.* Cambridge: Harvard UP, 1967.

Tatham, David. "David Claypoole Johnston's *Militia Muster.*" *American Art Journal* 19 (1987): 4–15.

————. "D. C. Johnston's Pictorialization of Vernacular Humor in Jacksonian America." *American Speech: 1600 to the Present,* ed. Peter Benes, 107–19. Dublin Seminar for New England Folklife: Annual Proc. June 25–26, 1983. Boston: Boston U, 1985.

————. *A Note about David Claypoole Johnston.* Syracuse: Syracuse UP, 1970. [Includes "A Checklist of David Claypoole Johnston's Book Illustrations."]

Thayer, Stuart. *Annals of the American Circus, 1830–1847.* Seattle: Peanut Butter Publications, 1986.

Thompson, Stith. *The Folktale.* New York; Holt, Rinehart, Winston, 1946.

Tierney, Frank, ed. *The Thomas Chandler Haliburton Symposium.* Ottawa: U of Ottawa P, 1985.

Todd, Henry Cook. *Notes Upon Canada and the United States.* 2d ed. Toronto: Rogers and Thompson, 1840.

Review of *Traits of American Humor, by Native Authors,* ed. Thomas Chandler Haliburton. *Irish Quarterly Review* 2 (Mar. 1852): 171–96.

Tupper, Frederick. "Royall Tyler, Man of Letters and Law." *Proceedings of the Vermont Historical Society* 4 (1928): 65–101.

Tuveson, Ernest. *Redeemer Nation.* Chicago: U of Chicago P, 1968.

Tyler, Moses Coit. *A History of American Literature, 1607–1765.* 1878. Rpt. New York: Collier, 1962.

"Uncle Sam's Peculiarities." *Bentley's Miscellany* 4 (July 1838): 40–48.

Valentine, Thomas W. *The Valentines in American, 1644–1874.* New York: Clark and Maynard, 1874.

Von Frank, Albert J. *The Sacred Game: Provincialism and Frontier Consciousness in American Literature, 1660–1860.* New York: Cambridge UP, 1985.

Voss, Arthur. "Backgrounds of Lowell's Satire in 'The Biglow Papers.'" *NEQ* 23 (1950): 47–64.

———. "*The Biglow Papers* in England." *AL* 21 (1949–50): 340–42.

———. "The Evolution of Lowell's 'The Courtin'.'" *AL* 15 (1953): 42–50.

Wadlington, Warwick. *The Confidence Game in American Literature.* Princeton: Princeton UP, 1975.

Walker, Nancy. *A Very Serious Thing: Women's Humor and American Culture.* Minneapolis: U of Minnesota P, 1988.

Walker, William. *James Fenimore Cooper.* New York: Barnes and Noble, 1962.

Walsh, Jim. "Favorite Pioneer Recording Artist, Cal Stewart." *Hobbies,* vol. 55 (Jan. 1951): 20–22, 35; (Feb. 1951): 20–25; vol. 56: (Mar. 1951): 18–23; (Apr. 1951): 18–24.

Ward, Edward. *A Trip to New-England with a Character of the Country and People, both Indians and English.* 1699. Rpt. New York: Columbia UP, for the Facsimile Text Society, 1933.

Ward, John William. *Andrew Jackson, Symbol for an Age.* 1955. Rpt. New York: Oxford UP, 1962.

Watts, Emily Stipes. *The Businessman in American Literature.* Athens: U of Georgia P, 1982.

Weber, Brom, ed. *An Anthology of American Humor.* New York: Crowell, 1962.

Weisbuch, Robert. *Atlantic Double-Cross: American Literature and British Influence in the Age of Emerson.* Chicago: U of Chicago P, 1986.

Weiss, Harry. "A Brief History of American Jest Books." *Bulletin of the New York Public Library* 47 (1943): 273–89.

Weitenkampf, Frank. *Political Caricature in the United States.* New York: New York Public Library, 1953.

West, James L. W. III. "Backwoods Humor in the Greenville *Mountaineer,* 1830–1850," TS, Furman U Library.

———. "Early Backwoods Humor in the Greenville *Mountaineer,* 1826–1840." *MissQ* 25 (1972): 69–82.

Williamson, Juanita V., and Virginia M. Burke, eds. *A Various Language, Perspectives on American Dialects.* New York: Holt, Rinehart and Winston, 1971.

Winter, Kate H. *Marietta Holley, Life with "Josiah Allen's Wife."* Syracuse: Syracuse UP, 1984.

"The World We Live In." *Blackwood's Magazine* 42 (Nov. 1837): 673–77.

Wortham, Thomas. "Introduction." *James Russell Lowell's The Biglow Papers [First Series,]* by James Russell Lowell, ix–xxxiv. De Kalb: Northern Illinois UP, 1977.

Wright, J. R. "Catalogue of the 16th Exhibition of Paintings at the Boston Athenaeum, 1852." *The Pioneer* 1 (Jan. 1843): 12–16.

Wyman, Mary Alice, ed. *Selections from the Autobiography of Elizabeth Oakes Smith.* New York: Columbia UP, 1924.

———. *Two American Pioneers: Seba Smith and Elizabeth Oakes Smith.* New York: Columbia UP, 1927.

Review of *Yankee Humor and Uncle Sam's Fun,* ed. William Jerdan. *Illustrated London News* 23 (3 Sept. 1853): 187.

"Yankee Humour." *Quarterly Review* 122 (Jan. 1867): 111–24.

Yates, Norris. *The American Humorist, Conscience of the Twentieth Century.* New York: Citadel, 1964.

———. *William T. Porter and the Spirit of the Times: A Study of the Big Bear School of Humor.* Baton Rouge: Louisiana State UP, 1957.

Zall, P. M. "The Old Age of American Jest Books." *EAL* 15 (Spring 1980): 3–13.

Ziff, Larzer. "Introduction." *The Simple Cobler of Aggawam in America,* by Nathaniel Ward. Lincoln: U of Nebraska P, 1969.

———. *Literary Democracy: The Declaration of Cultural Independence in America.* New York: Viking, 1981.

———, ed. *The Literature of America.* Vol. 1. New York: 1971.

Index